Developing digital scholarship
Emerging practices in academic libraries

Every purchase of a Facet book helps to fund CILIP's advocacy, awareness and accreditation programmes for information professionals.

Developing digital scholarship

Emerging practices in academic libraries

EDITED BY
Alison Mackenzie
Lindsey Martin

© This compilation: Alison Mackenzie and Lindsey Martin 2016
The chapters: the contributors 2016

Published by Facet Publishing,
7 Ridgmount Street, London WC1E 7AE
www.facetpublishing.co.uk

Facet Publishing is wholly owned by CILIP: the Chartered Institute of Library and Information Professionals.

The editor and authors of the individual chapters assert their moral right to be identified as such in accordance with the terms of the Copyright, Designs and Patents Act 1988.

Except as otherwise permitted under the Copyright, Designs and Patents Act 1988 this publication may only be reproduced, stored or transmitted in any form or by any means, with the prior permission of the publisher, or, in the case of reprographic reproduction, in accordance with the terms of a licence issued by The Copyright Licensing Agency. Enquiries concerning reproduction outside those terms should be sent to Facet Publishing, 7 Ridgmount Street, London WC1E 7AE.

Every effort has been made to contact the holders of copyright material reproduced in this text, and thanks are due to them for permission to reproduce the material indicated. If there are any queries please contact the publisher.

British Library Cataloguing in Publication Data
A catalogue record for this book is available from the British Library.

ISBN 978-1-78330-110-2 (paperback)
ISBN 978-1-78330-178-2 (hardback)
ISBN 978-1-78330-179-9 (e-book)

First published 2016

Text printed on FSC accredited material.

Typeset from editors' files by Facet Publishing Production
in 10/13 pt Minion Pro and Myriad Pro.
Printed and made in Great Britain by CPI Group (UK) Ltd, Croydon, CR0 4YY.

Contents

List of figures, tables and case studies vii
Editors and contributors ix
Introduction xiii

PART 1 A review of the landscape 1
  1 The university library and digital scholarship: a review of the literature 3
     Lindsey Martin

  2 Digital scholarship: scanning library services and spaces 23
     Alison Mackenzie

PART 2 The agile librarian 41
  3 Librarian as partner: in and out of the library 43
     Roz Howard and Megan Fitzgibbons

  4 **Novice to expert: developing digitally capable librarians** 61
     Charles Inskip

  5 Lean in the library: building capacity by realigning staff and resources 81
     Jennifer Bremner

PART 3 Digital spaces and services 103
  6 Digital scholarship centres: converging space and expertise 105
     Tracy C. Bergstrom

7 **Building scalable and sustainable services for researchers** 121
   David Clay

PART 4 Communications and social networking 139
8 **Social networking with the scholarly community: a literature review** 141
   Suzanne Parfitt

9 **Developing digital scholars: from the ivory tower to the Twittersphere** 157
   Alison Hicks

10 **Reflections on digital scholarship: so many reasons to be cheerful** 173
   Alison Mackenzie and Lindsey Martin

Index 179

List of figures, tables and case studies

Figures

2.1	Library engagement with digital scholarship services and systems	24
4.1	Assessment of the digital capabilities of staff whose core roles are student support and academic liaison: staff expertise	68
4.2	Assessment of the digital capabilities of staff whose core roles are student support and academic liaison: importance of staff developing expertise in this area	68
4.3	What is needed to ensure that library staff maintain and develop their digital literacies?	70
5.1	Macquarie University Library Service Model and Quality Enhancement Framework	85
5.2	The four central pillars of the Quality Enhancement Framework, including continuous improvement	89
5.3	Graphic created for the What We Do Matters communications	91
6.1	A floor plan of the Center for Digital Scholarship	112
6.2	Home page of the Center for Digital Scholarship web pages	115
7.1	University of Salford Research Data Repository home page	127
7.2	Cumulative downloads of open access research outputs from USIR between October 2010 and October 2015	129

Tables

1.1 Boyer as a framework for scholarly activity 5
1.2 Digital scholarship activity across Boyer's framework 19
2.1 Ownership/use of institutional business/enterprise systems (where available) 25
2.2 Use of digital scholarship services and examples of partnership working in delivery of services 26
2.3a Delivery of bespoke digital scholarship systems/services and comments 27
2.3b Delivery of bespoke digital scholarship systems/services and comments 28
2.3c Delivery of bespoke digital scholarship systems/services and comments 28
2.4 Delivery of experimental/innovative solutions by library services 33

Case studies

2.1 Hydra: a case study from the University of Hull, UK 29
2.2 Sussex Humanities Lab: University of Sussex, UK 30
2.3 Poetics of the Archive: Newcastle University, UK 33
2.4 Digitization of the Abbey Theatre Archive, National University of Ireland, Galway 35
2.5 Disruptive Media Learning Lab, Coventry University 37
5.1 Library shelving process 95
5.2 Library enquiry process 97
5.3 Library scanning and copying process 99
6.1 University of Notre Dame 110
7.1 Research data management at the University of Salford 125
7.2 University of Salford Institutional Repository (USIR) 129
7.3 Consultancy and training at the University of Salford 131
7.4 Meeting the challenges at the University of Salford 133

Editors and contributors

Tracy C. Bergstrom

Tracy C. Bergstrom is the director of the Specialized Collection Services Program within the Hesburgh Libraries of Notre Dame University, USA. As such, she oversees the Center for Digital Scholarship, Rare Books and Special Collections, University Archives, Preservation, and Digital Production. She is also the curator of the Zahm Dante and early Italian imprints collection at Notre Dame and is especially interested in the print history of Dante's *Divine Comedy*. She is a graduate of Smith College and Yale University and holds a bachelor's degree in Italian Studies and Art History, a Master of Arts degree in Archaeological Studies, and a Master of Library Science degree.

Jennifer Bremner

Jennifer Bremner has extensive experience in higher education and currently works as a Business Process Improvement Manager at Macquarie University in New South Wales, Australia. Prior to this she worked as the Macquarie University Library Quality and Planning Manager from 2011 to 2015. She has written conference papers and presents regularly at conferences. She is committed to continuous improvement and to Lean in Higher Education as a way of empowering staff to change processes and services for the better.

David Clay
David Clay is the University Librarian (Interim) at the University of Salford. David has over 15 years of experience working in academic libraries, having previously been Associate University Librarian for Learning and Research Support at the University of Salford and Head of Academic Liaison at the University of Liverpool. He is leading the development of Research Data Management services at the University.

Megan Fitzgibbons
Megan Fitzgibbons's career in librarianship focuses on learning and teaching, developed through multiple roles at McGill University (Canada) and now the University of Western Australia's Library and the Centre for Education Futures. She has also been a sessional tutor in Information Science at Edith Cowan University (Australia).

Alison Hicks
Alison Hicks is a PhD candidate in the School of Information Studies at Charles Sturt University, Australia and the Romance Language Librarian at the University of Colorado, Boulder, USA. With an MA from the University of St Andrews, Scotland, and an MSIS from the University of Texas, Austin, USA, her research centres on information literacy and digital scholarship practices.

Roz Howard
Roz Howard has over 20 years' experience working in Higher Education in both the UK and Australia. She has taken on a number of job roles from Librarian to ICT trainer. Relocated to Australia in 2012, she moved from a library management role to supporting education futures. More recently she has moved into a new career taking up a Director role in IT.

At the heart of all her roles have always been engagement and supporting staff and students in engaging with technologies in enhancing teaching, learning and research.

Dr Charles Inskip
Dr Charles Inskip is lecturer and currently programme director on the MA Library and Information Studies programme at University College London (UCL), teaching Collection Management, Information Sources, and Information Literacy. His research interests are around human information behaviour and information literacy. He is

particularly interested in identifying ways in which library and information professionals can support users effectively.

Alison Mackenzie

Alison Mackenzie is the Dean of Learning Services at Edge Hill University. Prior to taking up this post, she held the post of University Librarian at Bangor University, Wales and a variety of roles at Manchester Metropolitan University, and in her early career worked in art colleges and commercial practice. She has been an active contributor to the development of the profession, having held roles on the SCONUL Board, and as Chair of the Performance Measurement and Quality Strategy group. She is currently a member of the Northern Collaboration steering group (www.northerncollaboration.org.uk/).

Lindsey Martin

Lindsey Martin is the Assistant Head of Learning Services at Edge Hill University and is responsible for the learning technologies managed and supported by Learning Services. She has responsibility for the virtual learning environment and its associated systems, media production, classroom AV, and development of staff digital capability. She has worked in academic libraries for the past 20+ years in a variety of roles. She has been active on the Heads of eLearning Forum (HeLF) steering group (http://helfuk.blogspot.co.uk/) for a number of years and is currently its Chair.

Suzanne Parfitt

Suzanne has over 15 years of international experience in university and school libraries. Most recently she was Assistant Librarian at Tanglin Trust School, Singapore. Her role covered a variety of responsibilities; these included leading the reference team, developing the reference services offered by the library and supporting the creation of a makerspace. She was also responsible for the development of the school's online subject guides (libguides) collection. She has presented on school libraries' use of libguides for resource curation and was consulted on libguides by school librarians across SE Asia. This work has led to her interest in the benefits of online technology and library engagement through social networking sites. She is currently back in the UK undertaking a research project into this subject as part of a Master's degree in Information Studies (Applied Research) through Charles Sturt University, Australia.

Introduction

> Digital scholarship is an incredibly awkward term that people have come up with to describe a complex group of developments. The phrase is really, at some basic level, nonsensical. After all, scholarship is scholarship.
>
> (Lynch, 2014)

This is Clifford Lynch's response to the question 'how would you define digital scholarship?'

His response echoes in part our experiences when we started to examine how digital scholarship is interpreted. Scholarship is a dynamic concept, influenced by the demands of the environment it finds itself in, the ongoing debate about what it means to be a scholar in practice and what support and advice are needed by the digital scholar. There are no easy answers to this question but we aim to offer readers, through a collection of contrasting perspectives, contexts, insights and case studies, an exploration of the relationships between digital scholarship, contemporary academic libraries and professional practice. This will appeal to a readership from across the globe: practitioners, both academic librarians and managers; specialists in archives, special collections or learning technology; students, researchers and tutors of library and information science. Digital scholarship is arguably transformative and this timely publication will provide readers with insights into the changing behaviours of both scholars and librarians as they adapt to the impact that a digital environment has on skills, services, processes and systems.

Background

Toward the end of the last century a more inclusive view of scholarship emerged following Ernest Boyer's influential *Scholarship Reconsidered: priorities of the professoriate*, which recognized that knowledge is not only acquired through research but encompasses the full scope of academic work 'through synthesis, through practice, and through teaching' (1990, 24). Melanie Schlosser, digital publishing librarian at Ohio State University Libraries, has defined digital scholarship as 'research and teaching that is made possible by digital technologies, or that takes advantage of them to ask and answer questions in new ways'. In summary, it is perhaps a generalization but nonetheless true that 21st-century scholarship will be, by default, digital. 'It marks a move away from the passive, one-way form of communication from scholar to student or peer or novice. It is a new form of inquiry and practice that generates new questions, new evidence, new conclusions, and new audiences as it is used' (Ayers, 2012). The challenge for librarians and libraries is to identify how and where they can harness their skills and expertise in the creation of new knowledge from existing or new content, in partnership with researchers and scholars and through the utilization of new technologies and devices. These are the digital skills needed now. Whilst this may pose a challenge, it also presents opportunities to be bold, remodel, trial new approaches and reposition the library as a key partner in the process of digital scholarship.

'Fundamental aspects of university practices are being affected by the deployment of digital technology, including what it means to learn, the practices of academic reading and the way scholarship is conducted' (Jones, 2013, 171). For libraries the impact of digital technologies has extended far beyond the transformation of content. Services have emerged enabling new ways to access research, teaching and learning; the adoption of social media as a communication and marketing tool is accompanied by a growing focus on developing new customer relationships. The library itself aims to become embedded in the workflows and processes of its various communities of users. This has also led to a new generation of roles and new (shifting) responsibilities, with staff training and development often playing 'catch-up'. In this environment, which has seen the role of libraries in all sectors and across many countries change, one of the key challenges to emerge is how best to develop expertise in digital scholarship which draws on the specialist technical knowledge of the profession and maintains and grows its relevance for staff, students and researchers. As Panitch and Michalak assert, 'there may be many ways to be a scholarly digital library. We have an obligation to explore them, to integrate those values with our own, and to claim our place for the thoughtful, important, and scholarly work we do' (Panitch and Michalak, 2008, 62).

Chapter summaries

The opening chapters provide the context and landscape review for digital scholarship. In Chapter 1 Lindsey Martin delivers an extensive review of the literature associated with digital scholarship, examining it from a number of different perspectives. Starting with the question 'What is scholarship?' the chapter progresses to explore the nature of digital scholarship and the practices related to it. It highlights where, beyond the use of technology as a descriptor of digital scholarship – the characteristic which perhaps distinguishes digital scholarship from other forms – is an individual researcher's attitude to openness. The literature, however, offers little in the way of empirical studies to provide the evidence base to support this view; but anecdotal and small-scale studies suggest that scholars who are broadly in favour of open and networked practices will put effort into using technology where they can see discernible, personal benefits. The disruptive effects of enabling technologies are also discussed in relation to the requirement by funders to share underpinning research data – making data open and accessible is a focus of the review, but there is little evidence of new research practices emerging with the greater availability of open data. The role of libraries and librarians in support of digital scholarship is discussed, and although new, hybrid roles are described in the literature, equally, scholars are seemingly unaware of librarians' expertise, with the result that they will bypass the library and seek alternative sources of support. This is compounded by evidence which suggests that librarians are, on occasion, unaware of what their scholarly communities require in terms of expert guidance and support.

The review concludes with a re-working of Boyer's framework for scholarly activity, synthesizing what has been learnt to date from the literature, and concludes with the positive message that there are many opportunities for librarians to engage with digital scholarship activities, but action is required.

The theme of engagement is carried forward into Chapter 2 by Alison Mackenzie, who draws on the results from a small-scale survey to provide insights into the degree to which academic libraries are engaging with and using digital scholarship services and systems. The sample size of 20 is small, but luckily representative of the range of higher education institutions in the UK and Ireland. Based on the work of Vinopal and McCormick (2013), the survey's aim is to shed light on levels of engagement, from being an owner/user of an institution's business system, with an application relevant to digital scholarship, to a position where a library service could provide leadership and expertise in support of a research project. The results from the survey are supplemented by a number of case studies on the impact of digital scholarship and how it is shaping the role of libraries and librarians, and vice versa. These are success stories and illustrate where librarians have noted an opportunity and, in many cases, worked in partnership to develop a service that helps (re) assert their value as a strategic partner. One example, the Hydra repository at the University of Hull managed by the university library, provides a system and infrastructure capable of being sufficiently flexible to meet individual research requirements; at the University of Sussex, the newly formed Sussex Humanities Lab includes library staff as core members of the team. Both these case studies highlight the changing nature of the role of the library within an individual institution's scholarly environment. Moving on to specialized, experimental developments, the digitization of the Abbey Theatre Archive by the National University of Ireland, Galway is realizing the Archive's potential as a research source which would have been previously difficult to imagine. Staff use of new technologies at Newcastle University's library has transformed the approach to cataloguing literary archives and the case study, based on the Bloodaxe Books archive, is a showcase for serendipity over searching.

The final case study centres on the Disruptive Media Learning Lab (DMLL) at Coventry University, which is an example of multi-professional team working in an attempt to sustain innovation in teaching and learning practices. The digital skills of librarians are seen as essential to the potential success of this venture; but of equal if not more importance is the ability to flex, adapt and be willing to apply existing skills to new situations.

In summary, each of these case studies offers an illustration of the diversity of applications of digital scholarship, and in all instances the librarian, often in partnership and working collaboratively, is seen as an essential contributor.

The image of the librarian as 'agile' features across the following three chapters. The opportunities which new services present is a thread that flows throughout the chapters, and in Chapter 3 by Roz Howard and Megan Fitzgibbons its focus is on the potential of partnerships as a catalyst for the emergence of new roles which have the capacity to extend and enrich the profile and position of the profession. At the University of Western Australia the development of a multi-partner initiative to drive innovation in teaching and learning practices provided the Library service with an opportunity to reshape the role of the librarian, to further leverage pre-existing expertise in technology and digital literacy, and to apply and extend these into areas of curriculum development, learning design and learning systems. The power of these partnerships has the potential to dismantle pre-existing professional boundaries so as to create a new environment where librarians can transition their skills and expertise outside of the Library. This opportunity or necessity to forge new partnerships both individually and at a strategic level establishes the role of the Library in shaping and contributing to the future of its institution. The importance of grasping these opportunities is a key message which is revisited throughout the chapter and is presented as critical if librarians are to remain central and relevant to the university's vision for educational development.

The role of the librarian is further investigated by Charles Inskip in Chapter 4, which examines some of the key strengths and weaknesses of the profession operating within a digital environment. The need to recognize changes in the digital landscape, the emerging practices in support of digital scholarship and attendant digital literacies, require a suite of skills and competencies in which when it is surveyed, many librarians rank their own competency as novice. Inskip identifies projects and strategic approaches which have the potential to upskill librarians, ensuring that they have the confidence and digital capabilities to provide scholars with the advice and guidance required. The danger is that this is not regarded as a priority for investment and action, and that if these skills are not sufficiently developed users may go elsewhere for assistance or may not engage with the very systems, e.g. open access repositories, designed to support their digital scholarship. As staff costs will be the most expensive resource in an academic library, it is worth reflecting on whether skills gaps in key areas are limiting the capacity of the library to deliver its optimum services. As Heath has observed, 'Across all ARL libraries, personnel costs almost uniformly exceed the annual investment in resources for teaching, learning, and research. At the University of Texas, for example, in the last year for which data is available (2005), almost $20,000,000 was spent on personnel costs while $13,000,000 was invested in books, journals, and databases' (2006, 7).

How staff are deployed, the roles they undertake and how one academic library has refashioned its approach to service delivery is discussed in Chapter 5 by Jennifer Bremner. Focusing on Macquarie University Library, Bremner provides the reader with a strategic overview of how it has responded to the impact of digital scholarship on services and processes and examines how time and resources can be released through the use of lean methodologies. The principles of 'lean' focus on the customer and the practices which optimize the value and effectiveness of a process or service for the benefit of the customer. Employing a quality enhancement framework 'what we do matters', the university library has successfully engaged staff in cross-team working to improve staff skills, customer service, communication, co-operation and sharing of priorities. This fits in neatly with the view that academic libraries have to modify their service delivery and processes and (re)focus on their clients, systems and technologies, scholarly processes and learning environments if they are to be successful contributors to digital scholarship. The chapter selects a few processes to illustrate the positive impact of lean principles – reducing waste and improving perceptions of value are at the core, and are accompanied by the development of a workforce that is prepared and able to adapt and flex at speed – essential behaviours when responding to the changing digital environment.

The focus of the next two chapters shifts to examine the development of spaces and services which support digital scholarship. In Chapter 6 Tracy C. Bergstrom examines how the convergence of space and expertise across the USA has led to the formation of digital scholarship centres, many of which are located within a university library. The chapter considers the factors which have led to this and the importance of a library's reputation as a contributor to teaching and learning in new technology areas. The emergence of digital scholarship centres is also seen by many institutions as a reputational necessity and, as the factors which inform this view span departmental and disciplinary boundaries, the university library presents itself as a 'neutral' space. Bergstrom also draws attention to the fact that although the rationale which underpins the development of these centres across institutions may be similar, the services which are developed within centres are highly variable. Services may include planning digital projects, developing metadata, utilizing specialized software and tools, and the spaces may also include media production, digital visualization and 'makerspaces'. A case study focused on the development of a centre at the University of Notre Dame, Indiana provides an insight into the venture, the resources required and the benefits which can be accrued by the university library, in particular the opportunity to integrate librarians into scholars' research cycles utilizing existing expertise in new ways.

Constant attention to the need to remain relevant and extend the reach of the library to meet the needs of digital scholarship is a concern which is touched on by several contributors. In Chapter 7 David Clay examines the development of new roles and services that enable a library to become a successful partner in digital scholarship. Using the University of Salford as a case study, his focus is less on the development of physical space, but examines how digital and virtual services have been nurtured alongside the University's changing research agenda. The building blocks of robust technical infrastructures, supported by access to high-quality content and the ability to develop services which meet the needs of scholars, form the base. However, as Clay discusses, the challenge is to shift from delivering a collection-centric service to one which is largely based on engagement, working alongside scholars in the research process, providing consultancy and training as appropriate. Developing new services in support of digital scholarship is challenging, and recruiting staff with the appropriate skills base can prove problematic. Clay acknowledges all this, but provides the reader with insights into how one university has tackled the need to realign staff, services and resources so as to be better placed to deliver these services in an affordable and sustainable fashion.

The final section of the book is devoted to reviewing communication in a networked environment, looking at the role social media can play in forging new relationships and repositioning libraries and library services in the minds of their users. In Chapter 8 Suzanne Parfitt provides readers with a comprehensive review of the use of social networking sites by libraries and the methodologies used to measure the success or otherwise of their use. She explores in detail the approaches taken to engage users and the ways in which users engage with library services. Given the significance of the potential reach of social media, and in particular how it is being used, often ineffectively, as a communication tool to improve engagement with scholars, this chapter provides an objective assessment, based on the literature, of different approaches libraries could trial to ensure that investment in the use of social media delivers as far as possible an optimal impact.

In Chapter 9 Alison Hicks provides a structured and practical steer, based on her personal experience and informed by research, into the changing role of the librarian. Looking specifically at the concept of networked participation and paying particular attention to how the changing ideas of academic influence, reputation and identity impact on the traditional approaches to academic scholarship, Hicks explores the tensions that arise, and how the use of new technologies to build personal influence and reputation have a potentially disruptive (or emancipatory) impact on the research environment. Her focus is on the development of research practices, optimizing the use of Twitter, blogging platforms and social networking sites, with the aim of exposing researchers to new approaches to collaboration, profile building and reputational gain, while acknowledging the real fears associated with extensive public engagement and the accompanying risks. Focusing in on the activities at University of Colorado, Boulder, Hicks presents a persuasive argument for all librarians to become more actively involved in outreach activities, engaging their scholarly community in the use of social media, not simply as yet another set of tools, but with the aim of embedding their use into research workflows to promote an individual researcher's online identity, reputation and profile.

The upbeat tone of the final chapter to this book of contributed chapters presents a positive way forward for all librarians engaged in the support of digital scholarship. As Lankes (2014) comments,

> There is no one way to run or structure a library. The days when there was a single model for an academic library, if they ever existed, are gone. The idea that the academic library is a store house of books and materials is gone. The notion that a library can serve off to the side of the mission of the university is gone. What is needed today is a commitment by university administration and librarians to reinvent the whole concept of academic libraries.

Whether one concurs with this view or not, it is evident that the digital environment and the affordances of new technologies to open up research and new ways of working offer libraries and librarians opportunities to restate their value to their scholarly community and to continue to maintain their role as key contributors to the success of their institution's mission.

References

Ayers, E. (2012) *Discovery in a Digital World* [video], EDUCAUSE Annual Conference, 9 November.

Boyer, E. (1990) *Scholarship Reconsidered: priorities of the professoriate*, Princeton, NJ, Carnegie Foundation for the Advancement of Teaching.

Heath, F. (2006) *The University of Texas: looking forward. Research libraries in the 21st century*, www.lib.utexas.edu/symposium/symposium_white_paper.pdf.

Jones, C. (2013) Defining the Digital University. In Goodfellow, R. and Lea, M. (eds), *Literacy in the Digital University: critical perspectives on learning, scholarship, and technology*, London, Routledge.

Lankes, R. D. (2014) *Reinventing the Academic Library. Conclusion*, http://davidlankes.org/?p=6530.

Lynch, C. A. (2014) The 'Digital' Scholarship Disconnect, *EDUCAUSE Review*, **49** (3), 10–15.

Panitch, J. M. and Michalak, S. (2008) The Scholarly Work of Digital Libraries, *Journal of Library Administration*, **46** (1), 41–64.

Schlosser, M. (2013) Defining Digital Scholarship, [blog], *Digital Scholarship @ The Libraries*, https://library.osu.edu/blogs/digitalscholarship/2013/03/11/defining-digital-scholarship/.

Vinopal, J. and McCormick, M. (2013) Supporting Digital Scholarship in Research Libraries: scalability and sustainability, *Journal of Library Administration*, **53** (1), 27–42.

PART 1

A review of the landscape

1

The university library and digital scholarship: a review of the literature

Lindsey Martin

Introduction

Digital and web-based technologies have impacted on all aspects of daily life to the extent that it is almost becoming unnecessary to prefix terms with the word 'digital'. In the United Kingdom, the House of Lords Select Committee on Digital Skills concluded that the 21st century is experiencing a revolutionary period, which it calls the 'second machine age', driven by advances in digital technology to the extent that

> The whole economy has become digitised. It would be a mistake to take the 'digital sector' as our sole focus of interest. As digital is pervasive across most aspects of our lives, so the 'digital economy' is becoming synonymous with the national economy. Digital skills – the skills needed to interact with digital technologies – are life skills, necessary for most aspects of life.
>
> (Select Committee on Digital Skills, 2015, 20)

If digital is now the norm, then this suggests that there should no longer be any real distinction between scholarship and digital scholarship, and yet, according to Jones (2013) and Waters (2013), it is by no means a given that the use of new tools and technologies by scholars automatically results in digital scholarship. What technology does, they argue, is to create 'affordances' and 'possibilities' for new scholarly practices that scholars can then choose to make use of (Pearce et al., 2010; Weller, 2011; Goodfellow, 2013a; Scanlon, 2014).

The literature on the emergence, practices and impact of digital scholarship at the present time is neither broad nor deep. This review of the literature has revealed that there is little in the way of a shared understanding of what digital scholarship is, that there is a range of terminology and a variety of definitions dependent upon discipline and values, and that there is little that provides an insight into what it might mean to be a digital scholar in practice. Unsurprisingly, then, the role of libraries in responding to the emergence of digital scholarship practices offers a similarly slender literature of differing definitions and approaches to support for and engagement with scholars.

In order to gain a holistic view of the distance that has been travelled in the development of library support for digital scholarship, it was necessary to foreground any discussion of published work by and for librarians with that of the scholar's perspective: what does it mean to be a scholar in the digital age? Only by understanding the impact of the digital on our scholarly stakeholders can we begin to understand how well libraries have responded to the demands of digital scholarship, and to this end this review has identified three broad areas for investigation.

- What is scholarship?
- What is digital scholarship, and what are the scholarly practices associated with it?
- How have libraries and librarians repositioned themselves to better engage with and support digital scholarship and associated scholarly practices?

What is scholarship?

Whilst the activities and processes associated with undertaking scholarly work may vary according to discipline there is a general consensus that scholarship within an academic context is distinguished from other kinds of knowledge production by its shared values and behaviours, that 'it values critical reflection, the systematic and cumulative aggregation of knowledge and understanding over time, distinct modes of operation relating to the gathering of evidence and the warranting of its reliability, and the ethic of enquiry as a primary motivation' (Goodfellow, 2013b, 4).

Judging from this review of the literatures of scholarship and digital scholarship, the work that has seemingly had greatest influence in recent years is that of Ernest Boyer, a senior university administrator, who, using data gathered from more than 5000 academics, classified the types of activities that they regularly engage in. He was concerned about the evolution of a restricted view of scholarship that favoured research over other forms of scholarly activity, and his seminal work, *Scholarship Reconsidered*, on what it meant to be a scholar led him to conclude that there are four separate yet interdependent categories of scholarship: discovery, integration, application and teaching. His vision of an extended and inclusive view of scholarship argued for 'a recognition that knowledge is acquired through research, through synthesis, through practice and through teaching' (Boyer, 1990, 24). Boyer acknowledged that scholarship requires original research but that 'the work of the scholar also means stepping back from one's investigation, looking for connections, building bridges between theory and practice, and communicating one's knowledge effectively to students' (1990, 16). He argued that each of the four components should be valued equally.

Whilst it is frequently critiqued, Boyer's model continues to have resonance as a framework for understanding scholarly practice and is frequently used as the starting point for discussions around digital scholarship (Pearce et al., 2010; Weller, 2011; Veletsianos and Kimmons, 2012; Scanlon, 2014). Whilst Boyer's perspective was of the academic practices of individual scholars, his classifications continue to provide a useful benchmark for examining contemporary practices (Scanlon 2014). For ease of reference, Table 1.1 summarizes the activities that Boyer suggests are contained within the four components of scholarship.

Table 1.1 *Boyer as a framework for scholarly activity*

Discovery	Integration
Discovery is, for Boyer, what is usually referred to as 'research'. He describes discovery as disciplined, investigative efforts within the academy leading to the discovery of new knowledge.	Disciplined work across disciplines where fields converge that seeks to question, interpret, place one's own and others' research within a wider context and draw out new insights.
Application	**Teaching**
New intellectual understandings arise out of applying the outcomes of discovery to the real world – creating interactions between theory and practice that benefit government and society.	Beyond transmitting information to learners, teaching as scholarship is transformative through reading, activity, discussion. Teaching as scholarship shapes research and practice by extending the world view of both learner and teacher in creative new directions.

What is digital scholarship and its associated scholarly practices?

This review does not set out to recap the impact of digital and web-based technologies that has resulted in this 'information age', as this has been discussed widely elsewhere. It is, however, worth acknowledging the variable pace of technological adoption and change within what Pearce et al. (2010) describe as an inherently conservative higher education system. They caution that there have been 'extravagant claims about the transformational potential of computers' and that it is necessary to 'remain critical of much of the hyperbole surrounding new technologies, recognizing that previous technological revolutions have failed to transform most academic work'.

Nevertheless, it is fair to say that universities both as workplaces and as centres of scholarship have felt the impact of digital technologies. Pearce describes scholars' use of everyday web tools and technologies as pragmatic (Pearce, 2010). Weller (2011), however, argues that where the tools simply facilitate the 'business as usual' of publishing in traditional journals and creating teaching materials with PowerPoint, the digitally supported activity cannot, of itself, be considered digital scholarship. This, then, begs the question of to what extent digital scholarship can or should be regarded as an entity, as something separate from traditional scholarship.

According to Scanlon (2011), the nature of digital scholarship and the extent to which it has had an impact on scholarly practices is a contested area. Others describe the term digital scholarship as a 'catchall' or shorthand for a wide range of activities, attitudes and behaviours. Lynch (2014, 10) argues that 'the phrase is at some basic level nonsensical. After all, scholarship is scholarship. Doing science is doing science. We don't find the Department of Digital Physics arguing with the Department of Non-Digital Physics about who's doing real physics.'

So, whilst there is consensus that technologies have impacted on scholarly practices, there is no consensus among those scholars who are both engaged in and writing about it on what constitutes digital scholarship, and a large section of the literature on digital scholarship focuses on the use of technology within specific disciplines. Disciplinary differences are frequently portrayed as a binary divide between the disciplines. Scientists using specifically funded e-science tools use research groups for collaboration and networks of peers for support (Pearce, 2010), whereas humanists and social scientists, in contrast, are more likely to work alone, tending to rely on research-support professionals such as librarians as their primary collaborators (Goodfellow, 2013b). Pearce's (2010) review of the literature examining the factors that influence the adoption of technology by researchers reinforces the notion that they are a heterogeneous collection of individuals whose practices and workflows are strongly influenced by factors such as discipline, age and gender. Goodfellow (2013b, 4) also observes 'that the same characteristics of scholarship interpreted by different disciplinary and subject communities can give rise to distinctly different practices'.

However, the traditional notion of the lone humanities researcher has been challenged by the emergence of an area of activity known as the 'digital humanities', a term applied to initiatives involving 'digital libraries, visualisation, text mining, geographic information systems (GIS), multimedia, social networking, teaching with technology, open access and digital culture' (Rieger, 2010). Digital humanities projects are, by definition, 'collaborative, engaging humanists, technologists, librarians, social scientists, artists, architects, information scientists, and computer scientists in conceptualizing and solving problems, which often tend to be high-impact, socially-engaged, and of broad scope and duration' (Presner, 2009).

Weller (2011, 4) suggests that a simple definition of digital scholarship should be resisted, but that a useful starting point is 'someone who employs digital, networked and open approaches to demonstrate specialism in a field'. Goodfellow describes digital scholarship as 'the relatively recent invention of cross-disciplinary groups of individual scholars, particularly from education and the humanities who have begun to use technology to disseminate their own work outside of the formal academic publishing system' (2013b, 70) and Esposito (2013), describes research practices 'such as – information access, authoring, sharing, networking, publishing – mediated by technology'.

Digital scholarship as an ideology

Looking beyond the use of technology to support the scholarly day job in order to arrive at a definition of digital scholarship, Weller (2011) argues that it is only when three elements converge that scholarly practice has the potential to be transformed: digitization of content, networks (peers and content) and openness – which is both technical (open source software, APIs, standards) and values led (sharing of ideas, materials, data, discussions). Out of digitization, networks and openness, he suggests, it is openness that has the potential to be most disruptive in terms of changing existing practices. He goes on to extend his initial definition of digital scholarship as 'more than just using information and communication technologies to research, teach and collaborate; it also includes embracing the open values, ideology and potential of technologies born of peer-to-peer networking and wiki ways of working in order to benefit both the academy and society' (Weller, 2011, 50).

Those who adopt open practices are, according to Weller, adopting an increasingly political position. He goes on to describe principles that categorize openness and what is loosely considered to be the open 'movement', including being in favour of new rights, e.g. Creative Commons, and against proprietary copyright (Weller, 2011, 104). This ideological position is discussed further by Veletsianos and Kimmons, where they associate the 'movement' with the largely altruistic position that 'it is rooted in an ethical pursuit of democratisation, human rights, equality and justice' (2012, 181).

Burton (2009) makes his definition of open scholarship more personal but no less ideological. 'The Open Scholar, as I'm defining this person, is not simply someone who agrees to allow free access and reuse of his or her traditional scholarly articles and books; no, the open scholar is someone who makes their intellectual projects and processes digitally visible and who invites and encourages ongoing criticism of their work and secondary uses of any or all parts of it – at any stage of its development.'

The recipients of this discourse and these definitions appear to be an academic rather than a wider, popular audience, and it is largely but not exclusively confined to traditional academic publications where the focus is on the application of educational technology or alternative approaches to traditional educational practices. The discourse largely seeks to develop and, indeed, promote as a 'good thing' the ideas and values around open scholarly practices, including democratizing access to the scholarly output (Pearce, 2010; Pearce et al., 2010; Goodfellow, 2013b; Weller, 2011).

Scholarly 'islands of innovation' or large-scale transformation?
Whilst most of the authors discussed in this review confidently assert that there is a trajectory towards a digital, networked and open scholarly future, there are also warnings of the temptations of hyperbole. Goodfellow (2013a, 76–8) points out that 'Making a conventionally structured academic text accessible by publishing online for free does not, by itself, make the text more "open" in the sense of being more usable to a different or non-scholarly readership'. Rieger (2010) asserts that discussions by and about the digital humanities are 'spawning an ideology complete with advocates and pioneers' and suggests that there is a gap between how digital humanities pioneers are portrayed in the literature and those humanist scholars who continue with their traditional practice. This is supported by Weller (2011, 62), who, in an examination of recent studies exploring how researchers are using new technologies, concludes that technology adoption has been tentative, with only 'cautious experimentation'. He concludes that 'there are islands of innovation, but in general the attitude of the research community is one of caution and even occasional hostility'.

So, what can we learn from studies of how scholars are using technology? Rieger (2010), from the perspective of the digital humanities, is critical of published studies which she states 'tend to be descriptive and are often written in the form of self-ethnographies on the part of pioneers or advocates of digital humanities, illustrating how technologies are being used and their benefits and transformative nature'. Pearce's (2010) review of the literature found much that was dated, looking at scholars' engagement with more traditional technologies such as e-mail, subject repositories and groupware. He found few recent studies that examined how researchers engaged with Web 2.0 technologies, with his most recent example having been published in 2008. It can also be argued that this is true of the literature relating to digital and open scholarship, and this view is supported by Veletsianos and Kimmons (2012), who found few empirical studies to provide insight into digital, networked and open practices; and, indeed, this review has found little evidence of empirical studies and discovered nothing published after 2013.

Only five empirical studies of scholars' engagement with technology emerged from a trawl of the literature from 2010 to 2016. It is acknowledged that there may be others, and more recent, but, if so, they were not revealed by the discovery tools, databases and search engines used in the search. The largest study was a survey of 292 academic staff and research students undertaken by Pearce in 2007. Whilst he found limited evidence for disciplinary difference, he nevertheless found that 'the survey does still suggest that the heterogeneity suggested by the literature review does exist within a single institution, and the web and e-science tools are being pragmatically used by researchers when it enhances their research practice, collaboration or helps raise their public and professional profile' (Pearce, 2010, 1204).

The remaining four studies are small-scale and qualitative, and their authors caution against making generalizations from such small samples. They do, however, provide some insight into the mindsets and practices of the scholar participants. Studies undertaken by Rieger (2010) and Esposito (2013) sought to investigate the 'actual' digital research practices of scholars in order to add to what is known about this under-researched area. Rieger's (2010) study tracking 45 scholars over 22 months sought to better understand the different perspectives and daily practices of scholars engaged in digital humanities. She found that their daily academic practices had not significantly changed other than to incorporate commonly used tools such as search engines into their workflows and that they were not prepared to learn about or use new technologies 'unless they perceived a discernible benefit'. She concluded that her participants' routine practices occur in a heterogeneous ecology of analog and digital settings, tools and content'.

Esposito (2013) similarly aimed 'to understand whether evolving research practices enabled by technologies are merely improvements of pre-existing ways of enquiry conduct or whether they are disruptive breaks against tradition (e.g., open access repositories), which should be regulated and supported'. She found that the majority of her 14 subjects, who were distributed over four subject areas, were 'traditionally "digital", moderately "networked" and occasionally 'open'". Furthermore, most of her sample did not identify any clear benefits that would encourage them to adopt newer technologies or open practices, especially 'in the absence of information, institutional support, new rules within their own disciplines and any acknowledgement by peers'.

Scanlon (2014) and Costa's (2013) studies differ from those of Rieger and Esposito in that their subjects were chosen because they appeared to operate as digital scholars and could therefore offer some insight into how academic practice is being changed by technology. Both cases described the adoption of digital scholarship as a 'mindset' with a commitment to openness and open access as key to their practice. Scanlon (2014) studied 22 academics with expertise in educational technology and found that they tended to use technology to network and communicate with peers and to use a variety of publication formats from self-published blogs to formal journal articles and conference proceedings. She observed that the academics she interviewed were pragmatic, acknowledging that their publication practices were influenced by the UK Research Excellence Framework (REF) and the importance it placed on citation rates.

Costa studied ten researchers who were actively involved in what she terms the 'participatory web', which she describes as 'a set of digital communicating networks, applications and environments on which individuals act as active participants, contributors, and co-creators of information, knowledge and opinions' (2013, 1). She found that her participants' approaches to open practices in networking, communicating and publishing were characterized by their support for the open access movement, framing openness mainly within the context of publication in open access journals and alternative forms of publishing such as blogging that give others access to the process as well as the output of scholarly activity. Costa observes that her 'research participants are evoking their professional values that distinguish them from their immediate colleagues, given that they don't "feel like the people in [their] department"' (2013, 11). It is interesting to note that in Costa's study there are no references to pragmatism or to blended approaches to openness and formal publishing practices and to the tensions that may occur when the participants' values come into conflict with their institution's expectations regarding publication, engagement and impact.

Policy, incentives, pragmatism shaping scholarly practices

Whilst the small number of empirical studies into digital scholarship practices and the small sample sizes make generalizations unwise, they seem to paint a picture of scholars who are broadly in favour of open and networked digital practices but who publish their research where it will gain them the largest number of citations; who take a pragmatic approach to using technology where they can see a discernible, personal benefit. Despite technology use, the studies describe research practices that remain largely unchanged since Houghton. Steele amd Henty wrote how they were 'directly shaped by systems of evaluation, changing funding patterns and priorities. Existing evaluation and reward structures tend to lead to conflicting incentives in relation to scientific and scholarly communication' (2003, xi).

Weller observes that 'as with all such exercises they significantly shape behaviour, and do not simply measure it, so the message researchers may have gained from their institution that the exploration of new approaches is discouraged becomes reinforced at a national level', and that 'a cautious approach is therefore not surprising as researchers seek to understand where the potential of these new tools can enhance their practice, while simultaneously maintaining the key characteristics of quality research' (2011, 55). Scanlon (2014) also suggests that the reasons why many scholars might not engage with new technologies or open practices are due to the lack of encouragement within institutions, funding and evaluative bodies – for example, the REF in the United Kingdom, which still measures impact from metrics derived from the publication of research outputs in peer-reviewed journals. In the USA, issues around tenure seemingly impact on how far individual scholars adopt digital, networked and open practices.

Lankes (2014) describes it thus: 'Now a good part of this is a factor of being a tenured full professor. I have the liberty to publish in alternative venues than peer reviewed journals. I have the liberty to experiment with self-publishing.'

Does open data have the potential to change research practices?

Whilst scholarly publishing in academic journals remains the key means for determining researcher and research impact whether with traditional publishers or open access, the underlying data is becoming increasingly valuable in its own right. Davidson (2014) describes how a number of funding bodies in the USA and UK require data management plans to be submitted at the grant proposal stage to ensure that publicly funded research data remains accessible and reusable. She also notes that publishers are increasingly mandating that the underlying data be made available to peer reviewers and, upon request, to readers of the article. Noting that compliance with institutional, funders' and publishers' policies is not usually considered an attractive incentive for changing practices, Davidson describes Piwowar's research, which has revealed the significant benefit that 'researchers who share well managed and curated data can expect an increase of up to 69% in the number of citations they receive compared with those who do not' (Piwowar et al., 2007 in Davidson, 2014, 89).

Weller (2011), drawing on Boyer's description of discovery of new knowledge, discusses how his definition of digital scholarship as open, digital and networked could relate to the sharing of data in a way that was not possible previously and lead to changing research practices. Data itself has become a research output and digital datasets can be applied in contexts that were never envisaged by the original researchers. It can provide new insights by being combined with data from different fields and disciplines. According to Schmiede (2009), there are numerous examples of data availability and application in sciences and humanities but we do not yet have a realistic overview of instances and volume. Furthermore, the extent to which researchers are sharing data across academic disciplines is not yet clear (Goodfellow, 2013b) and there is, as yet, little guidance on how open data can be used (Atenas and Havemann, 2015). Davidson (2014, 83) asserts that 'there is a widespread lack of understanding and uncertainty about open access and self-archiving across the research communities'.

Scholars writing about open data tend to discuss it primarily in relation to its production, storage, licensing and accessibility, but there is little discussion about how it might be used thereafter. A series of illuminating case studies describe how open datasets can be applied in the scholarship of teaching and aim to justify the assertion that

> Students who are exposed to the use of Open Data have access to the same raw materials that scientists and policy makers use. This enables them to engage with real problems at

both local and global levels. Educators who make use of Open Data in teaching and learning encourage students to think as researchers, as journalists, as scientists, and as policy makers and activists.

(Atenas and Havemann, 2015, 23–4)

Have we learnt anything about digital scholars and their practices?

What we know is that the practices of digital scholars are an under-researched area. Whilst all scholars use technology to some extent, they tend to make pragmatic choices about which tools they investigate and invest time and effort in learning to use. Scholarly practices are shaped by disciplinary culture, institutional policies, reputational and financial incentives and external measures of esteem. Those who consider themselves to be digital scholars tend to adopt practices that match their personal values around openness and shape their scholarly identity. The types of digital tools and technologies used in the scholarly process and discussed by digital scholars are not the large-scale systems and infrastructures. There is a preference to use technology that encourages experimentation because it is usually free (or freemium) and outside formal institutional collections of paid-for, managed and supported tools. It is technology that is quick to set up, easy to learn and does not, in theory, require a training course or approval to set it up.

It is also interesting to note that within the literature identified in this review those digital scholars writing about their own practices, and those revealed through empirical research, make almost no reference to libraries, librarians and the skills, expertise and support they can offer. Rieger (2010), in contrast to Weller's view of scholars making use of easy, fast and free technologies, argues that 'For humanities scholars who are interested in engaging with ICTs, their institutions need to support this incentive with customized applications and services (such as those offered by digital humanities centres, libraries, learning and teaching centres, and academic technology units) so that scholars can continue to spend more time on research or teaching than trying to understand, manage, or sustain technologies'. It should be noted, however, that Rieger is a librarian for digital scholarship services at Cornell University Library and, whilst she is a scholar in her own right, is also closely attuned to the library agenda.

The other positive reference to libraries as enablers of digital scholarship is found in the guidelines provided by the American Historical Association (AHA), where historians using digital methodologies are advised that 'Most colleges and universities have staff in place whose job it is to monitor and promote new technologies. Librarians, in particular, have long been involved in professional conversations regarding new technologies of teaching and scholarship. Many of them will be delighted to hold workshops and address faculty in groups or as individuals' (AHA, 2015, 4–5). Whilst this is a pleasing endorsement of library and librarian expertise, its suggestion of an ad hoc approach to and from libraries does not suggest that they have yet had a wide impact upon this agenda in a strategic manner.

How have libraries repositioned themselves to respond to digital scholarship?

This section does not seek to revisit the changes wrought by digital technologies on academic libraries, as this has been undertaken widely elsewhere. Instead, it will focus on how academic libraries are responding to changes in research and researcher behaviours as a result of the impact on their workflows and outputs, from national and institutional changes to evaluation, policies and funding, as well as the adoption of technologies.

There is a striking similarity between the literature written by scholars on the emergence of digital scholarship and that written by librarians, in that there is limited research to provide an evidence-based understanding of practice. Much of what is written is what Schmiede (2009, 625) describes as having 'an essayist character rather than the shape of a solidly empirically and theoretically based analysis'. Apart from the work of Esposito (2013), the literature does not reveal librarians gaining a research-informed, direct understanding of the behaviours and workflows of researchers, nor does it show librarians engaging with the debate in the wider sphere of scholarly publishing beyond library and information science journals.

Both Schmiede (2009) and Borgman (2007) have identified that much of the library literature has focused on the importance of infrastructure – for example, research repositories. Schmiede observes that 'infrastructure is technology-based and/or institutionally based, but not shaped by and aligned to the varieties of the many scholarly cultures' (2009, 627). Discussion around developments and challenges with infrastructure that include digital collections, large-scale digitization projects and institutional repositories have been summarized elsewhere (Heath, 2006; Curtis et al., 2011), where it is clear that academic libraries have long been aware of their need to change and stay relevant in response to the disruptive influence of funding changes, rising costs and technologies.

Despite an awareness of the need for change, it would seem that there is much still to be done. However, the evidence to support this view is limited, drawing almost exclusively from a few large-scale library surveys, case study exemplars of digital scholarship projects or service initiatives, literature reviews and opinion pieces. Nevertheless, four recurrent themes have been identified:

- the emergence of digital scholarship centres
- changing roles, new roles and the emerging skills gap

- moving from a service model to engagement, partnership and collaboration with scholars
- strategy and leadership: balancing sustainable practices and innovation.

Shared spaces on campus: digital scholarship centres

Bryson et al. (2011) produced a frequently cited report for the Association of Research Libraries (ARL). The survey it conducted provided a snapshot of research library experiences of digital scholarship centres or services that support the humanities. With a response rate of 51% (64 out of 126 libraries completed the survey), its key findings were that this is an area of library activity that is mostly policy 'light', with staffing and support provided in an ad hoc manner. However, as demand for services supporting the digital humanities grows, many respondents expressed a desire to implement practices, policies and procedures that would allow them to manage expectations and cope with increased demand for services. The survey also provided a snapshot of digital scholarship centres and associated support services:

  5 (8%) libraries host a digital humanities centre
  30 (48%) provide ad hoc services
  15 (24%) host a multi-discipline digital scholarship centre
  4 (6%) reported no digital scholarship services offered at their institution.

Zhang, Liu and Mathews (2015) and Sula (2013) observe differences between where USA and European digital humanities centres are located on campuses. In the USA, nearly half of all such centres are located within libraries, and a further quarter maintain some form of relationship with libraries. In Europe (especially the UK), these centres are less likely to be located in libraries, and few mention libraries as collaborators.

Sinclair (2014) describes the inspiring work of 12 library-based digital scholarship 'incubators' in the USA and discusses the opportunities these spaces offer to all stakeholders, including undergraduates. He argues that such collective spaces engineer the serendipitous, interdisciplinary interactions that generate the creative thinking and innovation that are encouraged both by the big technology companies such as Google and by smaller, entrepreneurial start-up hubs.

Changing library roles, new roles and skills gaps

In describing the challenges of operating a digital scholarship centre, Sinclair (2014) argues that as a starting point, 'professional development opportunities must be there for existing personnel to adopt new skills and talents'. He goes on to write that at his university they 'rely extensively on bright student assistants'. It is interesting to note that in those universities with services aimed at supporting digital scholarship, the literature reveals the emergence of new, hybrid roles. Bakkalbasi, Jaggars and Rockenbach, for example, describe how Colombia's digital centres offer consultation services 'provided by librarians, technologists and student interns'. They have also created digital scholarship co-ordinator roles 'filled by recent PhD recipients who bring deep research and teaching expertise from the disciplines they support' (2015, 209).

Vandegrift and Varner (2013) observe that 'while the presence of scholar-librarians is not particularly new, the current crop of so-called Alt-Acs (alternative academics) is increasingly being called upon to occupy the space between the library and academic departments and serve as digital ambassadors and experimental researchers' (71). They also describe how alternative library roles such as 'digital humanities librarians, data librarianship, E-science, digital archivists, project-based appointments etc. is building the capacity for the library to be productively integrated into digital scholarship' (74). Zhang, Jaggars and Rockenbach also observe that support for digital scholarship will impact on library roles, blurring the lines between scholar, library and technical roles to the extent that 'looking ahead we will need hybrid professionals who possess both subject knowledge and technical expertise' (2015, 373).

The literature reveals a few vivid examples of innovative digital scholarship projects driven by libraries: Panitch and Michalak (2008) reflect on the scholarly work of their library in two contrasting digitization projects and relate their work to Boyer's concept of scholarship. Also of note are the University of Michigan library case studies that describe harnessing publishing as a pedagogical tool by connecting scholarly publishing and information literacy, working with undergraduate students in the process of publication and not simply with the product. Finally, Pun (2015) describes New York Public Library's projects that explore how librarians are utilizing the outputs of digitization projects to teach new data literacy skills such as data analysis and data management.

There is, then, some agreement that as a result of the changing research agenda and research workflows new library roles are emerging and existing roles are changing. It is argued, however, that the greatest impact of the digital scholarship agenda is on the subject librarian, a traditionally academic- and student-facing role. To this end, the publication *Re-skilling for Research* published by Research Libraries UK (RLUK) took this group as its focus because 'To date, Subject Librarians have supported the needs of researchers through relatively traditional services revolving around information discovery, collection development and some elements of information management' (Auckland, 2012, 2). Auckland's study included a survey of 169 subject librarians and their managers from 22 RLUK libraries and reviewed the skill sets of subject librarians against the emerging research needs of scholars, noting that

> A shift can be seen which takes Subject Librarians into a world beyond information discovery and management, collection development and information literacy training, to one in which they play a much greater part in the research process and in particular in the management, curation and preservation of research data, and in scholarly communication and the effective dissemination of research outputs.
>
> (Auckland, 2012, 5)

The study identified 32 skills and areas of knowledge that subject librarians need now, or will do in the future. Also revealed were gaps in nine key areas where involvement is required now and where demand is predicted to grow sharply, and it is interesting to note that four of the nine areas relate to data management in some form or another.

In the UK, a group of key stakeholders sponsoring the Libraries of the Future project argue that the issue of changing staff roles is not *if* but *when*. The project, which created scenarios to support strategic planning for a near-future of potentially disruptive challenges, predicted that

> at some point beyond 2020, the scenarios all suggest that the role of librarians will have changed radically (e.g. the embedding of specialist librarians as a team member within a research group or teaching and learning group, and the potential diversity of specialist librarian roles and skills) and they also pose these questions 'What is the set of skills and experience required of the librarians and how will this be met (e.g. recruitment, retention, redundancies, training)? What needs to be done to develop the skills of the current staff?'
>
> (Curtis et al., 2011, 22)

However, Auckland's (2012, 78) study noted that 'no obvious sources for the provision of this training and development were uncovered, and it is likely that new partnerships between research libraries, RLUK and various training providers will need to be forged to fully capitalise on the deployment of those people that already have the required skills and are able to impart them to others'.

There is, fortunately, some evidence in the literature of training and development programmes to ensure that librarians are able to meet the changing demands of digital scholarship on their roles (Posner, 2013; Davidson, 2014; Bakkalbasi, Jaggars and Rockenbach, 2015; Johnson et al., 2015; Zhang, Liu and Mathews, 2015). It is also possible, as suggested by Auckland (2012), that as much work has been done in recent years to re-energize involvement with learning and teaching, this slender literature on the role and skills of the subject librarian is supplemented in discussions elsewhere; for example, in relation to skills required for teaching information literacy, and working in multi-professional teams (Martin, 2008).

From service and support to engagement, partnership and collaboration

Dempsey (2013) writes about the challenge of greater engagement with users. For him, engagement is about libraries reallocating resource and effort to better engage with the learning and research lives of their users in order to add value, 'making research more productive and research outputs more visible'. There is some case study evidence in the literature that this is happening, particularly with reference to the introduction of digital scholarship centres and project work as discussed in a previous section. What is missing, however, is evidence of how librarians are deepening their engagement in scholarly workflows and of the added value or impact of that engagement. In spite of this, there are recommendations for practice drawn from experience that include: using marketing segmentation techniques and business intelligence to support outreach work (Wolski and Richardson, 2014); surveying user needs whether formally or informally (Sula, 2013); leaving the library, literally and virtually, to speak to researchers – attending events, joining networks and committees (Vandegrift and Varner, 2013; Zhang, Jaggars and Rockenbach, 2015). There are also tantalizing references to 'embedded' librarians who have left the library to work in other centres or faculties (Curtis et al., 2011; Auckland, 2012; Sula, 2013).

There are also words of caution amongst the advice. Marcum (2014) questions whether librarians fully understand what their users want and need. Posner (2013) is concerned that individuals who engage can become over-extended and become in danger of burn-out without top-down interventions and resourcing. Furthermore, Posner goes on to argue that librarians must learn to reframe their thinking away from service and support to partnership and collaboration, as 'the service-and-support approach, in which a scholar brings an idea to the library to build, often results in a less than optimal outcome' (2013, 46). Vandegrift and Varner see librarians' 'timidity', 'academic inferiority complex' and 'vocation of servitude' as being the key challenge to successfully engaging and collaborating with scholars (2013, 76).

Strategy and leadership: balancing sustainability and innovation

Much of the survey and case study evidence that provides a picture of how digital scholarship is supported in academic libraries points to an ad hoc approach to service provision and resourcing (Bryson et al., 2011; Posner, 2013). Marcum (2014) cites a 2010 Ithaka S+R survey of US academic library directors of whom nearly two-thirds reported that their libraries had not undertaken sufficient strategic planning to meet user needs and manage collections in the digital era. Whilst there are clearly case studies of innovative and forward-thinking services and practices in libraries, the overall message is of the significant challenges that libraries face in order to appear relevant to scholars. The findings of the 2015 *NMC Horizon Report* for libraries concur with this view, predicting that 'these centers for higher learning will become increasingly active, experiential environments where social, participatory, and collaborative interactions are at the forefront' and that, as a result, 'library leadership and missions must prioritize the continuous creation of innovative offerings' (Johnson et al., 2015, 30). Auckland acknowledges the scale of the challenges but offers reassurance that these could be reframed as opportunities 'by developing a unique role in consultation with their institution for the part they will play in the support of meeting researchers' information and related needs' (2012, 78).

Dempsey's (2013) observations on change are that 'emergent areas live beside established practices' and that it is at times difficult to determine which emergent areas are and will remain experimental, as compared to those that are sustainable (capable of being maintained over time) and scalable (can benefit as many other library users as possible). In terms of developing new services and staffing models, however, the literature revealed a recurring theme that libraries must also decide at a strategic, team and individual level what is no longer a priority and can be discontinued in order to redirect time or resource to new areas of importance (Dempsey, 2013; Posner, 2013; Vandegrift and Varner, 2013; Vinopal and McCormick, 2013).

These notions of sustainability and scalability have been elaborated by Vinopal and McCormick (2013) into a high-level service model describing how a library might organize support for digital scholarship. Such an approach, they argue, would avoid ad hoc projects that risk narrow-focused or short-lived solutions (unsustainable) and cannot be repurposed to benefit others (not scalable). The model and its potential for application are a valuable contribution to the literature on this topic and are discussed in greater detail in Chapter 2.

Concluding thoughts

As is evidenced in the literature, librarians have long been aware of the challenges posed by digital scholarship and there is clearly interesting work going on at institutional and practitioner level; however, there are too few critically reflective studies that evidence how, together, strategic leadership, new service models and innovative practice that is sustainable and/or scalable are having a real impact within their institutions.

Despite the limitations of the literature written by digital scholars and scholarly librarians, it is possible to highlight both the challenges and opportunities that academic libraries are facing. What is surprising is (i) that scholars are seemingly unaware of librarians' expertise and are uninformed about library services available to them, to the extent that they bypass the library as a source of support; (ii) that alternative service providers to libraries and librarians are emerging (Auckland, 2012); and (iii) that librarians tend not to fully understand what their scholars need (Lankes, 2014; Marcum, 2014). Certainly, there appears to be no exchange of ideas through the traditional channels of scholarly communication, as each tends to publish in academic journals aimed at their own kind. There is an opportunity here for librarians to publish case studies and other research in journals that can engage with a wider, scholarly debate as well as amongst themselves.

Whilst this literature review can offer only a snapshot of how libraries are responding to the demands of digital scholarship, there is a recurrent theme of ad hoc-ness in how service models and staff roles develop. Aside from the work of Vinopal and McCormick (2013), there is a significant gap in how libraries are documenting how they support digital innovation, scholarly activity and librarians' skills development in a strategic and systematic manner, which must be addressed.

Table 1.2 *Digital scholarship activity across Boyer's framework*

Discovery	Integration
New insights, cross-discipline, new knowledge created Sharing of data-sets and related activity: management, analysis, visualization Digitization of primary sources Networking and virtual communities of practice Visual and data literacy	Publishing models, open publication, peer review Collaborative working on texts, e.g. blogging Open access repositories for scholarly outputs and data Digital scholarship centres and makerspaces
Application	**Teaching**
Public engagement and influence via social media – blogs, Twitter, YouTube Personal 'brand', online persona and 'voice' – and identity management	Information literacy and digital skills Reproducible and sharable open educational resources and open data Open educational practices Digitization of primary sources Discoverability, discovery tools and repositories Undergraduate scholarship – students as producers – publishing

Nevertheless, to return to Boyer's (1990) framework for scholarly activity, Table 1.2 attempts to synthesize (i) what has been learnt to date about scholars' behaviours and workflows, and (ii) where libraries are already adding value to these workflows. It is encouraging to note that such activity and, indeed, librarians' involvement does extend across all four areas of scholarship.

References

AHA (2015) *Guidelines for the Professional Evaluation of Digital Scholarship by Historians*, AHA ad hoc Committee on Professional Evaluation of Digital Scholarship by Historians, American Historical Association.

Atenas, J. and Havemann, L. (eds) (2015) *Open Data as Open Educational Resources: case studies of emerging practice*, London, Open Knowledge, Open Education Working Group, http://education.okfn.org/files/2015/11/Book-Open-Data-as-Open-Educational-Resources1.pdf.

Auckland, M. (2012) *Re-skilling for Research: an investigation into the role and skills of subject and liaison librarians required to effectively support the evolving information needs of researchers*, Research Libraries UK, www.rluk.ac.uk/wp-content/uploads/2014/02/RLUK-Re-skilling.pdf.

Bakkalbasi, N., Jaggars, D. and Rockenbach, B. (2015) Re-skilling for the Digital Humanities: measuring skills, engagement, and learning, *Library Management*, **36** (3), 208–14.

Borgman, C. L. (2007) *Scholarship in the Digital Age: information, infrastructure, and the internet*, Cambridge MA, MIT Press.

Boyer, E. (1990) *Scholarship Reconsidered: priorities of the professoriate*, Princeton, NJ, Carnegie Foundation for the Advancement of Teaching.

Bryson, T., Posner, M., St Pierre, A. and Varner, S. (2011) *SPEC Kit 326. Digital humanities*, American Research Libraries, www.arl.org/storage/documents/publications/spec-326-web.pdf.

Burton, G. (2009) The open scholar, (11 August), www.academicevolution.com/2009/08/the-open-scholar.html.

Costa, C. (2013) The Habitus of Digital Scholars, *Research in Learning Technology*, **21**, 1–17.

Curtis, G., Davies, C., Hammond, M., Hawtin, R., Ringland, G. and Yapp, C. (2011) *Academic Libraries of the Future: how to use the scenarios*, sponsored by British Library, Jisc, the Research Information Network (RIN), Research Libraries UK (RLUK) and the Society of College, National and University Libraries (SCONUL).

Davidson, J. (2014) Supporting Early-career Researchers in Data Management and Curation. In Mackenzie, A. and Martin, L. (eds), *Mastering Digital Librarianship: strategy, networking and discovery in academic libraries*, London, Facet Publishing, 83–102.

Dempsey, L. (2013) *Three Challenges: engaging, rightscaling and innovating*, http://orweblog.oclc.org/three-challenges-engaging-rightscaling-and-innovating/.

Esposito, A. (2013) Neither Digital nor Open. Just researchers. Views on digital/open scholarship practices in an Italian university, *First Monday*, **18** (1), http://firstmonday.org/ojs/index.php/fm/article/view/3881/3404.

Goodfellow, R. (2013a) The Literacies of Digital Scholarship – truth and use values. In Goodfellow, R. and Lea, M. (eds), *Literacy in the Digital University: critical perspectives on learning, scholarship and technology*, London, Routledge, 67–78.

Goodfellow, R. (2013b) Scholarly, Digital, Open: an impossible triangle? *Research in Learning Technology,* **21**, 1–15.

Heath, F. (2006) *The University of Texas: looking forward. Research libraries in the 21st century,* www.lib.utexas.edu/symposium/symposium_white_paper.pdf.

Houghton, J., Steele, C. and Henty, M. (2003) *Changing Research Practices in the Digital Information and Communication Environment,* Technical Report, Department of Education, Science and Training, Canberra, Australia, http://eprints.vu.edu.au/456/.

Johnson, L., Adams Becker, S., Estrada, V. and Freeman, A. (2015) *NMC Horizon Report: 2015 library edition,* Austin, TX, The New Media Consortium, www.nmc.org/publication/nmc-horizon-report-2015-library-edition/.

Jones, C. (2013) Defining the Digital University. In Goodfellow, R. and Lea, M. (eds), *Literacy in the Digital University: critical perspectives on learning, scholarship, and technology,* London, Routledge, 162–72.

Lankes, R. D. (2014) *On Productivity: introducing a blog series on reinventing the academic library,* http://davidlankes.org/?p=6510.

Lynch, C. A. (2014) The 'Digital' Scholarship Disconnect, *EDUCAUSE Review,* **49** (3), 10–15.

Marcum, D. (2014) The Digital Transformation of Information, Education, and Scholarship, *International Journal of Humanities and Arts Computing,* **8** (supplement), 1–11.

Martin, L. (2008) Transforming Ourselves: developing the multiprofessional team. In Weaver, M. (ed.), *Transformative Learning Support Models in Higher Education: educating the whole student,* London, Facet Publishing.

Panitch, J. M. and Michalak, S. (2008) The Scholarly Work of Digital Libraries, *Journal of Library Administration,* **46** (1), 41–64.

Pearce, N. (2010) A Study of Technology Adoption by Researchers, *Information, Communication & Society,* **13** (8), 1191–206.

Pearce, N., Weller, M., Scanlon, E. and Kinsley, S. (2010) Digital Scholarship Considered: how new technologies could transform academic work, *in education,* **16** (1), 33–44.

Posner, M. (2013) No Half Measures: overcoming common challenges in doing digital humanities in the library, *Journal of Library Administration,* **53**, 43–52.

Presner, T. (2009) Digital Humanities 2.0: a report on knowledge, *Connexions,* http://cnx.org/contents/J0K7N3xH@6/Digital-Humanities-20-A-Report.

Pun, R. (2015) Conceptualizing the Integration of Digital Humanities in Instructional Services: possibilities to enhance digital literacy in the 21st century, *Library Hi Tech,* **33** (1), 134–42.

Rieger, O. (2010) Framing Digital Humanities: the role of new media in humanities scholarship, *First Monday,* **15** (10), http://firstmonday.org/ojs/index.php/fm/article/view/3198/2628.

Scanlon, E. (2011) Digital Futures: changes in scholarship, open educational resources and the inevitability of interdisciplinarity. *Arts and Humanities in Higher Education,* **11** (1–2), 77–84.

Scanlon, E. (2014) Scholarship in the Digital Age: open educational resources, publication and public engagement, *British Journal of Educational Technology*, **45** (1), 12–23.

Schmiede, R. (2009) Upgrading Academic Scholarship: challenges and chances of the digital age, *Library Hi Tech*, **27** (4), 624–33.

Select Committee on Digital Skills (2015) *Make or Break: the UK's digital future*, House of Lords Select Committee on Digital Skills, Report of Session 2014–15, www.publications.parliament.uk/pa/ld201415/ldselect/lddigital/111/111.pdf.

Sinclair, B. (2014) The University Library as Incubator for Digital Scholarship, *EDUCAUSE Review Online*, http://er.educause.edu/articles/2014/6/the-university-library-as-incubator-for-digital-scholarship.

Sula, C. A. (2013) Digital Humanities and Libraries: a conceptual model, *Journal of Library Administration*, **53** (1), 10–26.

Vandegrift, M. and Varner, S. (2013) Evolving in Common: creating mutually supportive relationships between libraries and the digital humanities, *Journal of Library Administration*, **53** (1), 67–78.

Veletsianos, G. and Kimmons, R. (2012) Assumptions and Challenges of Open Scholarship, *International Review of Research in Open and Distance Learning*, **13** (4), 166–89.

Vinopal, J. and McCormick, M. (2013) Supporting Digital Scholarship in Research Libraries: scalability and sustainability, *Journal of Library Administration*, **53** (1), 27–42.

Waters, D. J. (2013) Digital Humanities and the Changing Digital Ecology of Scholarly Communications, *International Journal of Humanities and Arts Computing*, **7**, Supplement, 13–28.

Weller, M. (2011) *The Digital Scholar: how technology is transforming scholarly practice*, London, Bloomsbury Academic.

Wolski, M. and Richardson, J. (2014) A Model for Institutional Infrastructure to Support Digital Scholarship, *Publications*, **2** (4), 83–99.

Zhang, Y., Liu, S. and Mathews, E. (2015) Convergence of Digital Humanities and Digital Libraries, *Library Management*, **36** (4/5), 362–77.

2

Digital scholarship: scanning library services and spaces

Alison Mackenzie

How is digital scholarship supported in practice? This chapter aims to respond to this question, informed by the results of a small-scale survey of 20 UK and Irish Higher Education (HE) libraries carried out in January 2016. The quantitative data generated by the survey is supplemented by a small number of case studies to provide a more detailed view of individual institutions' activities. The survey's aim was to capture the extent to which libraries are engaged with a range of services and systems associated with digital scholarship. Responses were gathered from institutions ranging from research intensive to small specialist, from different mission groups and locations.

The survey considered the impact a technology-rich learning and research environment has on the role of the library and, conversely, how libraries are optimizing their contribution to emerging digital practices and how this is helping to develop new expertise. It is evident that the skills librarians are developing are often in response to emerging service needs alongside new uses of library spaces, as Sinclair (2014) comments:

> Although the library incubator can be a catalyst, it is up to all of us – librarians, faculty, central IT staff, senior administrators, leading IT thinkers, alumni, and citizens, as well as our funding agencies and professional associations – to work together to encourage, promote, and support new forms of open scholarship over the more closed and insular forms of discourse from the past.

The context for the survey drew on the work of Vinopal and McCormick (2013), who in their article 'Digital Scholarship in Research Libraries' included a model for the delivery of scalable and sustainable services in support of digital scholarship. The model emerged from research, observation of trends and interviews with peer US institutions. The principles underpinning it have been adapted and reworked to fit the UK and Irish HE context and were used as a basis for the survey questions.

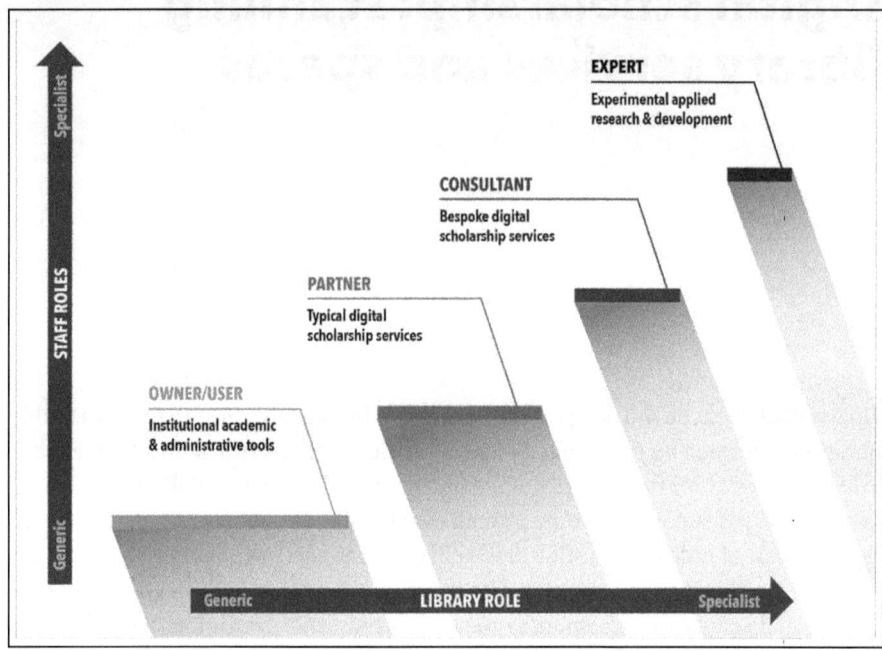

Figure 2.1 *Library engagement with digital scholarship services and systems*

The approach taken by Vinopal and McCormick places emphasis 'on developing, maintaining and integrating standard tools, platforms, and support services for a large community of users' and, as such, stresses the importance of scalability, reuse and impact. In recognizing the significance of scale in potential areas of high investment, the framework illustrates a strategic approach to the development of a coherent and systematic infrastructure in support of digital scholarship.

Of equal significance is the role libraries play in partnership with other professional and academic services within and beyond individual institutions and their contribution to the development of a strategic vision for digital scholarship at an institutional level (see Figure 2.1). Although it is self-evident, it is perhaps worth repeating that the menu of services and resources sitting under the banner of 'digital scholarship' will be informed by local mission, research expertise and interests. In turn, the external drivers of change – political, social and cultural – alongside digital developments will continue to transform scholarly practice.

Section one of the survey initially looked at institution-wide business systems and services with applications relevant to digital scholarship and asked respondents to identify whether their library/information service is the system 'owner' (is responsible for) or a user, where the system is available. The systems identified are described in Table 2.1.

Table 2.1 Ownership/use of institutional business/enterprise systems (where available)			
System	Owner/20	User/20	Not available/20
Text scanning services (print to digital)	12	6	2
Multimedia production	2	14	4
Media streaming services	2	16	2
Virtual learning environment	2	18	0
Institutional web services	2	18	0
Institutional blogging platforms	1	11	9
Institutional e-mail services	1	19	0
Project planning software	0	15	5

These services provide some of the key administrative and functional tools necessary for the success of scholarly practices, amongst others. The results provide an overview of library activity, from service owner to user, where those services are available. As expected, there is a high level of library engagement with these systems and the results broadly confirm this. In those few instances where the service is unavailable across an institution, it is likely that software may be held at a faculty or departmental level.

Section two of the survey examined services more directly associated with digital scholarship. Respondents were asked to identify whether they were the 'owner' or worked in partnership to deliver these services, where available. If in partnership, respondents were asked to list the key partners, as shown in Table 2.2.

Responses highlight the continuing importance of 'stewardship' and curation, advice and guidance in areas traditionally associated with academic libraries. However, there are new relationships and skills to be shaped, which can be helped by the fluidity of the digital ecosystem. The opportunities are there to forge new partnerships and identify where expertise can be grown or adapted to add value to scholarly processes. However, these processes are not linear or necessarily predictable and, as noted by Nowviskie (2013), 'we should recognize that walking any path is as much about the act as the destination. This one, in particular, requires that we engage as partners in messy, ongoing, and unpredictable scholarly processes.' The lack of certainty that on occasion characterizes the process may present a challenge for some libraries and their

Table 2.2 *Use of digital scholarship services and examples of partnership working in delivery of services*

Service	Owner/delivered in partnership/20	Partners (examples)
Institutional repository – publications	19	Research office; IT/computing services, academic schools
Institutional repository – research data	16	Research office; IT/computing services + external 3rd party suppliers
Copyright and publication advice	19	Legal services/university solicitor; governance units; research and enterprise units; finance department
Digitization services	17	Archives and special collections; governance units; business services
Data management services	10	University-wide initiative; strategy and planning unit; IT/computing services; research office
Data analysis tools/services	8	Data analysis research unit; research office; strategic development unit
Targeted staff development	16	Human resources; university staff training and development unit: quality enhancement unit; graduate school
Social media – news and information	16	Cross-university ownership; marketing department

staff, but it is not new. As Dempsey noted in 2005, 'libraries have always been eager to "fit in" to their users' lives. In a network environment, this increasingly means "fitting in" with evolving network workflows.'

The concept of being 'in the flow' has been and continues to be a frequent topic for discussion in the profession's literature. What is reassuring is that the results from this question highlight where libraries have successfully collaborated with partners, ensuring that they are far more 'in the flow' than a decade before. This is undoubtedly assisted by the environment for digital scholarship, which lends itself to serendipity and in which opportunities exist for libraries to present themselves as neutral spaces, ideal for forging new relationships or connections.

Section three of the survey examined in more depth the library's role in delivering bespoke digital scholarship services. The specialist nature of these services is closely aligned to an individual institution's level of engagement with digital scholarship and it is not surprising that research-intensive institutions that hold research-worthy special collections or archives are where significant progress has already been made, as is evidenced by the responses in Table 2.3a.

Table 2.3a *Delivery of bespoke digital scholarship systems/services and comments*		
Service description	**Delivered by the Library/20**	**Comments (examples)**
Providing an incubator space for testing new developments and technologies	10	1 Yes – but only informally. The Library is often the first to experiment with new technologies which others then take on board. 2 Library works closely with the Learning technology team to devise and test new developments. 3 Makerspace has just opened and we are planning a collaborative bid for a Digital Scholarship centre.

The comments indicate two distinct approaches taken by libraries in piloting and testing new technologies:

1 opportunistic, influenced perhaps by a local environment which supports an organic approach to development, recognizing that small-scale adoption, while not necessarily cost effective, provides a route to innovation
2 strategic and collaborative – the development of a successful makerspace requires up-front investment and a level of commitment at an institutional level.

In both instances the local environment will also need to support collaborative working, sharing of expertise and opportunities for interdisciplinary enquiry.

For those institutions that have funded a centralized system, this optimizes use and offers a cost-effective and sustainable approach to future development. Where responsibility is placed with the library for the delivery of these key services and systems, some of which may have significant reputational impact on their institution, this could be interpreted as an indicator of trust and the value accorded to the library and its staff by the institution. Conversely, where the library is central to the approach of small-scale innovation, this may also be regarded as a high-value contribution, if that is how an institution drives its approach to development.

It is evident from the survey responses that some colleagues have successfully secured this new responsibility and, in other instances (for example, copyright and publication advice), grown and expanded their roles, further establishing their contribution to wider institutional activities (Table 2.3b).

The results from both these questions indicate a correlation between the expertise within individual library services and their contribution to internal projects and grant

Table 2.3b *Delivery of bespoke digital scholarship systems/services and comments*

Service description	Delivered by the Library/20	Comments (examples)
Supplying consultancy services for internal projects	10	1 Yes, but only in relation to information literacy. 2 Provide advice on open access; research data; digital archiving. 3 We are invited to contribute to internal projects as appropriate where our expertise is relevant.
Supplying expertise to grant-seeking activities	10	1 We contribute to the development of data management plans and literature reviews. 2 A regular activity! 3 Occasionally with regard to grants that relate to possible research on our special or archive collections. 4 Digital preservation and management; research data management; metadata and discovery in general.

applications; the level of activity will also be informed by the extent to which library staff are integrated into teams with their research colleagues, as shown in Table 2.3c.

Table 2.3c *Delivery of bespoke digital scholarship systems/services and comments*

Service description	Delivered by the Library/20	Comments (examples)
Uses its existing expertise to design/deliver bespoke solutions	9	1 Current capacity limits availability. 2 Try to avoid anything bespoke – harder to maintain. 3 Yes, in relation to information literacy, e.g. reusable learning objects. 4 Digital literacies.

The comments suggest a pragmatic approach to where and how expertise can be deployed in support of small-scale innovation. Respondents noted a willingness to stretch their expertise but were reluctant to commit to initiatives which might be difficult to sustain and resource.

The following case studies pick up on the activities that are likely to be aligned to an institution's investment in digital scholarship at this stage. They illustrate how university libraries in the UK are responding positively to opportunities to assert their value and contribute to their individual institutions' strategic priorities.

CASE STUDY 2.1   Hydra: a case study from the University of Hull, UK
Chris Awre

Background
The University of Hull is a mid-size university (~14,000 students) covering a wide range of disciplines within six faculties. The University is research active, with pockets of excellence. As an institution it is keen to expand its research activity and find innovative ways of doing this. The Library is aligned with these research developments and is looking for ways to contribute where appropriate. One of the opportunities which continues to be fruitful is where Library expertise supports and guides the management of and access to digital outputs, including research, across all formats.

Hydra https://hydra.hull.ac.uk/ is the repository solution adopted by the University to support identified needs for managing digital content. This is an open source system, using the Fedora platform, originally developed through partnership with Stanford University and Virginia University in 2008, and is now maintained through a partnership of 30 institutions around the world. The project continues to host a collaborative set of pages at http://projecthydra.org to enable sharing and showcasing of information and examples of good practice and is sustained through an annual conference and regular communications.

The challenge
There was a need to provide a repository infrastructure that was designed to meet the multiple needs of managing, preserving and presenting structured digital collections generated within the University.

The intended outcome was, and still is, to provide the capability of managing digital content that is produced through scholarship and University administration.

The Library has led on this development from the start. As an early explorer of repository infrastructure and services it benefited from external funding from the UK organization JISC (Joint Information Systems Committee) and was initially supported by a special interest group located within the University Library. Over time, this unit has been disbanded and the service is now embedded into the mainstream Library service. Support from colleagues who have IT expertise is necessary for ongoing development and it is through these partnerships and others with researchers, academic developers and learning technologists that the shape of the repository service continues to keep pace with current requirements.

Benefits (achieved and potential)
The benefits for the Library service are visible but have not yet been fully realized. As new use cases emerge, the challenge is to find ways of making the repository fit to meet those

needs. Having Hydra in place allows Library staff to engage with academics about what they could do, knowing there is a system and infrastructure that is capable of being sufficiently flexible to adapt to individual requirements. It cannot be stressed more plainly that when the decision was made to establish the repository as infrastructure, it enabled it to be used as part of the research process and not solely as a repository for the research outputs.

Use of Hydra has extended beyond the initial scoping of research artefacts and now includes open content – such as dissertations, datasets, digitized texts and audio recordings – and restricted collections for University viewing only – for example, exam papers, committee papers and student handbooks.

In part, the adaptability of the repository is rooted in its open source origins and the associated benefits of collaboration. The community of Hydra users have established a solution which many institutions can use and, as numbers have grown, this has contributed to the project's ongoing sustainability.

However, maintaining such a solution does require IT and developer resource. These are specialist roles and not always easy to source but provide a vital investment if libraries are going to be able to fully engage in the management of digital equivalents of physical libraries.

Engaging with Hydra project partners has enabled the Library to generate a solution that it would never have been able to do independently and demonstrates how capacity can be grown through collaboration to provide innovative solutions to content management.

Summary

This case study highlights the role a library can play as a key partner in the scholarly process and how, on occasion, that role can extend into consultancy, providing advice to the University community on different approaches to managing their digital content. Being innovative and willing to take a calculated risk on the future adoption and development of Hydra to ensure its sustainability has afforded the Library a well deserved reputation for professionalism and as a provider of specialist advice within and beyond the institution.

CASE STUDY 2.2   Sussex Humanities Lab: University of Sussex, UK

Jane Harvell

Background

The University of Sussex, in the south of England, has over 14,000 students, of whom over a third are postgraduates. It has developed a reputation for innovation and inspiration and aims to attract academics and researchers from around the world to deliver high-quality teaching and learning programmes of study.

It has recently invested £3 million of funding to create a substantial research infrastructure – the Sussex Humanities Lab (SHL) – to support work to develop new forms of digital humanities. It is led by researchers from across the institution with direct contributions from the Library. The head of Library academic services and the special collections manager are core members of SHL, and in addition a research fellow has been appointed to work in Special Collections. This post holder will contribute to the development of SHL under the direct line management of the special collections manager.

The challenge

The development of the SHL in 2015 responded to the challenge to bring together researchers from across disciplines and units to embed and develop expertise both to lead and support research in the digital humanities. The aim is to generate a stronger institutional infrastructure, both technically and intellectually centred on the humanities lab.

The three goals of the SHL are to:

1 enable innovative work in digital humanities
2 capture major funding to further expand research capacity
3 ensure that these gains become sustainably rooted in the University infrastructure.

The last aim is important to the Library as the commitment to this development is significant. As core team members of the SHL, Library staff are expected to actively contribute to research bids directly through the work of the research fellow, and also serve as advisors and co-creators in areas such as digital preservation, metadata, discovery and archives.

Benefits (achieved and potential)

Senior managers within the Library are beginning to see exciting benefits as a result of the direct involvement with the SHL. These range from being part of a co-ordinated and much more supportive and knowledgeable approach to designing research bids that have a digital element and which involve deposit (and access) through the Special Collections, to the development of clear, well informed policies around digital preservation and access. Our work with the SHL has also given us the opportunity to reflect on the impact of digital scholarship on our own thinking process. The existence of the SHL is also acting as a catalyst. It is beginning to affect how the University makes decisions about its technical infrastructure to support research in this area and, of more significance, about the funding assigned to future developments. It is also having the knock-on effect of potentially delivering solutions to the challenge of long-term preservation of digital archival content.

As the SHL was launched only in 2015, relationships amongst all stakeholders are new and evolving. One key challenge is the employment of a research fellow as a member of Library staff. This is a new venture both for the service and for the member of staff employed as the research fellow. For the incumbent as well as the line manager, there have been a number of challenges to overcome, largely around objectives, understandings and reporting. The major risk, though, is that the Lab is funded by the University for only a certain number of years. Its continued viability is dependent on attracting significant research funding, which may be difficult in the increasingly crowded area of digital humanities.

On a more positive note, this is an exciting new area for the Library which, if successful, should make a constructive impact on future partnerships. The central involvement is a result of the close relationships fostered with academic colleagues over a number of years and is testament to the work done to ensure that Special Collections (collections and staff expertise) are valued by our institution. It also serves to highlight the importance of outreach activities and the profile of the service across the institution, both as a trusted partner and as an innovator.

Summary

Seizing the opportunity to become embedded in a research environment, but without any guarantee of long-term sustainability is now becoming less of a challenge for many librarians as being in the 'flow' becomes the norm. This case study illustrates the preparedness of colleagues to take a calculated risk, in particular when the potential reputational gains outweigh the lack of certainty over future funding.

The final section of the survey focused principally on the library's contribution to experimental digital scholarship. This section builds on the previous three sections and assumes that the library is in a position to lead or make a significant contribution to a particular research, discipline or institution-wide initiative. The results are summarized in Table 2.4. For the majority of institutions without extensive special collections or archives, it is unlikely that they will become strategic participants at this level of activity. This is also a tier of activity where external funding is likely to be sought and, if secured, may contribute to potential reputational gain for the library.

The next two case studies highlight the potential of developing innovative digital solutions using special collections and archive material as the focus for research. A central characteristic of both case studies is the successful groundwork that enabled collaboration between academics, librarians and specialists, using technology to surface and explore content that was previously difficult to access.

Table 2.4 *Delivery of experimental/innovative solutions by library services*

Service description	Delivered by the library/20	Comments (examples)
Delivering 'first of a kind' solutions	8	1 Using a portable Raman Spectrometer to do on-site spectroscopic analysis of other institutions' medieval manuscripts. 2 Managing the large-scale (c.1 million pages + A/V media) digitization of, and access to, the archive of the Abbey Theatre, Ireland's national theatre.
Leading on bidding process for external R&D funding	4	1 Yes, but limited to just 1 or 2 Digital Humanities projects. 2 Spectroscopic Analysis of Medieval Ink Pigment application (Arts and Humanities Research Council grant). 3 Through our research fellow in Digital Humanities (based in Special Collections).
Working on experimental developments	8	1 Collaborating with academics on novel textual analysis and presentation. 2 In areas of Special Collections – data mining, data manipulation and discovery, working closely with Digital Humanities scholars.

CASE STUDY 2.3 Poetics of the Archive: Newcastle University, UK

Ian Johnson

Background

Newcastle University's origins stretch back to the 19th century and today the University, in the North East of England, is home to over 16,000 undergraduates and 6000 postgraduates. As a member of the UK Russell group (http://russellgroup.ac.uk/) it is a representative of an elite group of UK universities, many of whom are leaders in global research.

The University Library's Special Collections' main principle is to support original research and teaching through the acquisition and curation of unique resources. A long-standing collection strength is contemporary literature, underpinning the relationship with the School of English Literature, Language and Linguistics (SELLS) as a major user, and the Newcastle Centre for Literary Arts (NCLA).

The challenge

In February 2013, Newcastle University acquired the archive of Bloodaxe Books, a poetry publisher of national and international significance, in a joint venture with SELLS. The central challenge was engaging scholarship within creative practice beyond traditional 'search and retrieve' interfaces. Additionally, this academic potential needed to be realized while the archive was being organized to best meet the research requirements for this specific user base.

This need was addressed through a major AHRC-funded project called The Poetics of the Archive (http://bloodaxe.ncl.ac.uk/explore/index.html#/splash). The process of cataloguing and digitizing the collection was approached as a genuinely collaborative activity, where archivists invited communities of poets and visual artists to respond to the concept of 'the archive'. These interpretations, underpinned by the Library's curation, rights clearance and unique access, informed a rich digital interface. This encourages innovation and serendipity as an alternative approach to research. This is aided by the approach taken to present the content of the archive using visual representation.

As a leading example of digital humanities at the University, the interface allows original manuscripts to be explored in multiple ways through content, context and structure. It also explicitly links them to creative responses, holistically linking current digital scholarship to unique research resources.

Additionally, it is intended to attract and inspire the wider public to engage with creative practice. Since its official launch in March 2015, the project website has attracted over 12,410 page views from users in the UK and abroad, with over 65% of usage coming from the United States.

Benefits (achieved and potential)

The enterprise has transformed the University Library's approach to cataloguing literary archives through a culture of seeking to involve stakeholders from the outset. It has also acted as a magnet for additional literary archives from publishers and writers which we plan to curate and celebrate in an equally engaging manner. Furthermore, it has enabled us to develop a truly collaborative partnership with the University's academics, with whom we are already developing plans for further digital humanities projects.

Reflecting on the success of the Poetics of the Archive, project leader Professor Linda Anderson observed, 'Library staff did far more than bring their undoubted archival skills and knowledge to the project; they were intellectual and imaginative partners, entering fully into the innovative scope of the project and recognising the potential for the archive to stimulate new creative as well as scholarly adventures. It has been a delight to forge this alliance which has influenced research plans for the future in the School of English...'

Summary

This case study illustrates how the Library has been a key influence on this project, confirming what Clifford Lynch commented in 2014: 'changes in the *practice* of scholarship need to go hand-in-hand with changes in the *communication* and *documentation* of scholarship. We're starting to see this phenomenon pick up steam. Increasingly, scholars want to include visualizations and interactive models and the like as part of the communication of their work.' The project has also been short-listed for the annual award of Outstanding Library Team, a UK-based competition organized by the sector publication, the Times Higher Education (https://www.timeshighereducation.com/). The Awards Committee recognized the Library 'for developing an innovative and engaging approach to digital humanities'.

CASE STUDY 2.4   Digitization of the Abbey Theatre Archive, National University of Ireland, Galway

John Cox

Background

The National University of Ireland is one of Ireland's oldest institutions. One of seven Irish universities, it has over 17,000 students, with a growing number of international students. Research is an institutional priority, with emphasis on selected areas of strength, building on its strategic partnerships in the performing arts and further developing its interests in digital humanities and associated data analysis. The Library (www.library.nuigalway.ie/) has developed a new Digital Publishing and Innovation Team and published a Digital Scholarship Enablement Strategy to engage with researchers across a range of initiatives. Co-location of the Library's archives and special collections with two major humanities and social sciences research institutes in a new research building has also opened up collaborative possibilities.

The challenge

The Abbey Theatre Archive (www.abbeytheatre.ie/archives/) contains over one million items and is one of the world's most significant theatre collections. It is described on its website as having 'a wealth of extraordinary and unique material providing a fascinating insight into Irish theatre, history, culture and society. The archival material ranges from posters, programmes, photographs and minute books to lighting plans, set and costume designs, sound cues, prompt scripts and audio files.'

The aim is to create a distinctive resource for scholarship in theatre and drama in particular, but also in other humanities disciplines, given the significance of the Abbey Theatre, as Ireland's national theatre, in shaping the country's history during the 20th century. The University also saw this as an opportunity to gain competitive advantage in student and academic recruitment, alongside enhancing its institutional profile and reputation.

Digitization of the archive began in 2012 and is due for completion in 2016. The scale is immense and some of the content is in a fragile condition, having been damaged by fire in 1951. From a process perspective the Library faces a number of challenges:

1. Time – the requirement is to complete the project in a maximum of 3 years out of a 26-year licence period.
2. Project management – this included procurement of and engagement with a service provider who executed c.80% of the project on Library premises, including development of search and redaction facilities.
3. Digitization – the fragility of some of the content added an extra challenge to the process, specifically the 20% that was digitized locally.
4. Metadata – this involves identifying and applying metadata to a previously uncatalogued collection, based on a productions database.
5. Rights management – this has led to the development of a digital rights asset management system designed to address, as far as possible, copyright and intellectual property rights.
6. Partnership – this involves maintaining effective partnerships with the Abbey Theatre as a national cultural institution and with academic staff to ensure that their use of the resource maximizes its research and teaching potential.

Benefits (achieved and potential)

The digital archive now enables new discoveries, connections and innovative forms of research across the entire corpus of artefacts. Single searches can now be conducted which will extract data that previously would have required multiple attempts. These functional benefits are significant and would be expected outcomes; however, some of the other benefits are perhaps more interesting.

The Library has been the 'glue' binding the whole project together, making connections across and beyond the campus. A very strong partnership with the Centre for Drama, Theatre and Performance in the University has been mutually beneficial. Previous projects had been small scale, but this one was very different and has had a positive impact in increasing Library staff confidence, developing new skills applicable to future digital projects and confirming the need to establish stronger and more lasting foundations to promote the contribution the Library can make. This is now achieved through the work of the Digital Publishing and Innovation Team, which acts as the Library's interface for engagement with new digital projects and partnerships and, as a result, is developing a higher profile and broader portfolio of Library services.

Looking beyond the immediate context of the project has been important. Building local capacity and expertise in managing and executing a large-scale digital humanities project has been proven and the potential to apply that to the future digitization projects for other theatre archives is now something that can be more realistically considered. This has led to connections with the University's data analytics unit to promote text mining of the archive, the co-organization of an international theatre archives conference and the hosting of a digital collections seminar. Publicizing the project to the full, and engaging with its strategic objectives for the University through annual reports and other engagements, has been key to securing funding for a complementary successor project.

Summary

The cultural significance of this undertaking cannot be understated and, as such, the benefits and risks associated with it are high. The experience gained by staff working on it illustrates not only the development of new digital skills but also their roles as partners and specialists working beyond the Library, as members of multi-professional teams. Culturally and practically, this shifts the focus of what it means to be a librarian, as the importance of being able to build productive relationships with new constituents takes on a heightened sense of importance.

The final case study, the Disruptive Media Learning Lab (DMLL) at Coventry University, provides a different insight into how digital scholarship has been conceived and nurtured. It marks a change of focus, with a greater emphasis on testing out the potential of new technologies for the purpose of developing innovative teaching practices.

CASE STUDY 2.5 Disruptive Media Learning Lab, Coventry University
Kirsty Kift

Background

Coventry University's roots can be traced back to the 19th century and today it is recognized as one of the UK's leading 'modern' universities, with over 28,000 students and a strong reputation for providing an excellent student experience. It won 'University of the Year' in 2015 and the judges praised the University 'for its student centred approach to learning, its efforts to make higher education more affordable and accessible; and the transformation in its research strategy'.

The Disruptive Media Learning Lab (DMLL) opened in the Lanchester Library, Coventry University in the autumn of 2014. The staff in the DMLL comprise a mix of practice specialists, project support workers, a learning technologist, educational researchers, student activators and administrative staff as well as the Library's Academic Liaison Team. Latterly the Office for Teaching and Learning has joined us, as innovation in practice is tied to quality assurance. Academic colleagues are also welcome to drop in and work in the space and use the teaching spaces. The Lab was envisioned by two academics, building on their innovative teaching practices within the then Media Department of the University.

The physical lab occupies the entire third floor of the Lanchester Library and comprises a series of alternative teaching and learning spaces. The Hill, an alternative to a traditional meeting space, is a five tier wood effect structure; The Grass, an astro-turfed semi-enclosed lecture space, provides an alternative venue for collaboration. These are accompanied by a configurable teaching room, exhibition space, project rooms and collaborative workspace for students, occupying two-thirds of the space. The rest is a glass-fronted staff space with no fixed workspaces.

The challenge

The key challenge that the DMLL seeks to address is how to embed and sustain innovative teaching and learning practice across a whole institution. At what point does the innovative become the mainstream and the established need reinventing? How can technology be used meaningfully in pedagogy and not just as a prop? Within this is the question 'why locate the lab in the Library?' The Library is central and popular, and the space was available. However, more than that, there was already a strong association with digital through the traditional lens of the 'e', and the Digital Production Office responsible for off-air recording and streaming was already present in the space. The Library was asked to place its teaching team of Academic Liaison Librarians permanently in the Lab. As the staff responsible for teaching digital and information literacy across the institution, they are unique in having contacts and teaching responsibilities in every faculty and school, providing a useful basis for promoting a fledging cross-institution concept.

The Lab provides a safe physical space where pedagogy can be continually explored and supported to disrupt existing practice. It aims to drive this by cross-university and external collaborations of not only staff but also students as key participants in pedagogic design. Underpinning this is a strong pedagogical research practice and a strong emphasis on transformative technology. Has the DMLL been a challenge for Library staff? Undoubtedly. The staff were asked to work in a hot-desking environment to encourage collaboration with DMLL and academic colleagues with laptops and no fixed desks. It has taken staff out of their comfort zone. They have been asked to examine their own teaching practice and use the opportunities offered by the Lab to inform future teaching. The Lab is digital heavy, with projects embracing flipped classroom, virtual reality and multiple forms of online collaboration and student engagement. What happens if the technology doesn't work? Staff have been asked to embrace failure and to learn from it. The Library team has collaborated directly with DMLL staff on a pre-arrival online induction package for international students, tried flipped classrooms and embraced student collaboration by working with the student poetry society and student activators, amongst other things.

Benefits (achieved and potential)

Being part of the DMLL has started to break down the preconceptions of what a librarian is and does. We are being asked to move into areas of teaching that are not traditionally ours, e.g. creativity vs enquiry and analysis, and to play a greater role in course teaching teams. The buzz of an open and multi-professional office has fostered better collaboration with partners and also within the Academic Liaison Team itself. Our Add+vantage module, part of the University's suite of vocational modules, is now being collaboratively delivered by the entire team. It is currently being rewritten to reflect changing skills and practice, with a much greater emphasis on digital literacy in both content and delivery and what that means to students and their future lives.

Change has not happened overnight and has taken more time to gain traction than perhaps we were expecting. To be disrupting is also disruptive, and inevitably some are enjoying the journey more than others. A lack of digital confidence on the part of some staff remains a barrier and new skills needs fostering and support. The Academic Liaison Team has not become 'DMLL staff' per se, as it became clear that we wanted and needed to retain our own identity and have a particular and valuable skill set to contribute. As anticipated, being exposed to new ideas and practices is the key driver for change.

To bring this back to the Lab's contribution to digital scholarship: its focus on the disruptive prompted Library staff to use the exhibition space within the Lab to display books that have been banned in various places and times through history. Thus we could draw a parallel, for those wondering what libraries have to do with disruptive practice, between the DMLL and our heritage: the book as a new 'technology' that has had the power to disrupt through history. In essence, we are still following that path into digital scholarship.

Summary

The development of the DMLL is a venture which features Library space and librarians as key contributors and the spaces present exciting examples of digital scholarship in practice. 'Sand box' environments, physical and virtual, for testing out technologies are common, but this approach, which encourages serendipity and can act as a creative catalyst, is very clearly aligned to their local institution's strategic intent. Keeping the creativity and energy flowing are two essential aspects of these spaces, and librarians can both contribute to and collaborate on using new technologies to progress scholarship across all aspects of teaching practice and research.

Conclusion

The outcome from the survey of UK and Irish HE libraries suggests that, unlike in institutions in the USA, investment in digital scholarship has not translated into a similar growth in digital scholarship centres in the UK or Ireland. Spaces such as the Sussex Digital Humanities Lab or projects such as the Poetics of the Archive are more common examples, where funding coalesces around existing expertise, particularly in support of research projects. Across the institutions surveyed, the level of engagement by the library services varied, with a noticeably higher correlation between digital scholarship, research collections and library participation.

The development at Coventry University provides a different perspective and it is clear that the librarians engaged in working in the DMLL are on a journey – one which will result in the acquisition of new skills and changed behaviours and attitudes through an evolutionary process, and on which also illustrates a real as opposed to theoretical example of how librarians are becoming digitally resilient, adaptable and confident when dealing the ebb, flow and unpredictability of the digital environment.

References

Dempsey, L. (2005) *In the Flow*, http://orweblog.oclc.org/in-the-flow/.

Lynch, C. (2014) The 'Digital' Scholarship Disconnect, *EDUCAUSE Review*, **49** (3), 10–15. http://er.educause.edu/articles/2014/5/the-digital-scholarship-disconnect.

Nowviskie, B. (2013) Skunks in the Library: a path to production for scholarly R&D, *Journal of Library Administration*, **53** (1), 53–66.

Sinclair, B. (2014) The University Library as Incubator for Digital Scholarship, *EDUCAUSE Review*, 24 June, http://er.educause.edu/articles/2014/6/the-university-library-as-incubator-for-digital-scholarship.

Vinopal, J. and McCormick, M. (2013) Supporting Digital Scholarship in Research Libraries: scalability and sustainability, *Journal of Library Administration*, **53** (1), 27–42.

PART 2

The agile librarian

3

Librarian as partner: in and out of the library

Roz Howard and Megan Fitzgibbons

Introduction

As was discussed in Chapter 1, the definition of scholarship has, since the work of Boyer (1990), moved from a narrow focus on research to incorporate the full scope of academic work; furthermore, the literature review also revealed tantalizing glimpses of how librarians are leaving their university library to become embedded in the workflows of academic departments. This chapter explores these two themes further by examining the impact of the digital on the scholarship of teaching and uses a case study of the University Library and Centre for Education Futures (CEF) at the University of Western Australia (UWA). The case study also explores how the transferable skills and expertise of librarians can be successfully extended in the development of digital learning and teaching design in a campus-based research-intensive university. It describes the collaborative partnership which incorporates services to academic staff and students and brings together two areas – library and education – in a practical and impactful approach to achieving the University's Education Futures Vision. Finally, the case study demonstrates how transferable skills and knowledge have allowed librarians to expand their roles within and beyond the Library, and have even led to library professionals changing career paths successfully.

More specifically, this chapter considers the following aspects of the partnership to demonstrate how librarians have a key role to play at the nexus of education technologies, learning design and scholarship in partnership with the CEF. It will examine how librarians are:

- experiencing change to their traditional roles
- contributing to learning design initiatives
- facilitating the implementation of a learning management system
- becoming embedded in the teaching and learning workflows of the CEF.

Looking towards the future of education at UWA

In 2012, following extensive stakeholder engagement, a UWA Leading Transformation Program group developed the 'University of Western Australia Educational Principles' with a focus on learning and teaching. The aim was to enable UWA to be a world leader in education and provide students with an exceptional, future-proofed, sustainable, world-class educational experience. The seven educational principles established in the University's strategic plan, 2014-2020 (2013) are:

1 Transformative teaching – practices that engage, challenge and transform
2 Evidence-based teaching – evidence based and quality teaching practices
3 Experiential learning – support staff to provide students with a rich variety of learning experiences
4 Integrated research experiences – learning and teaching experiences at UWA are integrated with, and informed by, research
5 Optimized resources – quality resources, facilities and technologies
6 Vibrant collaborative learning environment
7 Global Citizenship and Leadership – UWA students as contributing members and leaders of local, national and global communities.

In committing to innovation and the transformation of education at UWA, a key component of the University's Strategic Plan is greater utilization of effective, student-centred learning technologies, with strategic goals to ensure that 'UWA teaching and learning activities will be supported with an extended range of quality resources, facilities and technologies', with measures of success that include an 'increase in the utilization of education technologies'.[1]

UWA's CEF, established in 2015, has a key role in achieving UWA's 2020 Vision of gaining recognition as a global leader in education. The CEF supports educators at UWA to transform their teaching practices so as to promote more future-oriented, digital, student-centred learning. The Centre's key role is to work in partnership with faculties and service areas at UWA to transform and embed education technologies. The UWA Library is a key partner in supporting the many CEF initiatives to transform education.

The Centre for Education Futures (CEF)

The CEF is the lead centre through which transformative innovation in learning and teaching is achieved. Co-ordinating professional development and learning technology systems, the CEF provides information and support to staff to enable education innovation and futures thinking. It has responsibilities for:

1. implementation of innovations
2. increase in the use of educational technologies
3. increase in student satisfaction and achievements.

Operating under three main pillars of work, the Centre provides:

- learning environments: digital and campus learning environments enable the UWA community to engage fully in futures-orientated education;
- capability and capacity building: every member of UWA has the capability and capacity to design and deliver learning that is fully futures-orientated; learning technologists support the learning redesign of units and ensure that all staff are provided with the development opportunities to engage and embed education technologies;
- innovation and scholarship: UWA becomes known as a leader in educational innovation.

The Centre works to sustain and promote 'futures thinking' and to enable continuous implementation of new projects and processes, together with external partnerships and events. One of the ways it does this is through its Futures Observatory. This is both a concept and a space, demonstrating the use of disruptive and emerging technologies and their influence in the global educational community. It provides a physical space that evaluates 'over the horizon' technologies that can be adapted and adopted for pedagogical purposes, and enables staff to easily explore and experiment with the latest technology for learning and teaching. It also provides staff with new, supportive and inspiring pathways to contribute to the development of learning and teaching scholarship at UWA.

The University Library

The Library's aim as set out in the Library Strategic Directions 2015–2020[2] is 'to provide innovative and relevant Library services to support the University of Western Australia to be a leading global university. This will be achieved through the provision of excellent staff, services, collections and spaces and a focus on the deep understanding of user needs through collaboration and partnership.'

Five key strategic themes are outlined in the Library's vision, including the themes of 'Leadership in Education', where four priority areas are identified as follows.

1. To partner with the university community to design, develop and evaluate services and spaces that best support the University's education needs.
2. To develop high-quality, evidence-based collections that support the University's learning and teaching activities.
3. To make it easier to find and access information within the Library's collections.
4. To provide support for learning technologies which underpin the University's vision for education.

The University Library at UWA operates six libraries as well as functional departments for information resources management, scholarly communication and e-research. The strengths of the Library include the state-of-the-art Barry J. Marshall Library (opened in 2010), provision of an institutional publications repository and research data repository, a strong partnership with Student Services in supporting student learning and demonstrated success in engagement with students via the Library's social media channels (as described in Benn, Mills and Howard, 2015).

As well as the Barry J. Marshall Library, a recent investment was approved to refurbish the Reid Library. Located at the heart of the campus, the Reid Library opened in 1964 and is one of the most iconic and busiest UWA buildings, with over 1 million visits annually.

Students and staff from all faculties use the Reid Library, as well as a large number of community members. It provides a variety of learning spaces, including postgraduate research spaces, librarian and student IT support services and access to both online and print collections. It also houses a large collection of rare and valuable items available for access to library members. Undergoing redevelopment in early 2016, this library project is aligned to achieving the University's goal that 'teaching and learning activities will be supported with an extended range of quality resources, facilities and technologies' (UWA 2020 Vision, Strategic Plan 2014–2020 (2013)) as well as supporting the UWA Education Futures Vision. The redevelopment provides an enhanced range of facilities and services, along with spaces, including a learning suite to be used for teaching that is bookable by students when not in use.

Partnerships

For decades, academic librarians have strived to deliver services and promote information, digital and media literacy in a variety of environments, through a variety of approaches (Sapp and Gilmour, 2003; Rudin, 2008). At the present time, however, external pressures and the opportunities afforded by technology are driving academic libraries to re-envision their goals and their roles in relation to universities' overarching missions (Neal, 2010; Johnson et al., 2015), and this has involved working in partnership with their stakeholders. It has been argued that university libraries have a key role in delivering excellence in learning and teaching, both directly and in partnership with academic staff and the wider university community (Rockman, 2002). Similarly, Salmon and Angood (2013) note that partnerships between IT and Learning Development departments have proved to be highly productive. The Library already takes a partnership approach to its role in the University and has been involved in several fruitful collaborations (Sputore, Humphries and Steiner, 2015), but the partnership with the CEF is considered to be particularly relevant to the increasingly digital future of higher education.

The CEF's main responsibility is to develop staff with pedagogical transformation, and the Library has a key role in helping students to use new technologies in their curriculum. As the CEF has a complementary vision and goals to those of the Library, we sought to explore the full potential of a partnership approach with them and collaborative partnership between the two areas was therefore considered to be critical in delivering Education Futures at UWA. The partnership was further strengthened during the transition to a new institutional learning management system (LMS) or virtual learning environment (VLE) project (discussed later in this chapter). The Library's research and learning support assistant director, as a member of the University LMS/VLE transition project team, was responsible for organizing the creation of help guides and staff development programmes in order to engage University staff with this new technology. The assistant director was supported by a dedicated librarian to create media-rich, self-paced help resources and to organize library support for students in the new LMS/VLE. In subsequent months the assistant director was seconded to the project full time to manage the relationship with faculties and to manage the Centre's team of learning technologists. This also included implementing a series of the Centre's projects related to UWA's seven Educational Principles. From August 2015, the assistant director who had been seconded was appointed to the Centre as its Associate Director.

The partnership developments between the Centre and Library have been further reinforced by the appointment of an Education Innovation Librarian in the Centre to support scholarship initiatives, providing project management and research advice to scholarship grant awards. The Associate Director and Education Innovation Librarian positions have become seamlessly embedded into the Centre, providing both staff members with opportunities to become immersed in the transformation of education at UWA, and transforming librarians into futurists.

It should also be noted that opportunities to be involved in partnership activity were not restricted to these two library roles. All UWA research and learning support librarians have been involved in delivering a number of the Centre's transformation initiatives, which in turn have led to librarians developing new skills and knowledge.

Changing roles
Shifts in academic librarianship

This case study of the UWA should be understood in the context of the changing roles of librarians in universities, an evolution that mirrors shifts in the higher education sector worldwide. There have been several recent analyses of the environment that document changing roles and forecast future directions. For example, the Association of College and Research Libraries in the United States has published a series of essays called *New Roles for the Road Ahead* (Bell, 2015) that address the many ways in which librarians' skills are being redeployed or reimagined in response to the changing higher education environment. In the area of learning and teaching more specifically, it is argued across the compilation that librarians must go beyond putting all of their effort into information literacy development and instead become part of broader initiatives related to embedding and assessing graduate outcomes, knowledge creation and information policy in universities.

The 2015 New Media Consortium Horizon Report for Libraries, which monitors trends that affect higher education libraries concurs, saying that 'in addition to being digitally savvy, academic Library staff also have a responsibility to support alternative models of higher education, such as online and blended learning, which are materializing on campuses everywhere' (Johnson et al., 2015, 28), in order to maintain relevance and offer valuable contributions to their institutions. Jaguszewski and Williams, however, characterize the future as having 'an increasing focus on what users do (research, teaching and learning) rather than on what librarians do (collections, reference, library instruction)' (2013, 4). As learning and teaching are core functions of any university community, we take the view that librarians should be able to adapt and apply their roles and skills in the context of how learners learn and teachers teach in the current digital environment.

It has been argued that librarians frequently see their roles overlap with or morph into other roles in the university that both enhance the utility of their skills as librarians and allow them to develop new skills – roles such as instructional designers, information technologists and liaison librarians based outside the library (Cole, 2014; Delaney and Bates, 2015). Moreover, they can contribute to efforts in the scholarship of teaching and learning by encouraging collaborations across these various roles

(Neal, 2010; Otto, 2014). Overall, there are strong currents in the professional literature suggesting that as the entire enterprise of the university becomes digital, librarians have the opportunity as well as the necessity to embed and expand their skills through partnerships in the digital learning environment.

Professional development for librarians at UWA

To be effective in this changing environment, librarians must consciously develop their skills with regard to technology application and pedagogy. At UWA, the Library implemented a programme of professional development for its librarians taking on a new role in promoting learning in digital environments. These initiatives related to instructional design using technology for active learning, and 'flipped classroom' approaches and a series of tailored workshops for librarians on learning and teaching were organized and delivered in collaboration with the CEF. These workshops were delivered over a six-month period and subject librarians were encouraged to use 'real time' practices in developing content and collaborating with academics. Alongside this development, subject librarians were, for the first time, granted 'view only' access to all units in the LMS/VLE in order to assist students. This level of access meant that they were also able to engage with unit co-ordinators to develop LMS/VLE content when they were granted editing access to specific units on request.

Informal evaluation surveys conducted after the sessions reflected overall satisfaction with librarians' experience of the professional development sessions. They reported that they had increased their awareness of pedagogy and knowledge of practical tools. The flipped classroom component of the training, in particular, allowed librarians to work on an authentic project where they could apply what they had learnt and which led to changed practices. For example, some librarians now provide students with videos to view or tasks to complete before they attend face-to-face sessions, so that classroom time can be spent more on practising searching skills or discussions as opposed to demonstrations. The tailored workshops have been instrumental and timely in preparing librarians for understanding curriculum design and their subsequent contributions to collaborative initiatives with the CEF, as discussed below.

Librarian contributions to learning design initiatives
Overview

As has been found at the University of California Berkeley, 'the librarian's role as an educational partner is recognized as one area of strategic importance for the long-term vitality of research libraries and the effectiveness of campus teaching and learning initiatives' (Dupuis, 2009, 9; Kaufman, 2012; Giesecke, 2012). UWA also provides a strong example of educational partnership, by way of librarians' involvement in a key learning design initiative called Carpe Diem.

Carpe Diem, which is Latin for 'seize the day', is an active, team-based approach to learning design created by Gilly Salmon,[3] currently UWA's Pro-Vice Chancellor (Education Innovation). The Carpe Diem programme is an 8- to 12-hour workshop held over two days, in which each unit co-ordinator works with co-lecturers, learning technologists, librarians and administrative staff to redesign a unit with the aim of scaffolding student learning and implementing blended learning approaches. At UWA, the term 'blended learning' is generally used to describe a unit that includes both face-to-face learning on campus (usually in scheduled blocks of lectures and tutorials) and learning, interaction and assessment that takes place in the LMS/VLE or other online environment. Working through a six-stage design process, each unit co-ordinator works with their team to develop a 'blueprint' for the overall mission of their unit, draft a storyboard of the students' learning journey, prototype blended learning activities in the learning management system and create an action plan – all while sharing ideas and feedback with other workshop attendees and facilitators.

Carpe Diem: the librarians' role

Carpe Diem has been implemented at a number of universities worldwide, and at UWA librarians were involved from the inception of the methodology and their contributions are considered to be a valuable part of the process. In Carpe Diem workshops, one librarian is assigned to each 'pod' or unit design team and works to contribute to the overall unit redesign. The librarian's expertise may be drawn on to advise on copyright concerns, to identify resources that might support students' exploration of a topic or to suggest strategies for scaffolding students' development of information skills. More generally, the librarian works with the learning technologist to facilitate the pod/team through the process in certain aspects, serving as a sounding board, providing critiques to new ideas and assisting in the use of educational technology. The librarian's role, therefore, varies in each workshop depending on the unit, the lecturer's needs and the overall team dynamic. Adaptability, critical thinking and creativity have been identified as key dispositions that librarians must develop in order to contribute to the Carpe Diem learning design process.

Outcomes

Involvement in Carpe Diem actualizes the emerging role of the librarian as 'creative learning specialist' described by Bell (2015) in his conceptualization of librarians in the changing environment of higher education. In Carpe Diem, a virtuous circle has emerged as librarians contribute their broad general knowledge and technical capabilities as well as the 'soft skills' of being able to adapt quickly to the needs of the situation at hand and to have positive interactions with academics. In turn, they have developed a much richer understanding of learning design and educational technology by working with learning technologists. Moreover, they contribute in a tangible way to changing learning and teaching practices at the University through their input into the programme.

Outcomes of participation in Carpe Diem have been evaluated informally by CEF and the Library through surveys and large group feedback sessions in order to capture librarians' perceptions of their role and what they get out of the experience. Although some librarians have expressed concern about the time commitment of participating in Carpe Diem, the overall experience is usually found to be positive by all subject librarians. By working closely and intensively with unit co-ordinators, librarians learn more about the curriculum design and teaching practices at the University. The workshops also provide them with the opportunity to immerse themselves in someone else's knowledge and approaches, which broadens librarians' perspectives intellectually and creatively.

In addition, participants in Carpe Diem workshops (teaching faculty and professional support staff) are routinely surveyed after each session. Respondents frequently mention the value of the collaborative approach through which they can draw on the expertise of both librarians and learning technologists. In particular, faculties have commented that librarians are helpful and knowledgeable and are able to guide them towards student-centred, blended learning. The CEF has recently appointed a research fellow to undertake empirical research on the outcomes of Carpe Diem that will hopefully provide insight regarding what impact the collaborative approach has achieved. Overall, participation in Carpe Diem events has provided an opportunity for librarians to build trust and make connections with academic unit co-ordinators, raising the profile of their expertise and leading to future collaborations.

Implementation of a learning management system
Overview
In 2015, UWA transitioned to the Blackboard Learn LMS/VLE, having previously used a different system. The project was 'owned' by the CEF and the Library contributed to the project, opening new avenues for professional development, upskilling and collaboration. Since the Library's research and learning support assistant director was selected to step outside her usual portfolio to become a member of the LMS/VLE transition project team, she was able to closely integrate librarians' existing skills and relationships to meet the requirements of the project overall.

Librarians' role

There are discussions in the professional literature about strategies for incorporating libraries' services and information literacy-related teaching in LMS (Fabbro, 2013), but approaches are frequently one sided or ad hoc in nature unless there is a strong relationship between the university division that manages the LMS and the library (Farkas, 2015). At UWA, the Library's partnership in connection with the LMS/VLE implementation functioned on several levels:

- assistance with face-to-face staff training
- front-line support of students
- creation of online help resources and training guides
- librarians' personal development of skills in using Blackboard.

Support for UWA staff

The implementation of an LMS/VLE is a significant undertaking, both technically and culturally. It must be accompanied by training and assistance for the end-users of the technology, and by a sympathetic understanding of how the changes will impact upon behaviours, emotions and long-held ways of doing things. UWA took a number of approaches to working with end-users; for example, five full-day workshops were held for faculties to learn about the new LMS/VLE and be introduced to its basic functionalities. In addition, drop-in sessions were held twice daily in the lead-up to and early days of the LMS/VLE implementation, later dropping back to once per day on an ongoing basis, still allowing staff to get one-on-one advice for specific queries.

Librarians contributed to the face-to-face training efforts as one-on-one 'guides' for staff who had questions or difficulties with the system. Through this role, librarians have come to be seen as trusted advisors in relation to the LMS/VLE (in addition to their other areas of expertise). Although the Centre for Education Futures (CEF) is now ultimately responsible for LMS/VLE support, librarians continue to field queries and collaborate with academics with whom they have built relationships. For example, subject librarians for the Business School provided extensive assistance in the development of new, fully online units by providing technical advice/troubleshooting, setting up learning activities and suggesting resources. Librarians for music and law also are supporting their constituents by collaborating with faculty to set up Blackboard sites with resources (i.e. in music and law, respectively) for all students in particular degree programmes.

Finally, librarians also assisted in creating Blackboard help guides for staff and students and implemented the delivery of the guides to create 'help' sections for the system. An initial project sub-team with members from the CEF and the Library identified UWA's needs for online help materials, created and compiled guides and posted them on the website.

Support for students

In addition to working with staff, Library staff also supported (and continue to support) students' use of the LMS/VLE. Service points in the UWA Library are staffed by client support officers, who, in addition to handling circulation and basic reference assistance, also provide front-line technical assistance for students using University systems – for example, WiFi connectivity, network authentication, student e-mail, online enrolment. The new LMS/VLE therefore represented a new training obligation for Library staff as well as an increase in the need for student support during the transition period. All client support officers therefore underwent training on navigating and troubleshooting in Blackboard, led by a librarian who had developed expertise in the system. In addition, Library staff have ongoing access to general information and specific troubleshooting advice in a wiki-style knowledge base that was created by the Library's service delivery co-ordinator and a librarian.

Librarians' skill development

Most librarians at UWA did not have prior experience of using Blackboard and they therefore participated in an upskilling process so that they could assist academic staff and advise client support officers on difficult student queries. Given the 'all hands on deck' approach during the LMS/VLE transition, librarians participated in early-stage training offered by Blackboard, to learning technologists in the CEF. To demonstrate how important librarians' involvement in this project was, it was co-ordinated by the University Librarian and the Pro-Vice Chancellor (Education Innovation).

Beyond these initial workshops, librarians' training for Blackboard took a self-paced approach. A small group of librarians volunteered to develop a greater level of expertise on their own, using online tutorials and guides, and then acted as mentors and guides for other librarians in their subject areas. A site was set up in Blackboard to act as a sandbox where librarians could practise creating content, experiment using the various tools and share tips on using the system. Formal training and self-paced learning were mandated as part of librarians' workload.

This approach allowed librarians to focus on areas that were of particular relevance for their subject areas, both in terms of creating content in their own right and for fielding queries from academics. For example, librarians in the area of sciences looked into the use of symbols and formulas in the text editor in Blackboard, law librarians were particularly interested in how to develop the quizzes that they integrate into various units each year and librarians in the arts investigated how to embed videos from the Library's subscription resources. This ongoing upskilling effort took place in collaboration with the CEF as staff across the two areas shared knowledge, information and resources and worked together to support academic staff.

Outcomes

Overall, the LMS transition project proved to be a fruitful partnership between the CEF and the Library in collaborating on a priority project for the University and its Education Futures principles. Library staff in particular, especially the assistant director, were able to leverage existing relationships across the University to implement communication about the project and provide needed support. It was also an opportunity for librarians to develop new relationships with teaching staff and raise awareness of their expertise in other areas. One example of this is closer communication with administrative staff in the faculties (who also assist academics with Blackboard) via communications fora for Blackboard supporters. In addition, some librarians found new opportunities for collaboration with academics and administrative staff in their subject areas by assisting with initiatives related to the Blackboard implementation, such as creating standardized layouts and content for all units within a school or designing LMS/VLE sites with links and guides for students in particular courses.

The partnership also led to an enhancement to service, where the Library is now a 'one-stop shop' for students' Blackboard technical support as well as a resource point for staff. Librarians were able to contribute in this role because, even if they lack extensive technical knowledge, they are highly competent in finding resources and guides, troubleshooting difficulties and generally allaying the fears of those who feel less comfortable with learning new technical systems. Furthermore, librarians have developed Blackboard skills that they can use both to support academics and in their own teaching to a higher degree than they had done with previous learning management systems. They maintain current awareness and expertise in use of Blackboard through continuing involvement in the Carpe Diem learning design workshops and any follow-up contact with the academics with whom they have developed relationships.

Finally, the project also led to the transfer of two Library staff members into the CEF, demonstrating how the digital skills of librarianship can be applied across the dimensions of learning and teaching activities in a university.

Librarians embedded in the CEF

Librarians' expertise is increasingly relevant in the current digital environment, where technological platforms, provision of online resources and techniques for engaging students underpin learning and teaching activities. It is important that digital tools and materials that are the building blocks of teaching practice are not considered as add-ons or esoteric domains but, rather, as fundamental components of learning design. In recognition of the realities of the current landscape, and following on from the LMS and Carpe Diem partnerships discussed above, the role of Education Innovation Librarian, a full-time qualified librarian, has been embedded in the CEF. Key functions of the role include:

- advising on copyright and licensing issues
- co-ordinating the development and management of open educational resources (OERs)
- investigating and compiling information resources
- managing resources for staff development initiatives related to teaching
- supporting researchers who are conducting projects in the scholarship of learning and teaching, particularly in the terms of their use of information resources.

The University Librarian has also nominated librarians to be involved in other projects with the CEF (some of which took place before the Education Innovation Librarian role was created). These opportunities have allowed the CEF Librarian to leverage transferable skills developed in the field of librarianship, such as the ability to liaise with faculty members and knowledge of research processes, information organization and copyright, in order to contribute as a team member outside the Library context. Some examples of projects with an embedded librarian are provided in the following sections.

Learning and teaching development in the CEF

As its key mission is to promote innovation, the CEF has a number of activities related to the scholarship of learning and teaching. One initiative is the awarding of grants to academic staff to implement projects aimed at improving student learning. Grant recipients must evaluate the outcomes of their work, position it in the context of previous research in learning and teaching and disseminate their findings. Project leaders and teams come from nearly every faculty across the University, so their knowledge of resources and methods in education or social sciences varies so that the Education Innovation Librarian provides them with tailored advice on the identification and use of relevant resources for literature discovery, information about methodology and avenues for publishing their results. This support takes the form of workshops, one-on-one consultations and compilations of relevant databases and journals (including identifying open access journals, impact factor scores, etc.). By way of an example, the Education Innovation Librarian is involved in the development of a fully online 12-week unit for teaching staff that is intended to transform their approaches to learning and teaching. As a team member of the Transforming Teaching for Learning unit, she has contributed to developing the unit's structure and content, in addition to locating and organizing resources, managing copyright concerns and developing learning objects. When the unit goes live for delivery, she will be involved with tutoring and supporting students of this digital unit.

Massive Open Online Courses

Massive Open Online Courses (MOOCs) have been on the higher education scene for a few years now, heralded as a disruptive force in digital learning, and despite criticisms about their viability, they continue to be an important activity at many institutions. MOOCs are currently presenting a challenging area of copyright in Australia, as they do not fall under Australian statutory provisions for use of materials in an education context, nor are they strictly speaking commercial activities. It is therefore important to ensure that any third-party materials used in the MOOC are in the public domain, are appropriately licensed for reuse or have received such permission from their creator. Many university libraries are involved in MOOCs to varying degrees (O'Brien et al., 2014); it is clear that this is an emerging area of involvement for librarians.

Librarians at UWA have been involved in the development of its MOOCs, which were devised as a partnership between the Library and the predecessor of the CEF. UWA found MOOC development to be most effective when a librarian was involved as a team member from the very inception, so that copyright concerns could be incorporated into the design. It was found to be time consuming and counter-productive to consider copyright *after* content was developed if permission or licences could not be obtained for key materials. Librarian involvement has been found invaluable even where course designers intended to use only open access content; it is important to document sources and ensure that they are cited properly, particularly in the highly visible platform of MOOCs.

At UWA, a librarian working through a secondment agreement between the Library and the CEF developed a process for checking and recording the details and provenance of third-party materials used in MOOCs. She also carried out the work of recording the status of all content and managing permission requests and licences for two MOOCs and provided advice on others. Other Library staff have also been involved in formatting references, creating a subject guide and documenting the status of Creative Commons licensed images for MOOCs.

Managing resources and relationships

A further example of where a librarian has left the Library to work in another area of the University is the Associate Director for the CEF. The Associate Director's key responsibilities are to manage a team of learning technologists, keep an overview of the activities and projects of the whole CEF, build effective relationships with faculties, and deputize for the Pro-Vice Chancellor (Education Innovation). Building effective relationships and partnerships has been found to be key to engaging faculties with transforming their learning and teaching activities. The Associate Director's previous experience as a library assistant director for Research and Learning Support has combined her relationship management skills and knowledge, and has successfully integrated into the work of the CEF.

These examples of cross-fertilization of skills development highlight the agility of librarians and their ability to lead change. Furthermore, the Associate Director will be transferring to another role at another institution to take up a senior IT position as Director of Faculty Engagement and Systems Support, where her transferable skills will continue to be developed and applied.

Conclusions
UWA case study: lesson learned

The case study described in this chapter offers evidence of how partnerships are the key to extending librarians' roles in the digital environment for learning and teaching. The Library has a central presence in the University, as well as skilled librarians who have expert knowledge of information resources and well established relationships with the faculties and staff of the University. The CEF has a focused role at UWA, aiming to transform teaching practices with technology and to promote innovation in that space. It employs learning technologists who specialize in applying technologies in line with trends. Thus, the partnership between the CEF and the Library in the areas of learning design initiatives and the LMS/VLE transition has demonstrated how combining the skills and relationships of the two areas works to the ultimate benefit of the University.

Beyond the organizational partnership, the movement of individual staff members has also shown how librarians' skills can be reshaped and redeployed in the environment of digital learning and teaching. The role of a librarian embedded in the

CEF is quite different from the typical model of academic librarians who are physically based in a library and have clearly defined areas of responsibility (e.g. reference assistance, information literacy teaching, cataloguing). Instead, it is our experience that librarians can be effectively embedded in projects and workflows beyond the library and that, to be successful in this role, they must, above all, be flexible in contributing to whatever needs arise in the team.

Recommendations

In the increasingly digital and disrupted environment of higher education, it is crucial for different sectors of the university to form partnerships in order to leverage the diverse skills and areas of expertise of staff in different areas to form flexible teams that can adapt to the changing environment. We hope that the experience of UWA offers some insight that may apply to other institutions in similar circumstances.

Firstly, we have found that it is important for the parties in the partnership to have a shared understanding of the organization's larger vision (in UWA's case, the Education Futures Vision and Educational Principles). If a commitment to achieving this vision is shared, the priorities and approaches of the partners should also harmonize.

Secondly, as we have found at UWA and as argued in the literature (Dupuis, 2009; Jaguszewski and Williams, 2013; Cole, 2014; Bell, 2015), there is a significant opportunity for librarians to contribute in the increasingly digital environment of higher education. They can leverage their existing expertise in technology and information literacy and also extend their knowledge and activities in joined-up approaches to curriculum development, learning design and learning systems.

Thirdly, we have found that librarians' transferable skills in education and technology can be applied in emerging digital learning environments for the larger benefit of students and staff in the University. Their core professional skills, when coupled with a flexible approach and the ability to learn quickly, allow them to develop their roles and, in the process, learn new skills that are relevant to the future of learning and teaching.

As Dempsey (2015, 3) puts it, 'Academic libraries are a part of the changing education enterprise, and the character of that enterprise is what will most influence an individual library's future position'. We would also argue that librarians have much to contribute to the shape of their institutions' future by (i) cultivating partnerships with other key stakeholders and (ii) contributing their expertise where education and digital technology intersect. Moreover, librarians can have a broader impact by embedding their work in academic areas outside the Library, or even making the transition to a different career path, propelled by the core professional skills and knowledge they have developed as librarians.

Notes

1 UWA, *Achieving Success: strategic goals*, www.web.uwa.edu.au/university/executive/strategic-directions-2014/strategic-goals.
2 UWA Library Strategic Directions 2015–2020, www.library.uwa.edu.au/__data/assets/pdf_file/0003/2778114/University-Library-Strategic-Directions-2015-2020.pdf.
3 For more information, see Salmon and Wright (2014) or visit www.gillysalmon.com/carpe-diem.html.

References

Bell, S. (2015) Evolution in Higher Education Matters to Libraries, *New Roles for the Road Ahead: essays commissioned for ACRL's 75th anniversary*, **4**, http://acrl.ala.org/newroles/?page_id=237.

Benn, J., Mills, K. and Howard, R. (2015) *From Mediocre to Marvellous: SOCIAL media strategy to improve student experience at the University of Western Australia*, ALIA Information Online, Sydney, Australia, http://information-online.alia.org.au/content/mediocre-marvellous-social-media-strategy-improve-student-experience-university-western.

Boyer, E. (1990) *Scholarship Reconsidered: priorities of the professoriate*, Princeton, NJ, Carnegie Foundation for the Advancement of Teaching.

Cole, J. (2014) Instructional Roles for Librarians. In Blevins, A. and Inman, M. (eds), *Curriculum-based Library Instruction: from cultivating faculty relationships to assessment*, London, Rowman & Littlefield, 3–10.

Delaney, G. and Bates, J. (2015) Envisioning the Academic Library: a reflection of roles, relevancy and relationships, *New Review of Academic Librarianship*, **21** (1), 1–22.

Dempsey, L. (2015) Introduction, *New Roles for the Road Ahead: essays commissioned for ACRL's 75th anniversary*, **3**, http://acrl.ala.org/newroles/?page_id=239.

Dupuis, E. (2009) Amplifying the Educational Role of Librarians, *Research Library Issues: a Bimonthly Report from ARL, CNI, and SPARC*, **265**, 9–14, http://publications.arl.org/rli265/.

Fabbro, E. (2013) Seamless Integration of Library Service Points throughout the Learning Management System. In Daugherty, A. L. and Russo, M. F. (eds), *Embedded Librarianship: what every academic librarian should know*, Santa Barbara, CA, ABC-CLIO, 59–72.

Farkas, M. G. (2015) *Libraries in the LMS*, Association of College and Research Libraries, http://acrl.ala.org/IS/wp-content/uploads/2014/05/summer2015.pdf.

Giesecke, J. (2012) The Value of Partnerships: building new partnerships for success, *Journal of Library Administration*, **52**, 36–52.

Jaguszewski, J. and Williams, K. (2013) *New Roles for New Times: transforming liaison roles in research libraries*, Association of Research Libraries, University of Minnesota Digital Conservancy, http://hdl.handle.net/11299/169867.

Johnson, L., Adams Becker, S., Estrada, V. and Freeman, A. (2015) *NMC Horizon Report: 2015 library edition*, Austin TX, The New Media Consortium, www.nmc.org/publication/nmc-horizon-report-2015-library-edition/.

Kaufman, P. (2012) Let's Get Cozy: evolving collaborations in the 21st century, *Journal of Library Administration*, **52** (1), 53–69.

Neal, J. G. (2010) Advancing from Kumbaya to Radical Collaboration: redefining the future research library, *Journal of Library Administration*, **51** (1), 66–76.

O'Brien, L., Dorner, J., Porciello, J., Swanson, S. and Zisser, M. (2014) *Working Group on Models for Course Support and Library Engagement Report*, edX Libraries Collaboration, https://docs.google.com/file/d/0B4DgtXah7QuyQW5pQml3S0RoejBsOHpQWHps WkxGU3JKSEFz/edit.

Otto, P. (2014) Librarians, Libraries, and the Scholarship of Teaching and Learning, *New Directions for Teaching and Learning*, **139**, 77–93, http://dx.doi.org/10.1002/tl.20106.

Rockman, I. F. (2002) Strengthening Connections between Information Literacy, General Education, and Assessment Efforts, *Library Trends*, **51** (2), 185–98.

Rudin, P. (2008) No Fixed Address: the evolution of outreach library services on university campuses, *The Reference Librarian*, **49** (1), 55–75.

Salmon, G. and Angood, R. (2013) Sleeping with the Enemy, *British Journal of Educational Technology*, **44** (6), 916–25, http://dx.doi.org/10.1111/bjet.12097.

Salmon, G. and Wright, P. (2014) Transforming Future Teaching through 'Carpe Diem' Learning Design, *Education Sciences*, **4** (1), 52–63, www.mdpi.com/2227-7102/4/1/52.

Sapp, G. and Gilmour, R. (2003) A Brief History of the Future of Academic Libraries: predictions and speculations from the literature of the profession, 1975 to 2000 – part two, 1990 to 2000, *portal: Libraries and the Academy*, **3** (1), 13–34.

Sputore, A., Humphries, P. and Steiner, N. (2015) Sustainable Academic Libraries in Australia: exploring 'radical collaborations' and implications for reference services, *IFLA World Library and Information Congress*, Cape Town, South Africa, http://library.ifla.org/1078/1/190-sputore-en.pdf.

University of Western Australia (2012) *Education Futures Our Vision*, UWA, Australia, www.worldclasseducation.uwa.edu.au/__data/assets/pdf_file/0009/2789163/ UWA-Education-futures-Our-vision-2014.pdf.

University of Western Australia (2013) *UWA 2020 Vision, Strategic plan 2014-2020*, UWA, Australia, www.web.uwa.edu.au/__data/assets/pdf_file/0010/2538343/114085-VICCHA-StrategicPlan-v3.pdf.

4

Novice to expert: developing digitally capable librarians

Charles Inskip

Introduction

The estate of digital scholarship is expanding, the boundaries of academic librarianship are blurring and researchers and academic staff are widening their engagement in the process of creating and sharing new knowledge through the use of repositories and the adoption of emergent technologies. This has the potential to lead, on the one hand, to a lack of resourcing of support, which has traditionally been delivered by library staff and, on the other hand, to opportunities for forward-thinking professional services to revise their remit and add to their portfolio. The research discussed in this chapter was part of a (UK) nationwide Jisc-funded programme, Developing Digital Literacies (Jisc, 2014). Jisc (Joint Information Systems Committee) is a UK non-profit organization with the vision to 'make the UK the most digitally advanced education and research nation in the world' through 'exploiting fully the possibilities of modern digital empowerment, content and connectivity' (Jisc, 2016). It operates the national UK's higher education (HE) Janet network, negotiates collectively with vendors and publishers and provides training and advice within the education sector. This chapter explores the context of current conceptions of digital literacies and the growth in digital scholarship, which is defined here as 'the ability to participate in emerging academic, professional and research practices that depend on digital systems' (Jisc, 2011). It goes on to discuss issues around skills and competencies of librarians, focusing on how these relate to digital literacies and digital scholarship, particularly in university and research sectors.

Since the millennium, but more particularly over the last ten years, the impact of technology on the provision of library services in UK HE has been profound. Naturally, the increase in access to online resources within colleges and universities has affected budgetary and strategic considerations and the means of service delivery, while, on the front line, library staff now inhabit a complex and ever-changing information environment which would be almost unrecognizable to colleagues from the last century. Alongside these changes within the profession, the context and practices of users of all types have also developed apace. If libraries are to effectively support the needs of scholars, then it is important to recognize the changes in digital scholarship practices, and attendant digital literacies, and to map these to the skills and competencies needed by library staff to support them.

Digital scholarship

The availability of previously unfeasibly large amounts of data and literature at the click of a button has led to significant changes in research practices across the disciplines. Researchers are more visible in their creation of new knowledge through the use of social media and open repositories, and this is being shared seamlessly across collection boundaries which are now invisible and no longer bricks and mortar; the physical location (of researcher and collection) is often irrelevant to the user; access, rather than ownership, is now the key issue informing service provision; and, particularly, communication is central to digital scholarship (ACLS, 2006; Lynch and Carleton, 2009). Research practices which also involve the use of sophisticated software in the creation, organization and analysis of large datasets need to be supported by the library as it moves towards an information commons or 'scholars' collective' (Lewis, 2007). As this change is now impacting on the humanities as well as the early adopters in the sciences, the adoption of technologies is now all-pervasive in HE. Science's 'cyberinfrastructure' (National Science Foundation, 2003) is now the arts and humanities' 'digital humanities'.

The Jisc definition of digital scholarship referred to earlier goes on to identify some examples of practices:

> for example use of digital content (including digitized collections of primary and secondary material as well as open content) in teaching, learning and research, use of virtual learning and research environments, use of emergent technologies in research contexts, open publication and the awareness of issues around content discovery, authority, reliability, provenance, licence restrictions, adaption/repurposing and assessment of sources.
>
> (Jisc, 2011, 2)

It should be clear from these examples that although the role of the library in digital scholarship may be considered (by the library) to be central, there are other stakeholders within the institution that have an interest. These may include learning and teaching support, e-learning, academics, doctoral schools and technical services.

Efforts have been made at institutional level to reflect and support these changes in practice through the development of some libraries into learning centres or information commons. This has led to 'hybrid information jobs' (Corrall, 2010) for library staff within these new centres. Staff in these positions may suffer from skills gaps (Auckland, 2012). Addressing these gaps should be made a priority if services are to be provided which effectively meet this shift in provision. Problems can also arise if a library-centric approach is taken in this development. Open access repositories, for example, may be considered more important by the library than by the academics who, it is planned, will populate these repositories with their digital creations. Despite the importance (to the library) of a stewardship role in developing, making accessible and preserving these collections, time-poor researchers are reluctant to engage with what they see as administrative and bureaucratic interventions (MacColl and Jubb, 2011).

The growth in research data management (RDM), for example, has put these issues into focus. The activities around RDM involve drawing together policies and infrastructure to support data curation, sharing and reuse. While the role of the library in this context may be clear, there are difficulties in resolving what may be considered to be ambiguous roles when working in large HE institutions (Nielsen and Hjørland, 2014; Pinfield, Cox and Smith, 2014). Documented high-profile examples of these activities in the UK at University of Oxford (Wilson et al., 2011) and University of Edinburgh (Rice and Haywood, 2011) discuss some of the problems around skills gaps and collaboration, highlighting the 'interrelated nature of data management activities' (Wilson et al., 2011, 278) which require diplomacy and negotiation when navigating among the departments, services and, even, institutions.

Digital literacies

It is important to consider the digital literacies needed to maximize the potential return from investing in digital scholarship infrastructure. Jisc adopts a broad definition of digital literacy, considering the 'capabilities which support living, learning and working in a digital society' (Jisc, 2014). Its current model, the 'digital capability framework' (Jisc, 2015), comprises: information, data and media literacies; digital creation, innovation and scholarship; communication, collaboration and participation; digital learning and self-development; ICT proficiency; and digital identity and well-being. This framework has been adopted in the UK by the Quality Assurance Agency for

Higher Education (QAA) to support one of its review themes for 2015/16, digital literacy. These higher-level discussions of digital literacy (or capability) have been focused at the level of broad concepts and principles. In recognition that there is not a shared understanding of what it looks like in practice, Jisc has more recently produced a series of profiles that frame digital capabilities around the needs of scholarly 'tribes', e.g. teacher, researcher and learner, with the caveat that these profiles are examples of how the Framework could be applied in practice and should not be considered as definitive (Beetham, 2015).

While HE institutions have been developing student and staff information and digital literacies for some time, this has often been at an operational rather than strategic level. This delivery has generally been led by the library, but often involves wider stakeholders, particularly those responsible for learning and teaching (particularly e-learning) and for technical provision and support. The move towards measuring, or evaluating, the level of delivery and support for these literacies as part of formal external quality assessment has led to more widespread awareness, particularly at institutional management levels, of the importance of formally (and visibly) supporting these capabilities. This move has also coincided with a growing interest in and adoption of students' involvement in curriculum development and delivery as 'change agents' (Kay, Dunne and Hutchinson, 2010). A good-practice example of this approach is its adoption at Exeter University, where students have led and participated in numerous research projects – 'assessment and feedback, engagement in lectures, seminar provision, technology development (such as podcasting, video-streaming and the use of voting systems), learning spaces, sustainability, employability, cross-campus provision, personal tutoring, academic writing, and peer-tutoring' (Kay, Dunne and Hutchinson, 2010, 3) – which directly impacted on curriculum delivery in the institution. This holistic institutional approach to the delivery of digital literacy or capability appears to be gaining traction, drawing from the wealth of groundwork by committed networks.

There has been a surge in the adoption of digital scholarship practices by researchers, through the availability of electronic information sources (Lippincott, Hemmasi and Lewis, 2014) and tools that allow the asking of heretofore unimagined research questions. Centres for digital scholarship have been established, for example, at the Bodleian Library at the University of Oxford (Bodleian Libraries, 2015), University College London (UCLDH, 2015), the University of Edinburgh (University of Edinburgh, 2016) and the University for the Creative Arts (UCA, 2016). There has also been a raising of awareness and obligation at all levels to support the development of the literacies required to ask these questions, answer them and, notably, communicate the findings. The combination of these two factors means that information professionals need to reflect on their role in the delivery of information and skills.

Librarian skills and competencies

The role of librarians, and their attendant skills and competencies, were explored widely in the literature following the turn of the millennium. Partridge and Hallam identified two 'DNA strands' of the library and information professional: 'generic capabilities and discipline knowledge' (2004, 7), which intertwine as a genome. These strands reflect the wider literature on librarians' skills and competences (for example, Missingham, 2006; Orme, 2008), which suggests that the complexity of changes caused by the shift from physical to digital information requires a fundamental review of professional skills. These changes are leading to a need for the librarian to become a 'polymath' (Broady-Preston, 2010), enabling them to draw from a wide range of bodies of knowledge, or a 'blended professional' (Corrall, 2010) with a merged set of identities and practices which allow the information professional to cross contested jurisdictions of other ('rival') professional services in the institution (Cox and Corrall, 2013). The boundaries between libraries, technologists, administrators and academic staff are made ever more visible by the adoption of technology in the practices of digital scholarship – RDM, repositories, web-based materials, electronic resources, information and knowledge management and information literacy support are all considered by Cox and Corrall in their discussions. They conclude that:

> [t]he long-term success of such forays will be influenced by a number of factors, including the efficacy of the profession's knowledge base in that area or its ability to absorb other knowledge bases, the plausibility with which new roles can be equated to the existing public image of the profession, and the organization and posture of other professions that are jostling for position.
>
> (Cox and Corrall, 2013, 1538)

The complexity of navigating these bounded jurisdictions, and crossing them, requires motivated service leaders (on all sides), appropriately skilled staff, opportunities for negotiation and support from the institution.

There are numerous examples exploring the need to develop generic skills such as customer service and technology support (for example Haddow, 2012; Chawner and Oliver, 2013; Mamtora, 2013; Vassilakaki and Moniarou-Papaconstantinou, 2015). This widening of the skills net can be supported not only by library schools (Auckland, 2012), continuing professional development (CPD) (Mamtora, 2013), in-service training and professional organizations (Corcoran and McGuinness, 2014) but also by collaboration (Bonn, 2014) and institutional change (Vinopal and McCormick, 2013). If the move towards digital scholarship is to be facilitated by the library as a central player, leading to an increase in the adoption of digital scholarship centres

(Lippincott, Hemmasi and Lewis, 2014), then skills, collaboration and institutional change all need to be considered.

Looking at the complex changes in the digital information landscape, American College and Research Libraries (ACRL) discusses how 'the intersections between scholarly communication and information literacy' (ACRL, 2013, 1) offer the opportunity for collaboratively focused strategies which require a 'deeper knowledge of the life cycle of scholarship' (2013, 5) and information. They suggest that library and information professionals need to develop their own skills in pedagogy, curriculum development, advocacy and institutional change in order to meet the challenges created by these changes. Many of these issues were also drawn together by Research Libraries UK (RLUK) in its comprehensive report, *Re-skilling for Research* (Auckland, 2012; Brewerton, 2012). This work explored researchers' information needs and mapped these to subject librarian tasks in order to identify skill sets required to effectively support them. The findings identified nine key skills gaps relating to advice and support on: preserving research outputs; data management and curation; complying with funder mandates; data manipulation tools; data mining; use of metadata; preservation of project records; sources of research funding; and development of metadata schema (Auckland, 2012, 43).

These skills gaps relate very closely to the digital scholarship practices identified earlier (Jisc, 2011, 2) and the attendant growth in open access. The findings also relate closely to those identified in the wider literature, helping to further support the generally agreed view that the changes in the digital landscape and the attendant changes in research practices require a rethink on the development of staff to effectively support users in this complex environment.

SCONUL survey

A collaborative investigation of the support available to researchers in developing their digital literacies, Research Information Literacy and Digital Scholarship (RILADS, 2012), explored the range of skills and competencies of academic librarians suitable for these increasingly complex digital environments and linked them to the range of literacies required for this support. One strand of this work was led by SCONUL, the UK Society of College, National and University Libraries, whose role is to raise awareness, lobby stakeholders and support collaborative practices and service development (SCONUL, 2016a). SCONUL was a member of a nationwide Jisc programme Developing Digital Literacies (DDL), which aimed 'to promote the development of coherent, inclusive approaches to digital capability across institutions of further and higher education' (Jisc, 2014). An element of this project involved a survey of named heads of service and senior managers of academic libraries in the UK (SCONUL, 2012). The survey explored issues around the development of staff skills relating to the support of users' digital capabilities and identified gaps, good examples of current practice and opportunities for SCONUL, as a professional association, to support staff development.

The reason for choosing to approach named SCONUL members was that these participants would be in a position to engage practically with the survey findings once it was complete. Participants were asked to respond 'on behalf of the key group of staff responsible for the delivery of digital literacies' (Mackenzie, 2012), as it was felt that this would help to focus responses on the institutional experience, rather than generalizations. Fifty-three participants completed the survey, giving a response rate of around 30%.

The opening question of the survey drew from a Jisc definition of digital literacies, which identified six key capabilities: ICT/computer literacy, information literacy, media literacy, communication and collaboration, digital scholarship and learning skills (Jisc, 2011). The participants were asked to evaluate their staff's capabilities in relation to these criteria, identifying the level of staff expertise (expert/competent/novice/not applicable) and the importance of staff developing expertise in this area (essential/not a current priority/maybe in the future/not required). Freedom was given to the participants to provide qualifying comments. Participants were then asked to give feedback on a digital-lens iteration (SCONUL, 2016b) of SCONUL's Seven Pillars of Information Literacy framework (SCONUL, 2011) to determine its relevance and value as a staff development tool. They were then asked to provide information on the involvement of their service in the strategic development of digital literacies in their institution. Finally, they were asked to identify the level of prioritization for how staff development should take place, focusing on whether this should be local, role or sector specific, as part of an academic qualification, or by professional association or sharing experiences across professional bodies, giving examples and ideas for workforce development activities. The findings were then used to inform the development of a resources list (Inskip, 2013) that was designed to signpost resources, drawn from the Jisc DDL programme, that would help to support the development of digital capabilities in academic libraries.

A key finding of the survey was that although staff skills for digital scholarship had the highest number of responses showing staff to be 'novice' in this area (Figure 4.1), development was not considered to be as 'essential' as most of the other capabilities (Figure 4.2).

When qualifying their responses regarding expertise and the importance of staff digital scholarship skills, participants said that this was 'an area of growing importance for us', and that it was an 'emerging field but important to develop especially for staff support', although it might be 'not well understood or relevant to some student support'. Although there were deemed to be 'pockets of good practice in the service',

68 PART 2 | THE AGILE LIBRARIAN

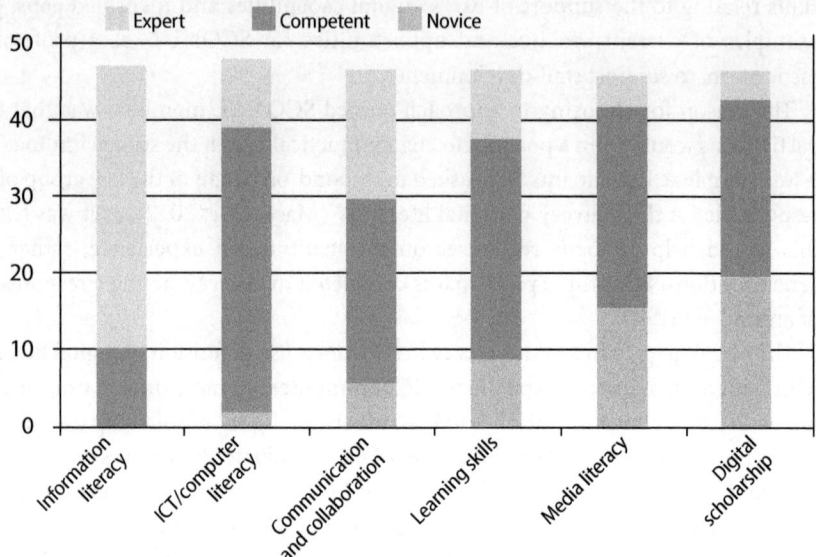

Figure 4.1 *Assessment of the digital capabilities of staff whose core roles are student support and academic liaison: staff expertise*

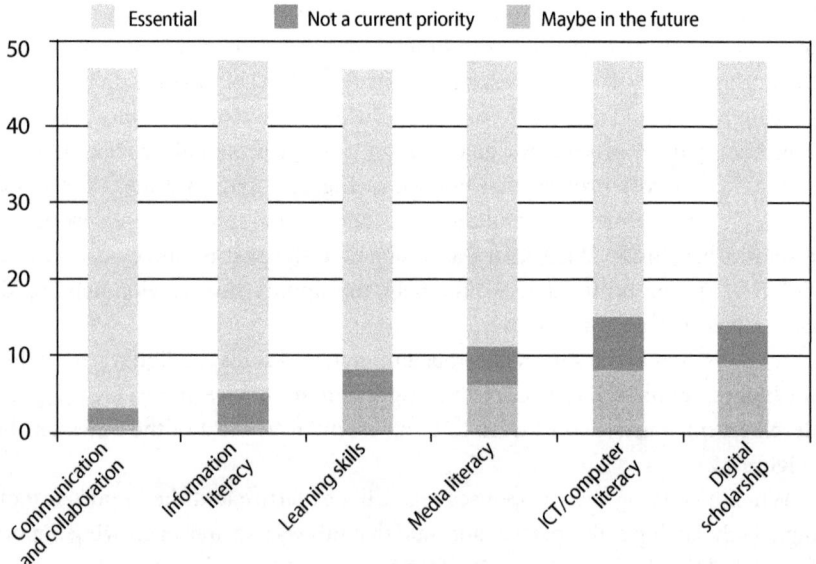

Figure 4.2 *Assessment of the digital capabilities of staff whose core roles are student support and academic liaison: importance of staff developing expertise in this area*

this might not be 'in the core roles with student support and academic liaison. Some knowledge sharing is needed.' Further to this, although 'librarians and learning technologists have an expert awareness' they may not 'have all the tools required to repurpose digital material'. These comments contrast with, for example, information literacy (which was considered a 'traditional library function') or ICT literacy, both of which are considered to be supported by higher-skilled staff; although even in these areas, skills cover a range of levels and the comments seem to indicate that despite these areas being considered generally more expert, they may be represented by pockets of good practice, rather than across the board.

When asked to describe how they were supporting the development of these digital literacies within their service, participants provided detailed evidence of good practice: 'Ongoing information, training and development opportunities for groups of staff' were very visible. Some took the approach of supporting 'a small team of digital skills supporters … supported by the centre for development of learning and teaching or 'internal and external training' and 'identifying in-house, free, and low-cost courses for skilling up staff.' Another means identified was the use of 'appraisals leading to individual action plans [with] external events and peer supported activity'. Links across services (to learning and teaching as well as faculty) were evident, as was high-level involvement in 'strategic changes to the student curriculum'. An urge to become paperless has involved 'trialling iPads' and other mobile devices. Another approach was to involve staff in decision making through 'involvement of the academic liaison librarians in the selection, implementation and promotion of digital resources and content; on the job experience of using digital tools' and working cross-sector with 'Technology Enhanced Learning team [who] are developing skills by using and promoting Blackboard [etc.]'. Linking appraisals with training, and the adoption of relatively low-cost internal peer-support were notable. Cross-service relationships, particularly with faculty and learning and teaching staff around curriculum development were also mentioned.

These answers led to an exploration of the level and type of involvement by the participants' services in the institutional strategic development of digital capabilities. They were asked how their service was contributing to the strategic development of their institutions' digital literacy. Again, it was apparent that there was a wide range of opportunities and challenges. A small number of services were contributing to strategic development, 'mostly ad hoc and largely dependent on personal contacts' and finding it to be 'slow work as current academics can be reluctant to change practices'. However, in the main, participants were involved at a relatively high strategic level, albeit in partnership, rather than leading, being included in cross-service working parties and learning and teaching committees. It was evident that 'digital literacy is a key priority'. Cross-departmental collaborations were evident and

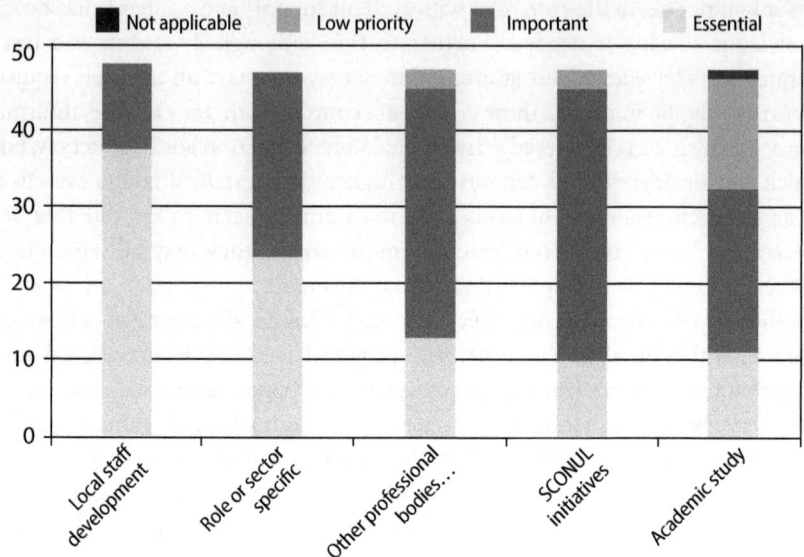

Figure 4.3 *What is needed to ensure that library staff maintain and develop their digital literacies?*

employability initiatives were broadening the area of digital scholarship skills to include wider services such as careers. However, in some institutions there was 'further work to be done to embed this in university priorities', as it was 'not seen as a current priority compared with other issues, though some academic staff are on board'.

Finally, participants identified that what was needed to ensure that library staff maintained and developed their digital literacies was a strong focus on local staff development initiatives, which were role or sector specific. SCONUL's input and that of related professional associations appeared to be welcomed more than support from academic library qualifications (Figure 4.3).

These findings were then used to focus on exploring action that was being taken to bridge the gap between novice and competence, examples of good practice in staff development for digital literacy, the value of the digital lens on the SCONUL Seven Pillars and opportunities for SCONUL to adopt a more strategic role in digital literacy. This led to a mapping exercise (Inskip, 2013), circulated to SCONUL members, which aimed to provide summary context for appropriate resources from the Jisc DDL programme which would be helpful in addressing the key challenges and issues which arose from the survey.

Resources

In terms of bridging the gap, resourcing in terms of funding for staff development can be more readily released through support at policy and strategic levels. It was suggested that organizations not benefiting from this support could explore resources which focus on institutional change and interdepartmental collaboration. Three projects from the DDL programme were identified as being appropriate here: Digidol (Cardiff University, 2013); Pride (University of Bath, 2013); Seedpod (Plymouth University, 2013). These initiatives particularly explored approaches to institutional change, notably through a holistic approach, enabling and encouraging conversations not only between services but also which bring in students and academic staff. It was suggested in these projects that, through these conversations, raised awareness and 'buy-in' to the importance of developing digitally capable staff and students would be much more easily generated, while supporting and recognizing the importance of contextual, or discipline-specific, needs and requirements.

This approach aligned closely to those resources focused on developing networks and collaborations. Recognizing that the digital landscape is shared, Heads of Educational Development Group (HEDG, 2013), Cascade (University of Exeter, 2013) and Standing Committee on Academic Practice (SCAP, 2013) resources particularly encouraged and reinforced the idea of engaging with students as change agents. Staff in other services across the HE sector face many of the same challenges as those in libraries, and these resources recognized that collaborative practice could provide insights into ways of working which could be adopted more widely.

It is generally agreed that good practice examples can support staff development. Here, the rise in importance of learning and teaching has become more apparent. Librarians are increasingly delivering information and digital literacy interventions to colleagues, staff and students. The studies by the Association of Learning Development in Higher Education (AldInHE, 2013) and Institute of Education (IoE, 2013) were highlighted for their potential in this support.

CPD was recognized in the survey as being important to staff development. Looking more widely across the institution to related professional associations' CPD frameworks, it was found that the Association of University Administrators (AUA, 2013), the Staff and Educational Development Association (SEDA, 2013) and the Digital Department project (UCL, 2013), as well as the Researcher Development Framework (VITAE, 2013), all addressed similar issues and challenges to those faced within the library service.

The preceding examples were focused predominantly on staff development and management issues such as strategic change. Numerous examples of specific tools, relevant to institutions already benefiting from a supportive infrastructure but searching for inspiration to continually develop a digitally literate workforce, were identified. Frameworks, mainly mapping skills to make comparisons, were considered quite widely to be of value. These enabled comparison between disciplines, services or faculties or, importantly, between service staff and user practices, helping to identify gaps in provision. Training programmes, tools and case studies are too many to mention here, but it is clear from their quantity and variety that there is widespread recognition of the value of resources in this area, many of which are sharable and freely available and in different formats – from online to face-to-face workshops.

Discussion

The digital capability framework (information, data and media literacies; digital creation, innovation and scholarship; communication, collaboration and participation; digital learning and self-development; ICT proficiency; and digital identity and well-being (Jisc, 2015)) recognizes the widespread nature of what users need to be able to do if they are to be digitally literate. These capabilities are contextual: they relate not only to what type of information landscape the user is a part of (school, university, workplace) but also to their discipline, and the particular culture of their institution. Librarians have been delivering and supporting what is currently called digital literacy (and springs from bibliographic instruction/user education/information literacy) for some time. The digital capabilities reflect the ongoing, complex changes in type and format of information and strongly suggest that the skills and capabilities of the librarian need to be constantly reviewed and refreshed to support these changes.

Although staff expertise and competence are in evidence, the survey showed (see Figure 4.1) that there is a low level of skills base in digital scholarship in particular. In the context of the definition of digital scholarship introduced earlier, the move towards access rather than ownership, and the increasing use by researchers of sophisticated tools to analyse large digital collections, is having a real impact on the delivery of support to these users. Clearly, if librarians and other stakeholders in the digital landscape are to effectively support users in their abilities to participate in the practices that depend on these new digital systems (Jisc, 2011), and if the skills of librarians are not sufficiently developed and supported on a continual basis, then the users are going to go elsewhere, or they may not engage with the very systems (open access repositories, for example) that are designed to support them in their activities. This was identified as an issue by MacColl and Jubb, who suggested that '[r]esearchers have little interest in the support services libraries have built for them in recent years, yet they are aware of support needs that are not being met' (2011, 10). Communications, as well as technical skills, need to be enabled by the institution if the benefit of these enhanced skills and services is to be fully realized. Reaching out and collaborating with partner services and departments is a vital strategy in enabling access to the users of these services, who do not care who provides these services – as long as they are timely, useful and reliable.

The level of 'novice' staff in the survey may have reflected the timing of the data collection. At the same time as this research, the RLUK findings of the nine key skills gaps (Auckland, 2012) and the ACRL intersections (2013) were also responding to a widespread perceived need. Other commentators referred to above also identified a need to review and develop the skills and competencies of library and information professionals to reflect the impact of digital information on practices across the board. Professional associations at the time were also actively developing and implementing new frameworks. In the USA, ACRL was setting out on its revision of the Information Literacy Competency Standards for Higher Education (ACRL, 2000) and in the UK, CILIP was launching its Professional Knowledge and Skills Base (CILIP, 2013), partly informed by the need to recognize the shift in the profession caused by the surge in digital information.

The results shown in Figure 4.2 indicate that the urgency around digital scholarship was not considered to be as severe as, say, learning, information literacy, or communication and collaboration. At the time, these three issues were more immediate, certainly in universities where teaching is prioritized over research. However, the combination of a greater proportion of novice staff with a lack of urgency in their development in the area of digital scholarship could be considered to be of concern. If the move towards digital scholarship is as significant as evidence from Auckland (2012), ACRL (2013) and Lippincott, Hemmasi and Lewis (2014) suggests, then this may be more urgent than was originally anticipated, particularly if we consider the surge in open access repositories prompted by the funder and evaluator obligation to the researcher to make their work available through these repositories (HEFCE, 2015). Unsurprisingly, it is the 'stick' of the requirement of depositing research that is having more impact on service development than the 'carrot' of universal access to knowledge. This can be used to the advantage of the library. It is not their requirement after all, but an external driver, which can be used to inform policy and strategy development and to lever funds which will enhance the position of the library within forward-thinking institutions.

The evidence in the survey (see Figure 4.3) of the range of sources of staff development initiatives supports the contextual nature of this need quite strongly. As we move across the options from 'local staff development' to 'academic study' it can be seen how, as the source moves further from the context, it is seen as being less important to the participant. Adoption of these strategies may also enable the cross-service collaborative conversations proposed by numerous participants in the DDL programme, leading to Broady-Preston's polymath (2010) and Corrall's blended professional (2010) becoming the norm. In-house staff development recognizes local context and builds more flexibly upon existing staff skills. In-house training can benefit from experiences from colleagues outside the institution through collaborative networks and formal and informal skills-sharing exercises supported by professional associations and library schools. Duplication of these skills within the institution, for example with IT or e-learning support, or academic departments, may cause difficulties and tensions – the contested jurisdictions mentioned earlier will come into play. Again, communication, negotiation and advocacy skills become increasingly important in supporting these developments.

The survey comments support the view that there is much already being done in this area, albeit often at a grassroots, ad hoc level. While there is some involvement at the institutional policy-making and strategic-planning level, the contested areas of digital literacy in general and digital scholarship in particular require a sustained higher level of recognition of the value of the library service on the part of institutional management. This will enable the release of resources to support staff development, on the one hand, and encourage a wider recognition of the importance of these capabilities, on the other hand. This is evident in the recent adoption by QAA, mentioned earlier, of the digital capabilities framework in their review process, which seems to be prioritizing their importance as part of the student experience and the related quality of university delivery. This adoption, if it continues, has the potential to help libraries to demonstrate their essential contribution to the mission of their institutions. It leads to awareness of digital literacy at the very top of the institution and provides a valuable opportunity for library advocacy.

If institutional policies and strategies recognize the importance of the value of digital literacies, then this is likely to facilitate the cross-service and inter-stakeholder conversations required to support strategic staff development, which may address the concerns expressed by these participants. Levering these literacies into long-term policy through evidence-based advocacy and wider institutional buy-in is key. Recent developments, however, show that the sustainability of even institutional-wide culture changes cannot be relied on. One of the DDL projects which focused on institutional change has since been disbanded because of changes at the top of the institution which led to a re-writing of strategies and a refocus away from digital literacies. This demonstrates that even institutional buy-in is fragile, and reliant on continuing support from the top, which is out of the control of even the most street-smart head of service.

Conclusions

As the academic digital landscape continually expands, information access widens and technology becomes more sophisticated and pervasive there is a constant need for all stakeholders to develop and progress. Librarians need the continuing development of skills and competencies to support their users. Staff may be expert in some digital literacies, and more competent or even novice in others. The recommendations that these challenges be faced by a combination of policy and strategic development and organizational change; supporting networks and collaborations; good practice case studies; and reference to continuing professional development frameworks from outside the library sector chime with similar work in related contexts, showing that this is a widely supported view. The creeping adoption of digital literacy by standards agencies is an opportunity that may enable library services to adopt some of these recommendations. Service development requires leadership from forward-thinking and politically engaged library management who are able to create and develop sustainable and resilient networks which will recognize the likelihood and impact of unforeseen strategic institutional and sectoral changes.

Acknowledgements

This research could not have taken place without the detailed contributions of the participants, who generously shared their time and their experiences. The survey was designed and administered by a small group of information professionals (Sara Marsh (University of Bradford); Alison Mackenzie (Edge Hill University) and representatives from the SCONUL Working group on Information Literacy, Cathie Jackson (Cardiff), Helen Howard (Leeds)), with direction, contributions and feedback from the SCONUL Executive Board. The work was funded by SCONUL through its participation in the Jisc DDL programme. The opinions expressed in this chapter are those of the author.

References

ACLS (2006) *Our Cultural Commonwealth*,
  www.acls.org/cyberinfrastructure/ourculturalcommonwealth.pdf.
ACRL (2000) *Information Literacy Competency Standards in Higher Education*, Chicago, IL,
  Association of College and Research Libraries.
ACRL (2013) *Intersections of Scholarly Communication and Information Literacy: creating
  strategic collaborations for a changing academic environment*, Chicago IL, Association of
  College and Research Libraries, http://acrl.ala.org/intersections.
AldInHE (2013) *Association of Learning Development in Higher Education*,
  http://jiscdesignstudio.pbworks.com/w/page/48783279/ALDinHE%20DL.
AUA (2013) *Association of University Administrators*,
  http://jiscdesignstudio.pbworks.com/w/page/48656386/AUA%20DL.

Auckland, M. (2012) *Re-skilling for Research: an investigation into the role and skills of subject and liaison librarians required to effectively support the evolving information needs of researchers*, Research Libraries UK,
www.rluk.ac.uk/wp-content/uploads/2014/02/RLUK-Re-skilling.pdf.

Beetham, H. (2015) *Framing digital capabilities for staff – deliverables*,
https://digitalcapability.jiscinvolve.org/wp/2015/11/10/framing-digital-capabilities-for-staff-deliverables.

Bodleian Libraries (2015) *The Bodleian's New Centre for Digital Scholarship*,
http://blogs.bodleian.ox.ac.uk/digital/2015/10/05/the-bodleians-new-centre-for-digital-scholarship/.

Bonn, M. (2014) Tooling Up: scholarly communication education and training, *College & Research Libraries News*, **75** (3), 132–5.

Brewerton, A. (2012) Re-Skilling for Research: investigating the needs of researchers and how library staff can best support them, *New Review of Academic Librarianship*, **18** (1), 96–110, doi:http://dx.doi.org/10.1080/13614533.2012.665718.

Broady-Preston, J. (2010) The Information Professional of the Future: polymath or dinosaur? *Library Management*, **31** (1/2), 66–78, doi:http://dx.doi.org/10.1108/01435121011013412.

Cardiff University (2013) *Digidol Project*,
http://jiscdesignstudio.pbworks.com/w/page/50732611/Digidol%20project.

Chawner, B. and Oliver, G. (2013) A Survey of New Zealand Academic Reference Librarians: current and future skills and competencies, *Australian Academic & Research Libraries*, **44** (1), 29–39, doi:http://dx.doi.org/10.1080/00048623.2013.773865.

CILIP (2013) *Professional Knowledge and Skills Base*, www.cilip.org.uk/jobs-careers/professional-knowledge-skills-base.

Corcoran, M. and McGuinness, C. (2014) Keeping Ahead of the Curve, *Library Management*, **35** (3), 175–98, doi:http://dx.doi.org/10.1108/LM-06-2013-0048.

Corrall, S. (2010) Educating the Academic Librarian as a Blended Professional: a review and case study, *Library Management*, **31** (8/9) 567–93, doi: 10.1108/01435121011093360.

Cox, A. M. and Corrall, S. (2013) Evolving Academic Library Specialties, *Journal of the American Society for Information Science & Technology*, **64** (8), 1526–42,
doi:http://dx.doi.org/10.1002/asi.22847.

Haddow, G. (2012) Knowledge, Skills and Attributes for Academic Reference Librarians, *Australian Academic & Research Libraries*, **43** (3), 231–48.

HEDG (2013) *Heads of Educational Development Group*,
http://jiscdesignstudio.pbworks.com/w/page/48783639/HEDG%20DL

HEFCE (2015) *Open Access Research*, www.hefce.ac.uk/rsrch/oa/FAQ/#deposit3.

Inskip, C. (2013) *Mapping Resources to Competencies: a quick guide to the JISC Developing Digital Literacies resources*,
www.sconul.ac.uk/publication/mapping-resources-to-competencies.

IoE (2013) *Digital Literacies as a Postgraduate Attribute project*, http://jiscdesignstudio.pbworks.com/w/page/50732695/Digital%20Literacies%20 as%20a%20Postgraduate%20Attribute%20project.

Jisc (2011) *Developing Digital Literacies: briefing paper in support of JISC grant funding 4/11*, www.jisc.ac.uk/media/documents/funding/2011/04/Briefingpaper.pdf.

Jisc (2014) *Developing Digital Literacies*, https://www.jisc.ac.uk/guides/developing-digital-literacies.

Jisc (2015) *Building Digital Capability*, https://www.jisc.ac.uk/rd/projects/building-digital-capability.

Jisc (2016) *Our Vision, Mission and Strategy*, https://www.jisc.ac.uk/about/corporate/strategy.

Kay, J., Dunne, E. and Hutchinson, J. (2010) *Rethinking the Values of Higher Education – Students as Change Agents?* Quality Assurance Agency for Higher Education, www.qaa.ac.uk/en/Publications/Documents/Rethinking-the-values-of-higher-education-students-as-change-agents.pdf.

Lewis, D. (2007) A Strategy for Academic Libraries in the First Quarter of the 21st Century, *College & Research Libraries*, **68** (5), 418.

Lippincott, J., Hemmasi, H. and Lewis, V. (2014) Trends in Digital Scholarship Centers, *EDUCAUSE Review*, www.educause.edu/ero/article/trends-digital-scholarship-centers.

Lynch, C. and Carleton, D. (2009) Lecture: Impact of Digital Scholarship on Research Libraries, *Journal of Library Administration*, **49** (3), 227–44.

MacColl, J. and Jubb, M. (2011) *Supporting Research: environments, administration and libraries*, Dublin, OH, OCLC Research, www.oclc.org/research/publications/library/2011/2011-10.pdf.

Mackenzie, A. (2012) *SCONUL: summary report on baseline survey of digital literacy; January 2012*, http://jiscdesignstudio.pbworks.com/w/file/fetch/66781051/SCONUL%20Baseline% 20summary.pdf.

Mamtora, J. (2013) Transforming Library Research Services: towards a collaborative partnership, *Library Management*, **34** (4/5), 352–71, doi:http://dx/doi.org/10.1108/01435121311328690.

Missingham, R. (2006) Library and Information Science, *Library Management*, **27** (4/5), 257–68, doi:http://dx/doi.org/10.1108/01435120610668197.

National Science Foundation (2003) *Revolutionizing Science and Engineering through Cyberinfrastructure: report of the National Science Foundation Blue-Ribbon Advisory Panel on Cyberinfrastructure*, www.nsf.gov/cise/sci/reports/atkins.pdf (accessed 15 January 2016).

Nielsen, H. and Hjørland, B. (2014) Curating Research Data: the potential roles of libraries and information professionals, *Journal of Documentation*, **70** (2), 221–40, doi:http://dx/doi.org/10.1108/JD-03-2013-0034.

Orme, V. (2008) You Will Be …: a study of job advertisements to determine employers' requirements for LIS professionals in the UK in 2007, *Library Review*, **57** (8), 619–33, doi:http://dx/doi.org/10.1108/00242530810899595.

Partridge, H. and Hallam, G. (2004) The Double Helix: a personal account of the discovery of the structure of [the information professional's] DNA, *Australia Library and Information Association Conference, Queensland, 21–24 September 2004*, http://eprints.qut.edu.au/1215/1/1215.pdf.

Pinfield, S., Cox, A. and Smith, J. (2014) Research Data Management and Libraries: relationships, activities, drivers and influences, *PLoS One*, **9** (12), e114734, doi:http://dx/doi.org/10.1371/journal.pone.0114734.

Plymouth University (2013) *Seedpod Project*, http://jiscdesignstudio.pbworks.com/w/page/50732781/SEEDPoD%20project.

Rice, R. and Haywood, J. (2011) Research Data Management Initiatives at University of Edinburgh, *International Journal of Digital Curation*, **6** (2), 232–44, doi: 10.2218/ijdc.v6i2.199.

RILADS (2012) *Research Information Literacy and Digital Scholarship*, https://rilads.wordpress.com/2012/10/26/rin-and-sconul-announce-rilads-project-into-information-literacy-and-digital-scholarship/.

SCAP (2013) *Standing Committee on Academic Practice*, http://jiscdesignstudio.pbworks.com/w/page/48784350/SCAP%20DL.

SCONUL (2011) *The SCONUL Seven Pillars of Information Literacy: core model for higher education*, www.sconul.ac.uk/sites/default/files/documents/coremodel.pdf .

SCONUL (2012) *SCONUL Digital Literacies Baseline Survey*, http://jiscdesignstudio.pbworks.com/w/page/50824902/SCONUL%20Baseline%20summary.

SCONUL (2016a) *About SCONUL*, www.sconul.ac.uk/page/about-sconul.

SCONUL (2016b) *Digital Literacy Lens on the SCONUL Seven Pillars of Information Literacy*, www.sconul.ac.uk/sites/default/files/documents/Digital_Lens.pdf.

SEDA (2013) *Staff and Educational Development Association*, http://jiscdesignstudio.pbworks.com/w/page/48784376/SEDA%20D.

UCA (2016) *Visual Arts Data Service Research Centre*, http://ucreative2.ucreative.ac.uk/article/39362/Visual-Arts-Data-Service-Research-Centre.

UCL (2013) *The Digital Department Project*, http://jiscdesignstudio.pbworks.com/w/page/50732785/The%20Digital%20Department%20project.

UCLDH (2015) *UCLDH*, www.ucl.ac.uk/dh (accessed 26 February 2016).

University of Bath (2013) *Pride Project*, http://jiscdesignstudio.pbworks.com/w/page/50732777/PRIDE%20project.

University of Edinburgh (2016) *Digital Scholarship*, www.digital.hss.ed.ac.uk/.

University of Exeter (2013) *Exeter Cascade Project*, http://jiscdesignstudio.pbworks.com/w/page/50732446/ExeterCascade%20project.

Vassilakaki, E. and Moniarou-Papaconstantinou, V. (2015) A Systematic Literature Review

Informing Library and Information Professionals' Emerging Roles, *New Library World*, **116** (1/2), 37–66, doi:http://dx/doi.org/10.1108/NLW-05-2014-0060.

Vinopal, J. and McCormick, M. (2013) Supporting Digital Scholarship in Research Libraries: scalability and sustainability, *Journal of Library Administration*, **53**, 27–42.

VITAE (2013) *Vitae DL*, http://jiscdesignstudio.pbworks.com/w/page/48785366/Vitae%20DL.

Wilson, J., Martinez-Uribe, L., Fraser, M. and Jeffreys, P. (2011) An Institutional Approach to Developing Research Data Management Infrastructure, *International Journal of Digital Curation*, **6** (2), 274–87, doi: 10.2218/ijdc.v6i2.203.

5

Lean in the library: building capacity by realigning staff and resources

Jennifer Bremner

Introduction

The body that represents the university sector in Australia, Universities Australia, has identified digital scholarship and operational efficiency as two key drivers for change in the Australian higher education sector. The strategy statement for 2013 to 2016, titled *A Smarter Australia*, recognizes 'the emergence of the digital economy and new technology, globalisation and the Asian century, economic and industrial restructuring and the need to improve productivity' (Universities Australia, 2013, 9).

In this strategy statement it situates digital scholarship within the context of the wider economy and government agenda for Australia:

> The digital economy and technology are transforming higher education, just as they have transformed media, retail, entertainment, finance and administration … These changing practices and cultures bring challenges and opportunities that change university teaching, research, structure and business models, and responding to them has been urged by both senior Labor and Coalition [Government] frontbenchers.
>
> (Universities Australia, 2013, 52)

In response to the drivers of the digital economy, including digital scholarship, and the need for greater productivity in the Australian university sector, it has adopted the policy principle that

> Universities need to continue to look for new ways to increase productivity and operational efficiency, including external benchmarking and innovative uses of new technologies.
>
> (Universities Australia, 2013, 49)

The strategic plan for Macquarie University has been formulated in response to extensive consultation conducted with staff and students after the arrival of the new Vice-Chancellor in 2012. As well as the drivers outlined in *A Smarter Australia*, the Macquarie University aspiration and vision is to be

> a university of service and engagement. We serve and engage our students and staff through transformative learning and life experiences; and we serve and engage the world through discovery, dissemination of knowledge and ideas, innovation and deep partnerships.
>
> (Macquarie University, 2013, 7)

There are strategic priority areas that support this vision. Strategic priority number seven in the plan is 'improving those aspects of our support services to realize this aspiration and vision' (Macquarie University, 2013, 23). This priority was designed to improve the University support services to enable research and teaching to deliver their potential for the institution and was formulated in response to staff feedback during the consultation phase, which identified that the University's processes and approaches were not sufficiently modern or efficient to support their academic purpose. Implementing this priority included a strategic Business Process Improvement Initiative 'to improve the quality and speed of the library's support processes to deliver on the University's strategic vision'.[1]

The digital environment facilitates new approaches to scholarly practice, which in turn initiates new ways of thinking, different skill sets and services that mean traditional ways of working often no longer make the most sense. Reviewing work activities and routine processes help to identify where outmoded approaches may be removed or replaced. The benefits of adopting such an approach will be explored in this chapter, but the overarching benefit can be realized through process improvements, freeing staff time and skills to address areas of emerging practices; because '[l]ibraries are experiencing the same kinds of transformational change our colleges and universities are encountering, digital technology fundamentally alters how services are provided, research is conducted and learning occurs' (Hawkins, 2000, 3).

In this chapter I will describe how Macquarie University Library has embraced business process improvement as an opportunity to redesign its processes and services in an environment of digital scholarship and fast-emerging, often disruptive, technologies. For the purposes of this discussion, digital scholarship can be described as 'shorthand for the entire body of changing scholarly practice, a reminder and recognition of the fact that most areas of scholarly work today have been transformed, to a lesser or greater extent, by a series of information technologies' (Lynch, 2014, 12).

Since the mid-1990s, Macquarie University Library has responded to the change in the way scholars research, teach, learn and communicate in a variety of ways that utilize technology. For example, an automated retrieval system (ARC), a robotic warehousing solution for storing the collection, was built into the new library building in 2010. Eighty per cent of the physical collection is now kept in the ARC storage bins, freeing up space for collaborative learning. The Library now has digital repositories, an electronic preferred approach to resource discovery, online service delivery and information literacy teaching, a new discovery system implemented in 2011 and a new library management system implemented in 2014; it has also worked to digitize some collections and integrate data, discovery services and resource management into wider university systems.

Despite the numerous changes implemented in response to the drivers of emerging information technologies, government policy, digital scholarship and scholarly communication, the Library continues to maintain some traditional – and often no longer valuable – processes, operations and services. We are now working to remove or redesign legacy processes and services to improve the user experience and also reallocate resources and staff to support new services and innovation. This involves a shift, as described by Dempsey (2013), 'from thinking about the library as a fixed set of services (bureaucratic) to thinking about it as an organization which configures to map changes in its user environment and expectations (enterprise)'. While this poses a challenge, there are also opportunities to be bold, develop staff and continue to position the Library as a key partner in the process of digital scholarship.

Macquarie University Business Process Improvement Initiative

The University commenced a Business Process Improvement Initiative (BPII) in response to feedback from the consultation process that resulted in the 2013 *Our University: a framing of futures* strategic vision. BPII works to simplify and clarify business processes for the whole Macquarie University community, endeavouring to empower both staff and students to identify improvements to organizational processes and then implement them. The BPII team facilitate projects which are run by cross-University and departmental teams who are tasked to implement improvements and act as change agents. The project teams work both to increase efficiency in processes and to provide value for the customers of those processes.

The BPII uses the Lean in Higher Education approach in order to improve the quality and effectiveness of University processes. Lean methodology originated in post-war Japan, when the car giant Toyota revolutionized the manufacturing process; its focus is on identifying just the right amount of resources required to complete an activity in a way that meets customer needs. Lean in Higher Education is defined as 'the application of lean principles and practices to higher education' (Balzer 2010, 14).

Lean in Higher Education is implemented in a wide variety of institutions globally and the model adopted by Macquarie University is the St Andrews model, adapted by the University of St Andrews, Scotland. The St Andrews model uses a specific methodology to apply the lean principles. It follows the path of request, scoping, planning, training, redesign (using a rapid improvement event [RIE]), implementation, review and feedback (Robinson, 2014). A key element of this model is the redesign phase, where RIEs are run over five days and the activities involved are: mapping the existing process, generating ideas for improvement and creating a new process for implementation.

The two fundamental concepts of lean are (i) respect for people and (ii) continuous improvement. Its principles and the identification of waste are the central elements of the process improvement methodology. Lean principles are about maximizing value in a process *as the customer sees it*. In practice this means improving the value and effectiveness of a process or service by focusing on the outcome that best meets the needs of the customer. This is done by consulting the customer and those who work in the process, and by removing waste within the process in order to increase its effectiveness and help to ensure the desired outcome.

Library business process improvement

Macquarie University Library has a Service Model and quality methodology that focuses on a 'one Library' approach. The one Library philosophy relies on collaboration, knowledge sharing and co-ordination across functional boundaries to deliver quality services. (Macquarie University Library, 2013). This approach encourages and supports cross-functional teams working together to meet client needs. Adopting the Lean in Higher Education methodology in improving processes and services is a natural fit with the one Library approach, as it emphasizes the need to work together across functional boundaries.

The current priority is to embed the management-based Quality Enhancement Framework and Service Model as practical operational elements which are meaningful for our staff and clients. The Quality Framework and Service Model (Figure 5.1) are designed to guide the way the Library works and to help it navigate towards its strategic goals. To be effective, they first need to be understood by the staff who are aiming for those goals. The plan is to create an organizational culture of deep staff engagement

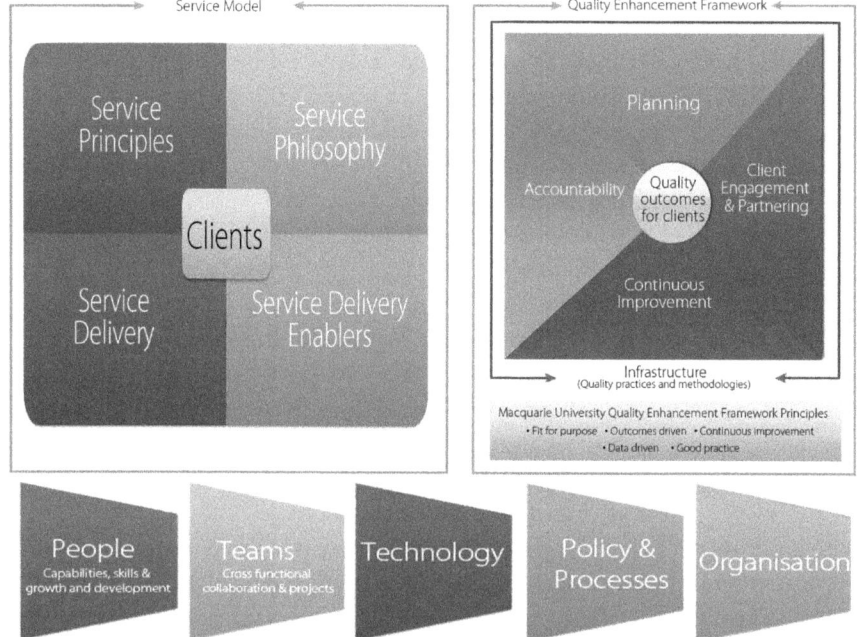

Figure 5.1 *Macquarie University Library Service Model and Quality Enhancement Framework*

with client-centred service delivery, where processes and client engagement are strengthened by continuous improvement. It is the staff that make a high-quality service possible and they, along with other colleagues working in the digital environment, must adapt to change and identify improvements as new ways of working emerge.

As part of implementing the Quality Enhancement Framework the Library introduced a business process management project based on the premise that it could not improve what it did not fully see or understand. This meant drawing maps of its current processes and services in order to ensure that they were effectively doing what they were intended to do, as well as to identify where processes intersect and where dependencies exist. During the discovery phase of this business process management project, the Library partnered with the BPII team so that it was using the University's preferred approach for improving processes.

The aim of the Library's business process management project was to move from functionally based (team) responsibilities to process-based (workflow) accountabilities. The project outcomes worked in concert with the Library's 'What We Do Matters' programme which was designed by the Library to embed the operational elements of the Quality Enhancement Framework and Service Model for its staff. This project established sustainable, holistic, end-to-end methods to better understand library processes into the future. The Library is combining the 'What We Do Matters' programme with lean principles to improve staff skills, customer service, efficiency, communication, co-operation, connections and understanding throughout the Library, and with other campus departments and areas.

A threefold approach was introduced for end-to-end cross-functional process management and improvement:

- *business analysis*: analysis of processes in liaison with departments and teams to identify, create and map them
- *process improvement*: partnering with the BPII in conducting process analysis and redesign using the Lean in Higher Education methodology; these redesigns are of processes recommended for improvement by the Library
- *process engagement*: encouraging empowered staff to ask 'is there a better way?'; to improve processes throughout the Library as part of the What We Do Matters programme; to implement the Quality Framework and Service Model in daily library practices.

This is only the beginning of a large, ongoing piece of work which has the potential to create lasting and transformative cultural change. In responding to digital scholarship, academic libraries have had to modify their service delivery and processes so as to adapt to challenges that are broadly 'focused around clients, systems and technology; the scholarly communication process and the learning environment' (Williamson, 2006, 551).

Using a process-based approach that

- encompasses value as the customer or client sees it
- encourages leveraging technology where possible and
- adapts to the cultural and organizational environment in which the process operates

provides a way of responding to these areas of challenge. Developing staff to work in an environment which focuses on process outcomes encourages them to see how all aspects of delivering a service interact together to either support or hinder a quality outcome.

Forming cross-functional teams which employ lean principles to improve processes and services reinforces the importance of providing value and reducing waste in all that the Library does. It also provides development opportunities for staff as they collaborate with their colleagues and identify how they can make a difference to their working environment.

Lean in Higher Education

The work of the BPII team, using Lean in Higher Education, has underpinned the ability of the Library to maximize value and reduce waste in the processes and services that have been reviewed. The lean approach supports flexible and creative service delivery in the fast-paced digital environment. The Library has been able to improve processes and services while removing unnecessary legacy activities. It has also enabled the Library to engage staff in collaborative teams and leverage existing digital service enablers more effectively. This has enhanced the way it works by promoting an understanding throughout the Library of work as a process and showing that processes can be improved effectively by the staff who work in them. This section describes how Lean has been applied in the Library.

Respect for people

Respect for people is a key concept in the lean methodology. Respecting all stakeholders in a process, listening to each voice and enabling individuals to be proactive and feel valued is part of this concept, empowering those who work in the process to redesign it and implement the changes. The Macquarie University Library What We Do Matters programme incorporates this concept.

This programme in conjunction with the BPII and the lean projects it has facilitated with the Library have enabled the Library to initiate and retire processes and services in response to customer needs and the current digital working environment. A key part of this approach is to employ cross-functional project teams who are focused on improving processes and services using a variety of lean and project management tools, which enable staff to learn from one another and to ask 'is there a better way?' A central tenet of this approach, respect for people and the What We Do Matters programme, is engaging with and empowering staff to suggest and enact improvements and to be flexible, innovative and responsive to change.

For the Library, quality outcomes are all about people working and learning together to achieve sustainable change and continuous incremental improvements. Our approach is to get the right people, including students and stakeholders, to work on projects, processes and service improvements. This dynamic approach has helped to foster a new relationship culture with academic colleagues, in particular those embracing new technologies in support of their teaching, learning or research.

Dealing with academics, researchers and cohorts of students who primarily work and communicate in a world which revolves around digital technology presents a number of challenges to the way the Library delivers services. It endeavours to hear and incorporate the voice of these clients as part of its development and continuous improvement of services. Lean focuses on value as the customer sees it and helps to keep the student and researcher experience at the forefront of decision making.

In order to adapt successfully and remain relevant in an environment of digital scholarship 'we must challenge our traditional cautious culture; our roles, systems, technologies, even language is changing. We must change our attitudes and skill sets. We must change our ideas and misconceptions' (Williamson, 2006, 556).

The staff in the project teams learn new skills, gain an understanding of lean principles and develop team working, collaborative and project management skills. They learn to see work as a series of processes, identify what clients value and recognize areas for improvement. They develop capabilities which enable professional growth and learn that it is acceptable, and even desirable, to let go of the things that are no longer effective or useful.

Continuous improvement

The final key concept of lean is continuous improvement, which is also a central tenet of the Library's Quality Enhancement Framework as shown in Figure 5.2.

The Library Quality Enhancement Framework and Lean in Higher Education methodology complement each other. It is self-evident that in order to improve we need to understand what we are doing. Viewing work as a process assists us with this and underpins the continuous improvement cycle. Many processes and services are improved either by using Lean in Higher Education RIEs or by applying lean principles to projects and daily work.

In order to improve incrementally and to manage change effectively we need to act based on a thoughtful assessment of evidence. Staff are encouraged to locate, identify and work together to fix problems and to make improvements. The Library has avenues in place for staff to raise issues, identify and implement improvements in their work areas and the processes they use. Stakeholder engagement is essential to ensure that changes are necessary, appropriate and co-ordinated.

Maximize value

The five principles of Lean describe value in the following terms.

1. *Value* – is what the customer determines it is as the customer sees it.

Figure 5.2 *The four central pillars of the Quality Enhancement Framework, including continuous improvement*

2. *Value stream* – is to find the best approach to any process and eliminate waste to enhance efficiency and improve the outcome.
3. Create *flow* – is to maintain a constant flow and deal with peaks in demand effectively.
4. *Pull* – is to create services and products based on what is in demand; give clients what they are asking for when they ask for it.
5. *Perfection* – is to seek perfection; you may not get there, but do not settle for the status quo if things can be made better – and things can always be made better.

The Library has begun applying these lean principles to maximizing value when assessing services or revising its practices. Using lean terminology, it wants to add value as the customer sees it. By doing this in the context of a mature culture of continuous improvement and client-centred staff engagement, the Library can demonstrate its value to the wider University. Reducing processes and services that do not add value enables it to focus on developing and demonstrating the roles it can play in supporting digital scholarship and other University initiatives; for example, redeveloping the website led to a focus on discovery, and removing legacy systems and pages has improved clients' satisfaction as they can more readily find what they are looking for – not necessarily what librarians want to tell them.

Reducing waste

As discussed earlier, the Library has been able to remove legacy approaches and unnecessary process steps. It has done this through the identification of waste as it is understood in Lean. Each process redesign identifies waste in processes and enables the team to see where things can be let go or retired. For example, waste might be getting multiple sign-offs for a blog post that delays the post going live and means that the blog is not responsive to client expectations of immediacy. Reducing this by entrusting social media communications to a few well-trained and informed staff enables the Library to be more relevant, timely and responsive to the digital environment.

Staff engagement – What We Do Matters

The What We Do Matters programme has four key elements in order to engage staff in the service and quality principles of the Library. The key elements of What We Do Matters are the following:

- Create positive experiences.
- Is there a better way?
- What I do matters.
- What we do matters.

These messages focus on the key concepts of Lean: respect for people and continuous improvement. Combining Lean with the staff engagement strategy has proved to be a sound and useful approach to developing and empowering staff. The ultimate goal is that these messages of better staff understanding, empowerment and engagement become embedded into the culture to the extent that they are regarded as 'the way things are done' at Macquarie University Library.

The What We Do Matters programme and its key elements support the strategic direction of the Library and the implementation of the service model and quality framework. It should be noted, however, that you will not find the terms *strategic, vision, principles, framework* or *model* used in this programme. Strategy, vision and principles still exist, but the way they are explained to staff and integrated into their daily work has been reshaped to be more accessible and relatable, as illustrated in Figure 5.3.

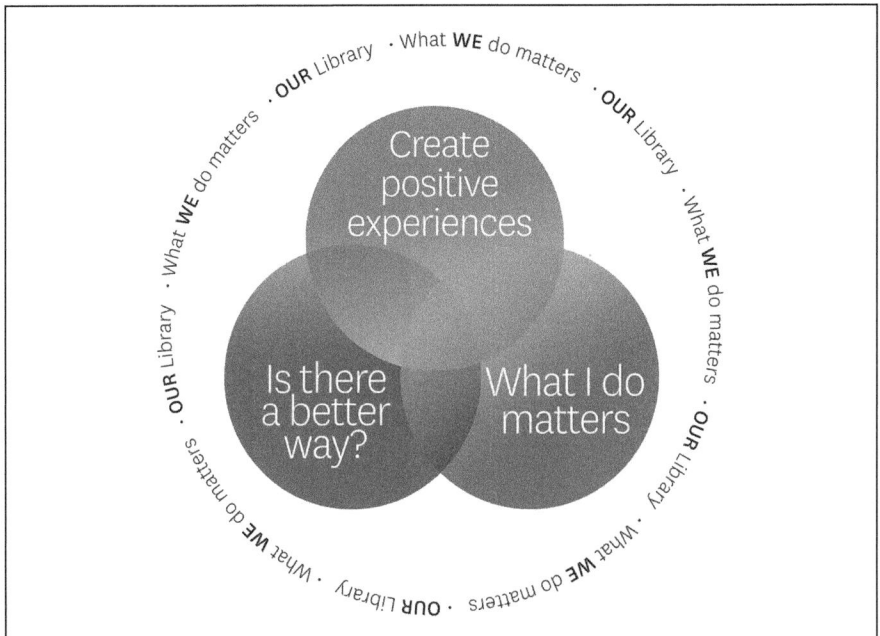

Figure 5.3 *Graphic created for the What We Do Matters communications*

Create positive experiences

The focus of the Library Service Model is on the customer experience, and in practice means being welcoming and client centred in all the Library does. Creating positive experiences for everyone is set out in the service principles of:

- responding to clients as individuals, as well as addressing their collective needs
- learning partnerships, learning together with clients and colleagues
- positive, proactive communication, client engagement and respect for others
- being responsive to client needs now and to future trends
- sharing knowledge and building relationships
- reflecting on and assessing services.

In practice this means staff:

- listening to clients
- responding to all requests and feedback with courtesy, patience, sensitivity and tact
- participating in the assessment of services
- adding value as the client sees it when suggesting improvements or changes to services.

Is there a better way?

By using evidence and encouraging staff to continuously improve services and processes, the aim is to create sustainable and agile enhancements. These incorporate quality principles:

- reflective practice to think about why and how we do things
- critically assessing what we do to see what is successful and what can be improved
- fit-for-purpose to ensure we can deal with fluctuations in demand, and create a smooth flow of work
- benchmarking to gather evidence, aid reflection and see if there are better ways of doing things
- evidence-based practice and decision making to inform recommendations.

In practice this means staff:

- providing meaningful feedback on services and processes
- participating in process improvement
- contributing to the development of new and improved services
- understanding the importance of reflection, assessment and continuous improvement.

What I do matters

Every staff member is an active participant in ensuring that services are relevant, provide quality and are user focused. Self-improvement and development are key to What I Do Matters, with its focus on accountability, skills improvement and professional behaviour.

In practice this means staff:

- being accountable and responsible for decisions and actions
- having direct engagement with client issues
- communicating and referring
- providing informed feedback and recommendations
- building expertise, engaging in training and development
- gathering evidence and reflecting on current practices to find opportunities to improve.

Our Library and What We Do Matters

We are one Library and rely on collaboration, partnerships, sound communication, teamwork, knowledge sharing and co-ordination across functional boundaries to deliver quality services. What we do daily as colleagues in support of our clients and one another matters. The aim is for us to achieve our strategic goals in a sustainable and synchronized manner.

In practice this means:

- participating in lean projects where staff collaborate to make improvements in response to user needs, strategic and environmental changes
- engaging clients through respectful, positive encounters and actively seeking their input
- creating and contributing to learning partnerships with colleagues and clients
- using established and clear referral mechanisms.

By adopting this clear What We Do Matters approach, demonstrating practical applications and keeping it very simple, we find that we are making inroads with most of the staff on the importance of a workable, practical model of quality and service.

To maintain momentum and engagement in the What We Do Matters programme the Library has undertaken:

- widespread coaching
- facilitation of group discussions
- regular briefing and debriefing sessions
- extensive internal communication
- a linked reward and recognition programme with both on-the-spot and annual rewards
- generic performance indicators for all staff
- guidance for team leaders and managers.

As a result of this programme and the associated application of lean principles using RIEs and projects it is pleasing that the Library is seeing deeper and more conscious staff engagement with service outcomes and continuous improvement.

In terms of the What We Do Matters programme there are a number of improvements which have been made without engaging the BPII while still applying Lean principles, where traditional approaches have been adapted to the digital environment and, as a by-product, staff have been released to deliver a more flexible and bespoke service which better meets clients' needs.

Some examples where changes to processes are now better aligned to clients' needs are:

- removal, and reduction in the number, of borrowing and loan categories. This has reduced confusion for clients and provided a more consistent service
- introduction of a single borrowing period for all clients, except for high-demand short loan items, with automatic renewals unless something is placed on hold by another customer
- streamlining of the way guests login to the guest PCs, with a significant reduction in paperwork
- redesigned approach to information literacy, with restructured online modules and video production in-house
- streamlined processing of materials for short loan, removing a large amount of manual handling and enabling the collection to be more responsive to client demand
- end to charging fines for late return of items (a replacement fee is still in place for lost items).

The speed at which these process changes can be implemented should aim to match the speed at which new skills, knowledge and technology enter the academic environment; for library services, the pressure is on to adapt quickly so as to remain relevant and valuable. 'If universities and libraries are to survive as institutions ... we must continue to adapt' (Williamson, 2006, 554).

The Library's approach to supporting and developing staff to be more agile and to understand work as a process enables it to identify how and where the staff can harness their skills in partnership with researchers and scholars and employ new technologies and devices to deliver a better experience for clients. Where processes are more effective and streamlined staff have been freed up to work on more value-added services such as the collaborative development of games to teach medical students about virology, the provision of learning skills and academic literacy support, and acting as researchers in the creation of systematic reviews for medical research.

Case studies

The following case studies illustrate how the Library has tackled three areas where legacy approaches were reducing the efficiency of a process. The RIEs and lean projects undertaken have been for processes where it was felt that significant gain could be made in areas under the Library's control and where small improvements would have large impacts on productivity or service delivery.

By redesigning these processes the Library has reduced obstacles and freed up staff time and skills to engage in more value-added work.

Each of the three case studies will outline one of the process improvement projects conducted by the Library and using BPII facilitated RIEs over a period of 18 months. Each will cover the context, problem, objective, resulting improvements and the impact of those improvements on service delivery. Whilst not describing digital scholarship initiatives, the case studies illustrate the lean process in action and show how the Library is applying strategy to reconfigure effort and services, and reallocate resource to better engage with service enhancements that are both sustainable and scalable.

CASE STUDY 5.1   Library shelving process

The context
In November 2014 an RIE was held with the objective of improving the processes for shelving items. The RIE was designed to look at how items used by clients, then either discharged or collected, could be most effectively returned to the correct physical locations. This was to facilitate better availability and use of the physical Library collection, to improve the client's experience of accessing items and provide quicker turnaround time for in-demand items.

The process
The shelving process includes activities where items are used by clients and then discharged or left for collection in the Library. These items then need to be returned to the correct physical location. Items being processed for other Library purposes were considered out of scope for this project.

The problem
Clients identified that multiple locations for shelving, the backlog with returns and items not being returned to the shelves quickly were the main problems with the process. A key

issue was the perception by clients that returns to the short loan collection were taking too long to be processed.

The objective
The express aim of the project was 'to make a process for shelving that is efficient, transparent and accountable and returns items to correct physical locations so clients can access these as required'.

The cross-functional team
The core project team that looked at the shelving process was primarily from one department; they consulted and worked closely with all library departments. The team consulted with academic staff and students and aimed to address the needs of the majority of clients.

The improvements
The redesign of the process allowed for the following improvements:

- a reduction of over 50% in process steps
- a 100% reduction in the backlog of items to be returned to the shelves on a daily basis
- students' ability to access short loan items as soon as they are discharged instead of waiting for a loaded trolley to be ready. Students no longer need to negotiate with staff for access to these items, nor wait unnecessarily
- process and workspace redesign to ensure that books to be shelved are moved only a short distance between the back office and their final location
- books sorted only once, directly onto trolleys, meaning a reduction in double and triple handling of items to be re-shelved, which enabled the removal of the sorting shelves
- removal of unnecessary counting of re-shelved items by shelving staff.

The benefits and outcomes
The key service improvements for clients are that they can access returned in-demand short loan items quickly and easily. They can collect their automated retrieval items themselves. They have more study space, as the sorting shelves have been removed and seating has been put in instead. Books are more likely to be on the shelves where they are supposed to be for borrowing and use.

Implementation

The new shelving process was implemented in January 2015, and as a result staff spend less time mediating collection access and shelving each day. This enables them to undertake other activities such as scanning for the digital repositories, dealing with enquiries and providing roving services in the Library. There is also a reduction in complaints about short loan items not being available.

CASE STUDY 5.2 Library enquiry process

The context

In February 2015 an RIE was held with the objective of improving the processes for Library enquiry management. The RIE was designed to look at how the Library answered, handled, managed, tracked and recorded incoming enquiries from all its clients.

The process

The enquiry process begins when an enquiry is received by the Library and ends when the client indicates that they are informed and are prepared to close the enquiry. Clients have the power to close the enquiry or leave it open depending on their level of satisfaction.

The problem

The problem identified with this process was the need to improve clarity and co-ordination in dealing with in-bound enquiries and referrals so as to provide a more streamlined service to clients with no gaps and duplication of effort or answers. Initially this problem was specifically focused on the 'virtual' enquiries, those coming in from sources other than face-to-face, such as chat, phone and e-mail. However it was quickly realized that clients would benefit more if all enquiries were included, no matter where or how they arrived.

The objective

The objective was to create 'an integrated, coordinated, consistent, accurate and timely enquiry process that gives clients a clear pathway to have their information needs met'. The investigation of the enquiry process showed that it was not managed holistically. This RIE enabled the process to be redesigned as a cohesive whole.

The cross-functional team

The project team for this RIE included representatives from all five Library departments and involved the largest range of roles of any RIE to date. The focus was on matching the incoming enquiry process to clients' requirements based on the service philosophy that all Library staff are directly engaged with clients and their needs.

The improvements

The improvements from this RIE so far include:

- a clear, consistent process with streamlined referral
- a transparent, smooth process for the client with reduced barriers to service
- a reduction in double handling, so that clients do not have to make multiple enquiries to get answers
- the introduction of a customer relationship management system, leveraging on the University system
- a new, co-ordinated telephone system with appropriate checks and balances
- clear guidance for staff on how to handle client enquiries and improved staff training
- centrally gathered and analysed information to identify recurrent enquiries and self-service options created for recurring enquiries.

The benefits and outcomes

The key service improvement for clients is that they have a central online place to ask questions, provide feedback and find FAQ information. A consistent level of service is provided and they do not have to repeat information they have already given about an enquiry. They can check their enquiries to see progress.

The new enquiry management process has led to:

- enquiries being handled and tracked more effectively
- more telephone enquiries being answered, with reduced queues and fewer turned-away calls and hang-ups by clients
- better support for digital scholarship by more appropriate referrals to qualified staff
- staff with appropriate expertise having more time to actively support digital scholarship and partner with scholars in their research and teaching.

Implementation

The new process was implemented in July 2015 and a staged release of the changes with incremental improvements is continuing. A review of the new process was due to take place in April 2016. Looking at how the new process works during a peak time, the beginning of session one in February and March 2016 aimed to fully test it and its capacity to handle a large volume of enquiries.

CASE STUDY 5.3   Library scanning and copying process

The context
In October 2015 an RIE was held with the objective of creating an improved scanning and photocopying process. This process used a number of paper forms and was very manual. Clarifying the roles and responsibilities within the process was essential.

The process
The process begins when a client or staff member makes a request for an item to be scanned or copied and ends when the copy or scan is made available. It should be noted that this service is provided for access to restricted collections. If clients need to copy or scan books on the open shelves they are asked to do so themselves.

The problem
The main problems were the inconsistency in approach between departments and the fact that the Library was not effectively leveraging technologies and systems to support clients or generate usable statistics to inform planning and evaluation.

The objective
The RIE and lean project were intended to provide an 'efficient, coordinated and consistent process with clear ownership and responsibilities so that scans and copies are made available within agreed time frames and to agreed quality'. Meeting deadlines was particularly important for in-demand items, for clients with specific due dates and for the digital repository. Quality was essential for all users, and particularly for those who required specific formats and accommodations to use print materials.

The cross-functional team
The core project team was drawn from three Library departments, with essential critical friends representing the whole Library. The team consisted of those who worked with the

Library systems and technology and those who performed scanning or copying as part of their work.

The improvements
The improvements implemented to date include:

- reduction in the number of steps from 75 to 30
- reduction in paper forms and manual handling
- the creation of a central scanning facility
- improved staff knowledge about the scanners
- reprogrammed scanners to improve scans and reduce double handling.

The outstanding improvements still to be implemented from the RIE include:

- replacing all paper forms with a central online request form
- looking at ways in which the scans can completely replace photocopies for clients, as they have for the collections
- clients being able to make their own digitization requests directly into the system.

Intended benefits
Key benefits are a reduction in paper forms, improved scans and faster response times.

- Statistics are kept and are available for analysis.
- Informed and well trained staff provide a better, more timely service.
- Co-ordination, ownership and responsibilities are clear.
- Existing technology and systems are used to generate and collate the majority of requests.

Implementation
This new process and the service of digitization were planned go live in early 2016, the staff side being fully enacted and the client option being introduced later and given a limited pilot to test its viability. So far, staff involved in the scanning process have been able to create a team where they share knowledge and several members of the scanning team have taken on new roles and responsibilities in dealing with clients and services.

To date, half of the Library staff have participated in lean RIE redesign and implementation projects. In November 2015 the first four teams won the Vice-

Chancellor's Excellence Award for Professional Staff in the category of innovation and process improvement.

Conclusion

To be regarded as an asset in the digital environment, the Library must demonstrate that it can deliver on the University's vision and address the challenges faced by the whole organization. It must prove that it can provide valuable strategic and tactical advantages to the University and to scholars working in a ubiquitous digital milieu. Macquarie University Library has worked to support the University's vision to 'be a university of service and engagement' (Macquarie University, 2013, 7) by practising service and engagement in concrete and measurable ways.

The Library has three strategic priorities that align with the University strategy. These are:

- enhance research performance
- provide an inspiring learning experience
- establish and foster distinctive and purposeful partnerships.[2]

Through collaboration with the BPII the Library has established and continues to foster a distinctive and purposeful partnership. This partnership is supporting the client-centred service model and greatly enhancing the Library's ability to undertake continuous improvement.

In order to actively support the university and proactively engage with digital scholarship, the Library recognizes that its key asset is its people. Implementing a strategic staff engagement approach, encouraging collaboration and empowerment has enabled it to develop a workforce that is more agile, ready for the rapid pace of change in the digital environment. The Library uses staff engagement and lean principles to adapt its ways of working and increase its effectiveness in response to the digital economy and the need for greater productivity in the Australian university sector.

The Library has demonstrated (and continues to do so) that it is an asset to the University by engaging with its clients to give them what they tell it they need, what is of value to them and, through them, to the organization. The Library demonstrates that it is an asset by improving its productivity and by doing more with what it has. Using Lean in Higher Education to redesign processes and reposition its resources allows the Library to let go of the activities that absorb resources without providing a corresponding benefit to the University. As it realigns its resources by removing legacy activities it can make space to introduce appropriate new approaches to continue to position the Library as a significant partner in digital scholarship.

Notes

1 www.mq.edu.au/about/about-the-university/strategy-and-initiatives/strategic-initiatives.
2 www.mq.edu.au/about/campus-services-and-facilities/library/about-us/strategic-planning/strategic-priorities-2014-2016.

References

Balzer, W. K. (2010) *Lean in Higher Education: increasing the performance and value of university processes*, New York, CRC Press, Taylor & Francis.

Dempsey, L. (2013) *Three Challenges: engaging, rightscaling and innovating*, http://orweblog.oclc.org/three-challenges-engaging-rightscaling-and-innovating/.

Hawkins, B. (2000) Libraries, Knowledge Management, and Higher Education in an Electronic Environment. In *ALIA 2000. Capitalising on knowledge: the information profession in the 21st century, Conference Proceedings, Canberra, Australia* (ERIC Document ED 425865).

Lynch, C. (2014) The 'Digital' Scholar Disconnect, *EDUCAUSE Review*, May/June, http://er.educause.edu/~/media/files/article-downloads/erm1431.

Macquarie University (2013) *Our University: a framing of futures*, www.mq.edu.au/our-university.

Macquarie University Library (2013) *Macquarie University Library Service Model 2013*, https://www.mq.edu.aug/_data/assets/pdf_file/0005/98582/143232.pdf.

Robinson, M. (2014) The University of St Andrews Lean Journey for Macquarie University, Sydney, Australia, https://www.youtube.com/watch?v=MtC4WToqVv0.

Universities Australia (2013) *A Smarter Australia: an agenda for Australian higher education 2013–2016*, Canberra, Australia.

Williamson, V. (2006) Surviving Change and Growing the Profession Together, *Library Management*, **27** (8) 548–61.

PART 3

Digital spaces and services

6

Digital scholarship centres: converging space and expertise

Tracy C. Bergstrom

Introduction

Within the USA, the emerging currency of 'digital scholarship' within the academy can be demonstrated through various metrics. With support from the Andrew Mellon Foundation, Bucknell University in Pennsylvania offers an annual academic conference solely devoted to topics in digital scholarship. The conference held in 2015 attracted over 150 attendees from across the USA (Bucknell University, 2015). Many professional organizations now provide guidelines for evaluating academic work in specific disciplinary fields of digital scholarship for the purposes of hiring, promotion and tenure (see, for example, the guidelines of the Modern Language Association, 2012). Academic job advertisements seeking digital scholarship knowledge have increased drastically in the past decade; in the field of history alone there was a tenfold increase from 2003–4 (three postings) to 2012 (34 postings) with at least some mention of digital scholarship. Of the academic positions in history (tenure-track, academic administration, or non-tenure faculty) advertised in fall 2013, 5 mentioned 'digital' in the title and an additional 11 required or preferred it. These prodigiously growing numbers in the above categories do not begin to reflect the broader opportunities for recent graduates with specialized digital scholarship skills outside of the traditional academy.

At many institutions, the university library fills the role of training and supporting individual researchers and students with an interest in digital scholarship. While teaching and research faculty are eager for their students to apply technology-based methodologies to research questions, they themselves are often unable or unwilling to devote class time to the acquisition of such skills. In many academic environments, therefore, including large research universities and small liberal arts colleges, the university library has increased its support for teaching and learning in new technology areas. In a workshop that brought together members of 24 digital scholarship centres from across the USA, Lippincott and Goldenberg-Hart (2014) identified common factors across institutions that led to the formation of a centre. These include a growing awareness by faculty or administration that students are graduating without the acquisition of contemporary skills sets; apprehension that peer institutions will eclipse the support or facilities offered at a particular university; and institutional assessment that affirmed the need or desire for services potentially offered by a digital scholarship centre. As these factors span departmental and disciplinary boundaries from pedagogical, financial and administrative concerns, the university library is well suited to adopt this new concept.

Digital scholarship centres

As one of the few organizations within a university with the potential to interact with all academic departments, the library also has the responsibility to democratize its services to address the greatest needs within the environment. While the motivations to establish digital scholarship centres across institutions are often similar, the suite of services offered by individual centres is highly variable. As Posner (2013) points out on behalf of digital humanities, establishing the appropriate administrative and technical infrastructure and support is crucial to success. Thus, although many academic libraries in the USA now support digital scholarship centres, each offers a unique programme of services based on the capacities of librarians who support services, the availability of space and resources, the library technology infrastructure and the existing technology support landscape of the university. Lippincott, Hemmasi and Lewis (2014) compiled a brief list of some of the most frequently supported activities of digital scholarship centres. These include planning digital projects; utilizing specialized software and tools; developing metadata and helping patrons to understand standards; answering intellectual property questions; planning for preservation; digitizing collections; and understanding scholarly publishing opportunities. A quick survey of digital scholarship centre websites also demonstrates that the support areas that the above categories apply to are highly variant and may include GIS (geographical information systems), text mining, digital exhibit design, data visualization, usability studies and makerspace or media production environments. Most digital scholarship centres offer a mix of services from these, but in no two instances are the precise service models exactly the same.

As mentioned above, many digital scholarship centres currently offer elements of a makerspace that potentially provide creative, design-related or engineering tools and applications such as 3D printers or modelling applications, robotics or computing kits.

A makerspace environment is therefore of potential interest to students across a wide range of disciplines including studio art, architecture and design, computer science or engineering. A makerspace environment in principle, however, operates on an entirely different model from a digital scholarship centre. A makerspace is intended to be a creative, open environment in which researchers can experiment with new ideas in a communal atmosphere (New Media Consortium, 2016). While makerspaces may be staffed, the emphasis is on individual growth through praxis; the creation of new products or ideas through prototyping; and community learning. In contrast, digital scholarship centres often are constructed as more formal environments in which the generation of new knowledge through technology is supported via partnerships with on-site staff, formal collaborations on projects with specific desired outcomes or the pursuit of articulated research questions. While some digital scholarship centres clearly mix elements of the two models, the tone of the space differs between a digital scholarship centre that includes makerspace elements and a true communal makerspace. The needs of the local university environment must guide each institution in determining exactly what mix of elements is appropriate when designing new library spaces.

Considerations in forming a new digital scholarship centre

The availability of librarians and other professionals with training commensurate to digital scholarship is the first of several considerations for academic libraries contemplating the formation of a centre. In Lippincott and Goldenberg-Hart's survey (2014) of the factors that led to the foundation of a new centre, no institution gave the rationale that funding had been set aside or raised specifically for the purpose. Therefore the majority of institutions that are starting digital scholarship centres are doing so with existing staff and resources. Paramount is the question of who will staff a new centre and what skills are appropriate to their new roles. Expertise in some aspect of emerging technology is obviously critical, but just as important are soft skills, or what Lewis et al. (2015) have defined as collaborative competencies. Digital scholarship projects are highly collaborative by nature, and are often accomplished with a small team that includes individuals with disciplinary knowledge, project management experience and the appropriate technology skills. A new centre will also be flooded with requests that are out of the scope of its services, and it will be necessary to use librarians who can either work collaboratively with researchers to find a middle ground or politely say 'no'. Centre policies that define the scope of services are useful, but many projects fall into troublesome grey areas in which individual judgement is needed about how a centre defines the limits of its support.

Librarian skills

A robust body of literature exists to document the recommended technology skills for 21st-century librarians, but critical to the issue of digital scholarship centres is individuals' time for speculative work and growth. The 20th-century model of faculty or researchers approaching the library for assistance and the library then performing a finite service in support of this request is unsuitably dated for digital scholarship services. Librarians and staff who operate digital scholarship centres must have the time and flexibility in their schedules to act as partners on projects, not just service providers. Many patrons approach a centre with projects that can be classified as consulting work that occupies five hours or less of staff time; in these instances, often the patron's desired outcome can be matched with appropriate, low-barrier technology tools. The more time-intensive projects, however, involve scholars with promising ideas but little practical knowledge on how to functionally organize and execute digital project work. For digital scholarship centre staff who work in this capacity as collaborators, these projects are time consuming because of the amount of work to be accomplished, and also because projects need added buffer time for trial and failure. In many respects, digital scholarship librarians perform an extension of a library's traditional responsibilities: helping patrons to access data and the tools that enhance its legibility; matching resources in a variety of formats to scholars' needs and interests; and ensuring that research output is preserved and accessible for the future. The concept of speculative, theoretical work that may result in failure is new but imperative to the capacities of a digital scholarship librarian, and must be recognized and protected. In their survey of global scholarship centres, Lewis et al. (2015) also specifically note the importance of the leader of the initiative to set a collaborative tone, establish expertise and encourage curiosity within the centre.

Use of space and resources

Accessible space and resources are a second consideration when building digital scholarship services within an academic library. The websites of current digital scholarship centres illustrate that the amount of physical space devoted to centres varies considerably. Targeted spaces such as visualization or multimedia labs, classrooms or collaborative workspaces also vary by institution. Indeed, most new centres are retrofitted into existing libraries in which space is at a premium. McCullough (2014) has documented on behalf of the University of North Carolina-Charlotte what seems to be a relatively standard prioritization for new centres: to begin with staff were collocated in the same space to increase visibility and then some physical modifications were made to provide initial services. These changes were made while funding was sought for the creation of more extensive lab and specialized spaces, with additional equipment being purchased through each subsequent budget cycle. This iterative build-up of services makes sense, especially when considering the cross-disciplinary role that a centre is expected to fill; from a resource perspective this often translates to expensive hardware and software licences for which individual departments are unable to bear the cost. A library therefore cannot expect to build a functional centre by solely committing librarian time, but must also commit increased resources for the acquisition and support of new technology.

Technical infrastructure

The technical infrastructure of the overall library into which a new centre will fit is another important consideration, as a digital scholarship centre must be able to be flexible when supporting new technologies. Requests to support trials of software or to test hardware before it is implemented on a larger scale by a departmental lab are not uncommon, as a digital scholarship centre is perceived as a potential sandbox environment. However, these kinds of requests are relatively new to libraries, which may not be well suited to respond nimbly. Some of the responsibility to manage complex and changing suites of software on the digital scholarship centre's hardware falls to IT staff. Related work lands with staff or librarians in the centre, who must be ready to learn new products quickly so as to be able to support patrons' usage. Also of principal importance is the administrative understanding that providing such an environment within a library raises complex policy questions that must be answered with specific reference to the needs of a digital scholarship centre; for instance, what are the centre's long-term responsibilities for maintaining individuals' research products on library servers or in other local environments? Nowviskie (2011) has written about 'skunkworks' at the University of Virginia's Scholars' Lab as an extreme form of this work, in which small teams of developers are exempt from the usual constraints of administrative oversight in order to increase their innovation. While this example is not found in practice in all digital scholarship centres, it illustrates the overall necessary principle for digital scholarship centres in libraries: if you expect innovative results, you must be willing to adjust and accommodate to provide an innovative environment.

Aligning to institutional needs

A thorough understanding of the existing technology support landscape within the larger university is also critical for a library that is about to undertake a new digital scholarship centre. As already mentioned, while numerous academic libraries in the USA now feature digital scholarship centres, no two offer exactly the same suite of services. This is in part because numerous organizations within a university, including the IT office, departmental labs or discipline-specific centres or institutes may support related services. Once the library has developed an understanding of the institution's needs, this can then be assessed in regard to the availability of librarians who might implement new services and the resources that could be directed towards a new centre.

CASE STUDY 6.1   University of Notre Dame

Background
At the University of Notre Dame Libraries, a Center for Digital Scholarship (CDS) was constructed in the summer of 2013 with funding from the University President to advance the vision to redefine and transform library services and spaces for the 21st century. During implementation, the Center's staff, service model, physical space and website were carefully positioned to signify an evolution of library services. Located on the ground floor of the main campus library, the CDS incorporates state-of-the-art technology, high-end software and research data-sets for analysis and visualization, and discipline-specific consulting and support. The Center currently supports GIS, digital humanities, data analysis, text mining, digitization, metadata services and data management planning, all formerly unavailable to the broad campus community. In 2015 the CDS received a $10 million gift, which is intended to support continued growth, technology enhancements and physical space development (University of Notre Dame, 2015).

Identifying and aligning with institutional needs
Initial internal funding was received for the construction of the CDS at Notre Dame in the summer of 2012, with a targeted opening date of August 2013. In the spring of 2013, the Libraries' Digital Initiatives Librarian conducted an environmental scan of services and support for digital scholarship activities on the Notre Dame campus. The resulting gap analysis indicated that while many digital scholarship services were offered in a wide variety of locations to various sub-groups of the campus population, such as support for data mining within Notre Dame's Mendoza College of Business or data visualization through the University's Center for Research Computing, two major campus needs fell within the Libraries' aegis: while specialized support services existed on campus for faculty or upper-level researchers, the Libraries should provide 'gateway' services geared toward introducing undergraduate and graduate students to the concepts and tools of digital scholarship; and the Libraries should act as a nexus of information regarding digital scholarship support and services within campus, providing a first point of contact and learning for researchers seeking information. In interviews, the Digital Initiatives Librarian gauged interest in areas

identified by the Libraries as those in which existing personnel could offer expanded services, namely GIS, statistical analysis and metadata enhancement/data management. Surveys and conversations with other institutions that offered these services revealed the necessary basic hardware and software packages needed to support these services, which were then acquired and put into place over the next six months.

The staffing model

Three years later, the staff of Notre Dame's CDS is composed of a Program Director for Digital Initiatives and Scholarship who leads the Center, a Digital Initiatives Librarian, a Metadata and Digital Projects Librarian, a GIS Librarian, an English and Digital Humanities Librarian, an Economics and Social Science Data Librarian and a Digital Scholarship Coordinator. The Libraries' digital projects staff, including a Digital Collections Librarian, a Visual Resources Curator, two Media Digitization Specialists, and two CLIR (Council on Library and Information Resources) postdoctoral fellows, one for Data Curation for the Sciences and Social Sciences and one for Data Curation for Visual Studies, also fall under the auspices of the CDS. Of all of these positions, only the Digital Scholarship Coordinator role was created specifically to support the initiative; this position includes responsibilities for promotion of the space, cultivating external relationships crucial to the advancement of the Center and keeping metrics on usage, workshops and other activities. Since the Center's construction in 2013, the Digital Collections, GIS, Digital Humanities and Economics and Data librarians were added to the Libraries' personnel roster; all other positions were pulled from various units within the Libraries into the CDS as it was formed. In departments where personnel were removed to join the CDS staff consolidated workflows to allow for the loss of an individual. All librarians within the Center's staff are expected to teach workshops and engage with patrons on behalf of individual research projects (Bergstrom and Papson, 2016).

Support for research and enquiry

Notre Dame's CDS supports research and enquiry by several broad means: providing individual project consultations to any interested member of the University community; educating the community in tools and best practices appropriate to digital scholarship through workshops, which vary from one-hour introductory sessions on topics such as GIS or 3D printing to multi-day 'boot camps' targeted to advanced researchers; partnering with academic departments and centres to host talks and other events that explore trends in technology and scholarship; and offering access to specialized hardware, software and facilities within the central campus library. While access to services is provided through a website with an embedded chat box and a vanity e-mail address, most enquiries are made directly to personnel associated with the Center, either in person or to their individual e-mail addresses. Like the majority of current digital scholarship centres, the CDS thus offers an evolution of the Information Commons service model, in that librarians and specialized staff are on hand and virtually available to assist with enquiries that merge informational and technological questions (Lippincott, 2006). Blended with this model, however, are more contemporary service concepts found within the Library 2.0 model of service, specifically that the CDS must be able to change with the evolving community and has the responsibility to engage with users directly to set the future directions of services (Kwanya, Stilwell and Underwood, 2012).

The floor plan for Notre Dame's CDS combines a number of different functional spaces that were intended to be a prototype in which to refine how the Libraries interact with researchers within the context of emerging technologies (Figure 6.1).

Constructed in the summer of 2013, the Center occupies 410 square metres on the central library's ground floor, with an additional 120 square metres elsewhere in the central library devoted to staff-only digitization and production areas. While the initial build-out focused

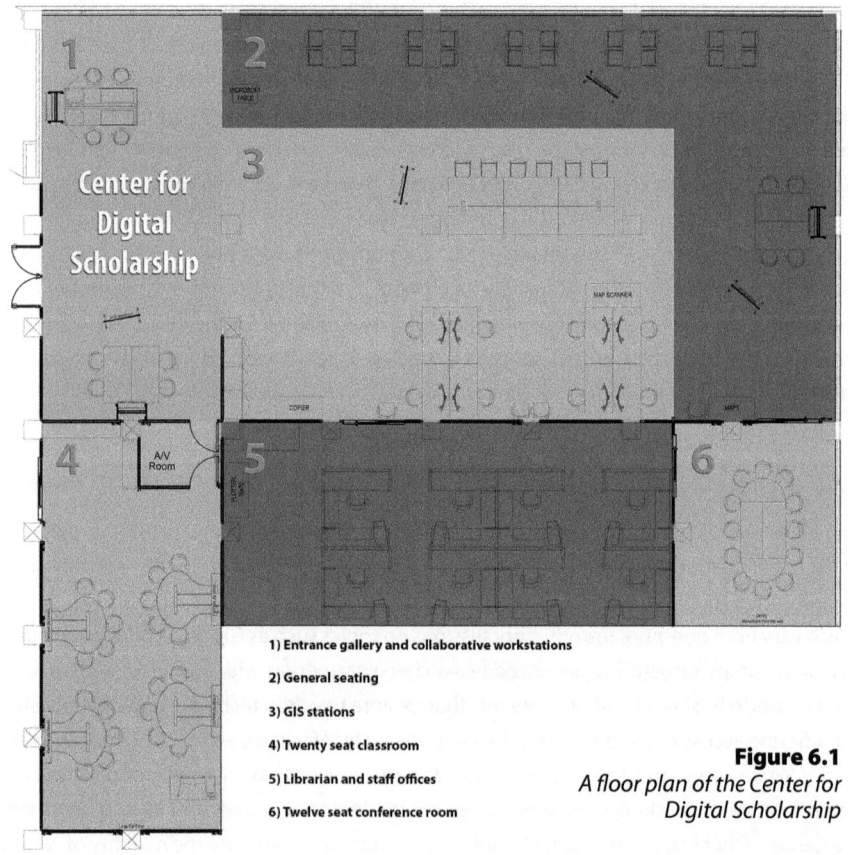

1) Entrance gallery and collaborative workstations
2) General seating
3) GIS stations
4) Twenty seat classroom
5) Librarian and staff offices
6) Twelve seat conference room

Figure 6.1
A floor plan of the Center for Digital Scholarship

on open spaces, additional demand for soundproof recording spaces expanded the Center's service offerings within two years to include a single-user sound studio and a 170-square foot One Button Studio, or digital video production studio that requires no prior video experience. Part of the job description of the Digital Scholarship Coordinator is to keep meticulous statistics on which areas are most heavily utilized, so as to inform future development. The Center's various technology spaces see equitable usage, with the GIS workstations being utilized most frequently, at 22% of overall space use. The collaborative classroom and collaborative workstations, which were planned in direct response to feedback from faculty and students, are utilized relatively infrequently, at 14% and 13% of overall space usage, respectively (Vecchio, 2015). As the Center will move to a larger location within a forthcoming library renovation, this data is instrumental for confirming which technology zones should be expanded. In particular, it illuminates that patrons use the Center primarily for individual rather than collaborative computing, in contrast to what pre-launch focus groups suggested would occur.

Reflections on the Center's first 12 months

Within Notre Dame's CDS, many of the first year's challenges related to inhabiting the Libraries' first open-concept space. Areas normally found behind solid walls, including a classroom, collaboration spaces and librarians' offices, are intentionally open to patrons via glass walls within the Center. Librarians' offices especially are integrated with public spaces to encourage users of all levels that support is present and at hand. As each person who occupies these open offices had formerly sat in private, enclosed spaces, this transition was not an easy one. The Center is designated as 'collaborative' space within the central library, meaning that students are encouraged to converse and work together on projects at appropriate noise levels. However, what constitutes acceptable noise levels, between student groups and individual researchers, occasionally demands intervention by librarians to defuse tensions. Faculty, many of whom were delighted with the new space, were initially frequent offenders of the Center's noise and collaborative space use policies as they informally co-opted media-integrated workstations for teaching. Noise that travelled between student spaces, offices and the classroom was greater than expected, and had to be mitigated by the installation of sound buffers and a white noise system. Executed in the second year of the Center's operations, this sound-dampening work was expensive, but the space had proved to be especially troublesome for librarians and staff to work. The cost of the sound buffers was considered an acceptable alternative to librarians' disappearing into the stacks with their laptops to work, diminishing the intended effect of their presence in the space.

These combined factors often left the Center's librarians, several of whom had formerly held behind-the-scenes technical positions, with more policing and policy work than expected during the Center's first year. One of the first tasks given to the Center's Coordinator, hired in December 2013, a few months after the public opening, was the creation of written policies to guide space usage and provide direction for staff who might be called upon to resolve issues. Three policies in particular were important: noise guidelines, procedures for students to be able to reserve spaces and 'bump' policies for specialized equipment. The noise guidelines clarify that some noise fluctuations should be expected in an environment that is conducive to collaborative research and scholarship. They request patrons be mindful of limiting personal conversations, to utilize headphone while listening to media, to silence electronic device notifications and to take personal cell phone calls outside of the CDS space, as these were the activities about which staff received the majority of complaints. The student room reservation procedures clarify that while library and teaching faculty usage of the room is prioritized during business hours, students may book the Center's rooms on weekends and evenings. Students are, however, responsible in these times for their own technical support and contacting Center staff during business hours for assistance. A 'bump' policy also proved important, especially for the Center's dual-monitor GIS machines, which students quickly realized were perfect for simultaneously displaying both academic assignments and a Facebook feed. This signage simply states that a user may be asked to vacate a station in order to allow another patron access to GIS software. All policies invite users to contact any CDS employee to help facilitate a resolution of conflict.

The CDS's web presence

The website for Notre Dame's CDS is also a departure, in terms of both appearance and features, from the sites of other library services (University of Notre Dame, 2016). In conversations with the Libraries' Director of Communications and Marketing in planning the website, she advocated that the Center should have a web presence that is immediately distinct within the University to signify the evolution of library services that the CDS represents. While initial conversations focused on the aesthetics of the site, once the Center had opened it was important to have a flexible infrastructure to support the various technologies and spaces. A patron can submit a 3D or large-format print job via ingest forms that utilize survey software or can book the sound studio or other spaces via embedded calendaring and space management systems (Figure 6.2).

Technical guides are embedded throughout the site to provide assistance and include patron satisfaction surveys. Patrons can easily browse open hardware and specialized equipment before arriving at the library. Deliberate language such as 'expertise' is also utilized throughout the site to reinforce the professionalism of the services offered by the library and the collaborative partnerships between librarians and researchers that are critical to digital scholarship projects.

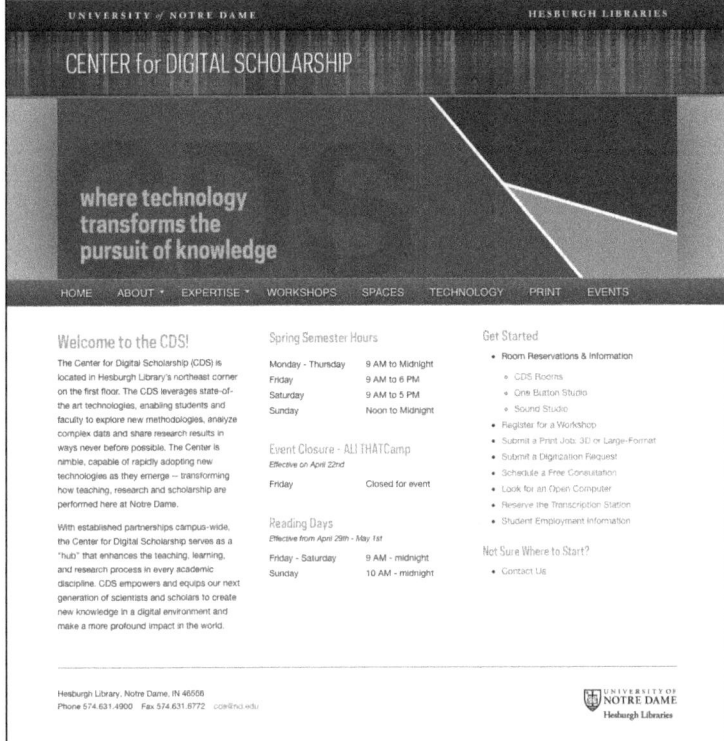

Figure 6.2 *Home page of the Center for Digital Scholarship web pages*

Marketing the CDS

A marketing strategy on behalf of the new CDS was also implemented thoughtfully in regard to multiple potential audiences. The Center opened its doors in August 2013 and held a grand opening celebration in November, which featured informal demonstrations of new technologies by librarians and attracted over 250 people into the space. Additionally, open houses with demonstrations were promoted to all faculty. While attendance at these open houses was sporadic, faculty who attended became early adopters and supporters of the concept; this was especially important in that while the opening celebration brought people into the space, word-of-mouth marketing between faculty colleagues was much more important in building a reputation and attracting projects. The University Librarian spoke about the Center's services at meetings with deans and department chairs from across the University to build awareness and support at administrative levels. Graduate students, who make up the vast majority of the Center's clientele, often initially discovered the CDS through workshops and then requested help with research on the basis of connections formed within this setting. With this in mind, librarians offered workshops on 4 areas of interest (GIS, text mining, data analysis, metadata) in the Center's initial year, but increased this to 11 areas (including data modelling, usability and visualization) of interest within the following two years. Total counts of users within the space, taken throughout the day to track where individuals and groups prefer to sit, indicate an annually increasing attendance, with 18,304 individuals tallied in the Center's first year, rising to 27,610 in the third year of operations.

Responsiveness to emerging technologies

The difficulty of maintaining currency for researchers and students is a critical challenge faced by the University of Notre Dame's CDS and many others. Within a digital scholarship centre a significant amount of funding has been invested in particular services, including the purchase of specific hardware, licensing of software and the training of support personnel. Requests for new areas of support are brought to a centre with some frequency, and the capacity to be responsive to emerging technologies is greatly dependent on personnel time and available funding. At many centres, student employees are utilized to provide front-line patron support, to investigate the local applications of new technologies and to contribute to projects within their areas of interest and specialization. Emory University's Digital Scholarship Internship Program documents the competencies that graduate student employees are expected to acquire as part of the programme and how this manifests into support of the work of Emory's centre (Emory University 2015). Students in later phases of the programme are proficient to provide front-line support to centre patrons and join project teams, thus removing some of this time-intensive work from librarians. This model, closely related to that of the University of Virginia's ground-breaking Praxis Program, prepares its student participants for new positions within the academic job market and alternative academic careers in a manner that strengthens the services of the library and its users (University of Virginia, n.d.). This model also provides additional capacity for centres to be more flexible in their service offerings and development, as students with different interests become involved on an annual basis and provide skilled labour in new and changing areas.

Postdoctoral fellows represent another opportunity for digital scholarship centres to increase their personnel in emerging technology areas. In the USA, the CLIR supports one- and two-year fellowships for recent PhD graduates in a variety of disciplines (Council on Library and Information Resources, 2014). The fellowships encourage symbiotic relationships between host institutions and recipients, in which the institution benefits from fellows' expertise while the individual participants have a funded opportunity in which to explore possible career paths within libraries. Supporting postdoctoral fellows also presents the library with an additional opportunity to expand its reach within a university community. The University of Notre Dame's CDS has hosted three CLIR postdoctoral fellows to date: a fellow for data curation and GIS from 2013 to 2015; a fellow for data curation and visual studies from 2015 to 2017; and a fellow for data curation for the sciences and social sciences from 2015 to 2017. From the Center's opening in 2013 through to 2015, the postdoctoral fellow provided the majority of patron services on behalf of GIS, including teaching a credit-bearing class and workshops on the topic and acting as the primary support for patrons. Throughout this fellow's funded postdoc, the Center's metrics showed that GIS was the most popular service, receiving 34% of overall enquiries. This data compelled library administration to create a new librarian position dedicated to this service, and the CLIR fellow was hired into this permanent position at the conclusion of his fellowship.

The University of Notre Dame's CDS's two current CLIR fellows are also dedicated to building and exploring the needs for new services. The fellow for data curation for the sciences and social sciences works in particular to establish data management support on behalf of the overall library. This service addresses potential data concerns over the lifecycle of a research project, including formulating and applying appropriate metadata standards, complying with policies on reuse and sharing of data and preserving data in an appropriate environment. While library personnel had already provided consulting support on these topics, the service model was ad hoc. The fellow works to formalize the workflow and personnel involved with the service, which includes a variety of subject librarians on behalf of individual disciplines. The Center's current fellow for data curation and visual studies serves to establish better support from the library on behalf of digital visual exhibits. In this area in particular the Center had experienced difficulty in establishing an understanding and policies around the scope of support for exhibits, in particular in regard to what the library's role should be in supporting and preserving exhibit content in the long term. As such, this fellow's work involves exploration and research of various tools as well as development of internal best practices and policy documentation. In both of these instances, the Center will be much more strongly prepared for expanded service offerings in these areas at the conclusion of the fellows' two-year terms.

Sustainability

Securing the funding to allow flexibility is also a major concern for digital scholarship centres. As previously noted, most digital scholarship centres to date are established without the benefit of an influx of funding to support additional personnel or new space. Therefore, centre staff must think creatively about ways in which their service model can be nimble, but also continually engaged and innovative as Dempsey (2013) has suggested. Critical to this effort is a ruthless assessment on an annual basis of patron priorities and usage patterns: is the centre paying licence fees on under-utilized software that can be dropped, or offering frequent workshops with moderate attendance that could instead be offered on demand? Student roles should also be re-evaluated on an annual basis: are there new areas of support consuming significant librarian time that can be shifted to student assistants, or is there administrative work pertaining to the running of the centre itself with which students can assist? A continual evaluation of a centre's usage illuminates areas in which services can be halted or shifted to meet patron demand, thus potentially freeing up funding or time to investigate new areas of interest. In a model in which centres seek to be responsive to patrons' needs, librarians also bear the responsibility to be mindful of work they can potentially stop doing, as well as to use conference attendance and other external opportunities to become cognizant of potential future opportunities. As such, everyone involved with the centre must be conscientious of the need to remain current and the responsibility each member of the team shares to make this feasible.

Conclusion

With new digital scholarship centres opening at increasing numbers of institutions, the near future promises increased engagement and collaboration. As funding agencies look to prioritize cross-institutional ventures and projects that result in impact across universities, digital scholarship is an area in which libraries can partner together and with a variety of others within a university, including faculty and IT staff, to pursue new developments and tools. This is especially important when considering the long-term viability of digital scholarship centres for which stable funding is unclear; the more a centre can establish itself within the local and broader community as a distinct and valuable unit, the better its chances of survival will be through funding fluctuations. An institution contemplating the formation of a new centre for digital scholarship thus faces many points of consideration. Resources at various levels, including new models of staffing and targeted funding, must not only be devoted to the initiative, but also carefully balanced in recognition of a wide variety of demands and the complexities of dividing resources across needs. New potential services, including support for emerging publishing models, consideration of leading-edge technologies and their scholarly applications, and assistance with copyright and reuse questions that continually evolve with new technology are a significant investment for a university library to sustain. Librarians and other professional staff must additionally be supported with funding and time for continuous learning. The benefits of a centre for digital scholarship, however, are manifold for a university library. Not only does a centre bring new services to a university community, but it repositions librarians into scholars' research cycles in new and opportune ways. A centre increases potential opportunities for librarians and professional library staff to be collaborators on innovative research as well as on projects seeking high-profile grant funding. It also partners scholars and librarians in seeking technical solutions to emerging research questions and greatly increases the library's reach within an academic community.

References

Bergstrom, T. C. and Papson, A. (2016) Promoting Digital Library Services through Workshops. In *Creating the 21st Century Library. Vol. 7: Marketing and Outreach for the Academic Library: new approaches and initiatives*, Lanham MD, Rowman & Littlefield, 71–80.

Bucknell University (2015) *Collaborating Digitally: engaging students in public scholarship*, https://dsconf.blogs.bucknell.edu/.

Council on Library and Information Resources (2014) *General Information*, www.clir.org/fellowships/postdoc/info.

Dempsey, L. (2013) *Three Challenges: engaging, rightscaling, and innovating*, http://orweblog.oclc.org/three-challenges-engaging-rightscaling-and-innovating/.

Emory University (2015) *Digital Scholarship Internship Program*, http://digitalscholarship.emory.edu/about/internship%20program.html.

Kwanya, T, Stilwell, C. and Underwood, P. G. (2012) Library 2.0 Versus Other Library Service Models: a critical analysis, *Journal of Librarianship and Information Science*, **44** (3), 145–162, doi:10.1177/0961000611426443.

Lewis, V., Spiro, L., Wang, X. and Cawthorne, J. E. (2015) *Building Expertise to Support Digital Scholarship: a global perspective*, Council on Library and Information Resources, CLIR Publication 168, www.clir.org/pubs/reports/pub168.

Lippincott, J. (2006) Linking the Information Commons to Learning. In Oblinger, D. G. (ed.), *Learning spaces*, EDUCAUSE, 7.1–7.18, http://net.educause.edu/ir/library/pdf/PUB7102g.pdf.

Lippincott, J. and Goldenberg-Hart, D. (2014) *Digital Scholarship Centers: trends & good practice*, Coalition for Networked Information Workshop Report, https://www.cni.org/wp-content/uploads/2014/11/CNI-Digitial-Schol.-Centers-report-2014.web_.pdf.

Lippincott, J., Hemmasi, H. and Lewis, V. M. (2014) Trends in Digital Scholarship Centers, *EDUCAUSE Review Online*, http://er.educause.edu/articles/2014/6/trends-in-digital-scholarship-centers.

McCullough, H. (2014) Developing Digital Scholarship Services on a Shoestring: facilities, events, tools and projects, *College & Research Libraries News*, **74** (4), 187–90.

Modern Language Association (2012) *Guidelines for Evaluating Work in Digital Humanities and Digital Media*, https://www.mla.org/About-Us/Governance/Committees/Committee-Listings/Professional-Issues/Committee-on-Information-Technology/Guidelines-for-Evaluating-Work-in-Digital-Humanities-and-Digital-Media.

New Media Consortium (2016) *The NMC Horizon Report: 2016 higher education edition*, http://cdn.nmc.org/media/2016-nmc-horizon-report-he-EN.pdf.

Nowviskie, B. (2011) *A Skunk in the Library*, http://nowviskie.org/2011/a-skunk-in-the-library.

Posner, M. (2013) No Half Measures: overcoming common challenges to doing digital humanities in the library, *Journal of Library Administration*, **53** (1), 43–52.

University of Notre Dame (2015) *Hesburgh Libraries Receive Largest Gift in History from*

Navari Foundation, http://news.nd.edu/news/59492-hesburgh-libraries-receive-largest-gift-in-history-from-navari-foundation/.
University of Notre Dame (2016) *Center for Digital Scholarship*, http://library.nd.edu/cds/.
University of Virginia (n.d.) *About Praxis*, http://praxis.scholarslab.org/about/.
Vecchio, J. (2015) *CDS Annual Report AY 2014–2015*, doi:10.7274/R0MG7MDW.

7

Building scalable and sustainable services for researchers

David Clay

Introduction

The role of the library in support of research is changing. Lorcan Dempsey (2010) has traced the shift in focus away from outside-in resources, where the library is buying or licensing materials, to 'inside-out' resources that may be unique to an institution. This has led to the library supporting creation, not just consumption, of scholarly outputs.

This is reflected in the new roles and services libraries are developing around digital scholarship. Weller (2011, 41) identifies different flavours of digital scholarship; one 'refers to the curation and collection of digital resources, which places it in the information sciences, whereas others use it in a broader sense to cover a range of scholarly activities afforded by new technologies'.

This chapter explores the background to the development of these new roles and services and looks at how libraries are supporting different flavours of digital scholarship, using examples from the University of Salford in the UK and other academic and national libraries. It examines scholarly communication initiatives; research data services; digitization, curation and preservation activities; consultancy and training. The relationship of the library with faculty and other support services is considered, as are the challenges in developing new roles and services that enable the library to become a partner in digital scholarship.

Background
Liu and Thomas (2012) state that we

> are in the first phase of a digital revolution in higher education. Much of the teaching and learning apparatus has moved online. Computational technologies and methodologies have transformed research practices in every discipline, leading to exciting discoveries and tools. New interdisciplinary initiatives, exploiting the digital, such as bioinformatics, human cognition, and digital humanities, are bringing faculty members together in ways never before attempted.

The key drivers behind this change are the digitization of content and the development a global, social network (Weller, 2011). The internet has removed barriers to communication and collaboration and enabled the development of new tools and techniques to interrogate the abundance of scholarly information and knowledge that is now available online.

Lynch (2014, 12) suggests that digital scholarship can be used as shorthand for this 'entire body of changing scholarly practice, and recognition of the fact that most areas of scholarly work today have been transformed, to a lesser or greater extent, by a series of information technologies'. There is no fixed definition of digital scholarship. The American Council of Learned Societies Commission on Cyberinfrastructure for the Humanities and Social Sciences (2006) notes that digital scholarship has meant several related things:

1. building a digital collection of information for further study and analysis
2. creating appropriate tools for collection building
3. creating appropriate tools for the analysis and study of collections
4. using digital collections and analytical tools to generate new intellectual products
5. creating authoring tools for these new intellectual products, either in traditional forms or in digital form.

Borgman (2007) suggests that the preservation and management of digital content are the most difficult challenges to be addressed in building support for digital scholarship. However, while the building of digital collections and the tools to interrogate and use them are seen as important scholarly activities, the generation of new intellectual products such as data visualizations, databases, blogs, wikis, games, videos and other new forms of digital publication should be seen as the core meaning of digital scholarship.

The preservation and management of content are frequently cited as being central to the mission of a library. Alexander et al. (2014) suggest that 'collections are the foundation of all libraries' but that, as both curators and creators, 'librarians view the scholarly record as more than just repositories – they see it as a building block for creating new knowledge'. Libraries contribute to digital scholarship both by curating and collecting digital resources and by using them to create new scholarly applications and knowledge.

Dempsey and Malpas (2015) suggest that the collection should be seen as a means to an end rather than an end in itself. In a pre-digital world researchers organized their workflows around the library. The library collected the outputs of research, such as books and journals, and enabled their consumption, but there were limited opportunities for engagement with the wider research lifecycle. In the digital environment, the focus has shifted from enabling consumption to enabling creation. The library has to organize itself around the workflow of researchers and, in doing so, has opportunities to engage with them at all points in the research lifecycle. This drives 'a deeper engagement with the research and learning behaviors of the institution and individual researchers' (Dempsey, Malpas, and Lavoie, 2014, 399).

This shift in focus from a collection-centric approach to one based on engagement is leading libraries to develop new expertise in research support and digital scholarship.

Libraries and digital scholarship

The expertise developed by libraries in research support and digital scholarship will vary according to their institutional mission, research and learning and teaching priorities. De Belder (2013) states that the library at the University of Leiden 'is becoming an expert centre [of] digital information for research and teaching'. It is developing expertise in new areas including data management and curation, text and data mining, geographic information systems (GIS), copyright and publication support, with further areas to be identified through engagement with researchers.

The University of Leiden is not unique in developing support for digital scholarship. The development of library expertise and services for the digital scholarship activities identified by the American Council of Learned Societies Commission on Cyberinfrastructure for the Humanities and Social Sciences (2006) will be explored in the following four sections. These sections will consider the different ways in which libraries are building digital collections, creating tools and enabling the generation of new intellectual products.

Digitization, curation and preservation

Hughes (2014) states that 'the use of digital collections – primary sources that have been digitized; online reference resources, including catalogues and scholarly journals; and born-digital material from publishers – is now a critical part of the scholarly life cycle, as is the underlying digital infrastructure that delivers this content to the widest possible audience'. These digital resources have been created through a mix of boutique or small-scale digitization projects aimed at creating material around a specific theme or research question, and mass digitization projects aimed at digitizing whole collections or general-interest content such as books and journals.

Libraries have developed mass digitization strategies and have facilitated boutique digitization projects. This content is made available through a digital library service, such as the Digital Bodleian Library,[1] and through portals such as Europeana[2] and the Hathi Trust[3] that aggregate content from a range of different libraries and cultural heritage institutions.

The National Library of Wales (2011, 4) developed a digitization strategy that commits it to creating a 'critical mass of digitized content relating to Wales and the Welsh', taking the library's 'digitized collections to existing and new users regardless of their location' and enabling 'use of the Library's digitized collections in new ways for research and learning'. Coble, McCormick and Vinopal (2014) note that digitization workflows in libraries, like the National Library of Wales, have usually been developed around the mass digitization paradigm and providing a boutique service to facilitate the research and engagement activity of individual scholars is a challenge. Libraries need to be able to meet researchers' requests for the selective digitization of material from their own collections, for assistance in combining content from their collections into a new resource, or for combining content from multiple library or cultural heritage collections to create new knowledge. The National Library of Wales has focused on the digitization of its own collections, and now offers access to millions of pages of Welsh newspapers, journals and archives.

It also supports, through its Research Programme in Digital Collections, 'projects that develop *new* digital content that addresses specific research or education needs in partnership with academics and other key stakeholders' (Hughes, 2014). An example of this is Echoes and Traces project, a digital approach to Welsh traditional music (Cusworth, 2013), which is bringing together relevant items from the collection of the National Library of Wales to create a new online multimedia resource that will enable the exploration of the soundscape of Wales in the 19th and early 20th centuries. Hughes (2014) believes that digital content can 'create a transformation of scholarship, through research that would otherwise be impossible or that addresses research questions that could not be resolved without digital approaches'.

Data services

The Royal Society (2012, 10) recommended that

> scientists should communicate the data they collect and the models they create, to allow free and open access, and in ways that are intelligible, assessable and usable for other specialists in the same or linked fields wherever they are in the world. Where data justify it, scientists should make them available in an appropriate data repository. Where possible, communication with a wider public audience should be made a priority, and particularly so in areas where openness is in the public interest.

For this to be possible, institutions would need to develop the capacity to curate and manage data resources and support the data needs of their researchers.

Alongside this growing recognition of the importance of open data, research funders have started to mandate that data 'be made openly available with as few restrictions as possible in a timely and responsible manner' (RCUK, 2011). Journals such as *Nature* (2013) have also started to require authors to disclose data, code and protocols as a condition of publication.

The ACRL Planning Review Committee identified library involvement in research data management as one of its top ten trends in 2012. Tenopir et al. (2014) distinguish between informational and technical research data management services. Informational services provided by libraries include consulting on the development of data management plans or metadata standards, providing guidance on data citation, data licensing and finding datasets. Technical services include developing and managing data and code repositories, assistance with preparing, appraising, selecting and deselecting datasets and enabling data impact to be tracked and measured. While providing informational services can be seen as an extension of existing research-support services, developing technical services requires closer engagement with the research community, and significant investment in staffing and infrastructure (Rambo, 2015).

CASE STUDY 7.1 Research data management at the University of Salford

The Library at the University of Salford has responded to the research data challenge by leading the development of an institutional Research Data Management Policy (University of Salford, 2015a) and a Research Data Management service, providing researchers with both informational and technical support. The Research Data Management Policy affirms both researchers' and the University's responsibilities for managing research data. Its primary application is to ensure that research data is managed effectively throughout the lifecycle and is discoverable and accessible.

The Research Data Management Service supports both the mission of the University and the expectations of funders who require that 'effective data curation is provided throughout the full data lifecycle' and 'adequate resources are provided to support the curation of publicly-funded research data' (EPSRC, 2014). It addresses the requirements of researchers and research students, enabling them to manage their data on a day-to-day basis, and to store and share their data, in ways that are compliant with legislation and funders' requirements.

The development of the Research Data Management Service brought together researchers with staff from the Library, IT Services and the Research Office to create a service that works across the research lifecycle and, as far as possible, fits into researchers' workflows. The pooling of skills and experience into a multi-disciplinary team approach was crucial to the development of the service. It better positioned the team to tackle the cultural, behavioural, policy and technical challenges that arose as the Research Data Management Service was being developed. It ensured, for example, that the policy, support and technical solutions addressed critical information governance issues.

The Research Data Management Service meets key challenges such as securely storing and preserving research data and making it reusable and discoverable. It has five components.

- The Research Data Collaboration Space functions as a dashboard to the other research data management systems and supports project management, document creation, management and sharing.
- The Research Data Storage Service enables researchers to store, sync and share files or folders with internal or external collaborators, across a range of devices.
- The Source Code Repository provides researchers developing software with collaboration, code review and code management tools.
- The University of Salford Data Repository (Figure 7.1) enables researchers to store, share and make their data discoverable, citable and available for reuse.
- The Research Data Management Support Service provides support, training and guidance for researchers to help them manage and share their research data.

The Research Data Management Service was launched as a pilot service in November 2015.

The time spent interacting with researchers and understanding how they work was invaluable and is reflected in the positive way the service has been received. The different components of the service have been incorporated into the workflows of researchers and research teams from a number of different subject disciplines since launch. The Research Data Storage Service has seen the most uptake as the element of the service researchers might be expected to interact with on a daily basis. Researchers are depositing their datasets in the Research Data Repository and are reserving digital object identifiers for inclusion in data access statements.

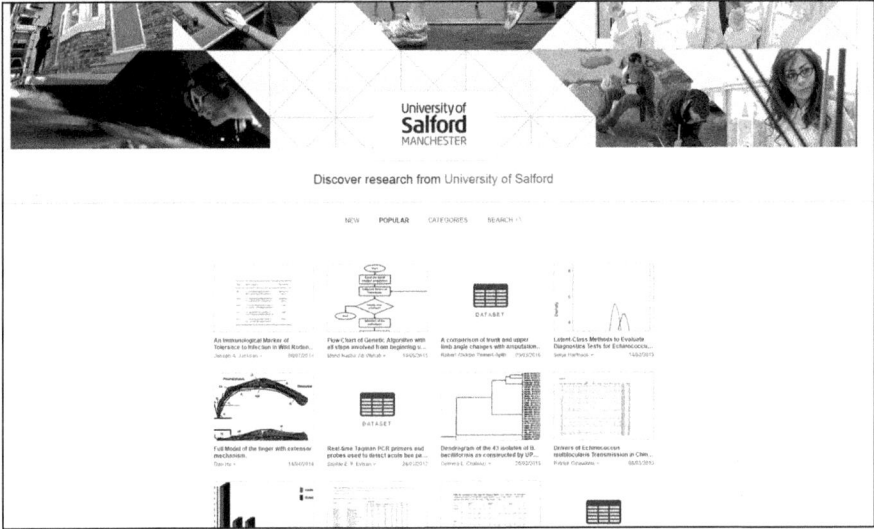

Figure 7.1 *University of Salford Research Data Repository home page*

The number and complexity of enquiries to the support service is growing as researchers become aware of the assistance available when preparing their data management plans or archiving their data. The uptake of the training is increasing as it is embedded into existing school and University programmes.

However, it is too early to draw any firm conclusions about the impact of the Research Data Management Service. The next steps for the University of Salford are to continue to grow the service and to evaluate its impact and effectiveness at the end of the two-year pilot period.

As well as supporting the curation and management of research data, libraries are also developing what Wang (2013) defines as data computing services. These services include statistical software support, data analysis services, data visualization and geospatial information services. For example, New York University's Data Services (2016) 'support quantitative, qualitative, and geographical research' by providing access to specialty software packages for statistical analysis, GIS and qualitative data analysis as well as support and training.

Scholarly communication

The ACRL (2003) defines scholarly communication as 'the system through which research and other scholarly writings are created, evaluated for quality, disseminated to the scholarly community, and preserved for future use. The system includes both formal means of communication, such as publication in peer-reviewed journals, and informal channels, such as electronic listservs.' The formal elements of this system are known to be in crisis for reasons that include the economically unsustainable increase in journal costs and the barriers to accessing publicly funded research that impact on researchers in less well-funded institutions and anyone without an affiliation to a higher education institution (Gross and Ryan, 2015).

Libraries have responded to this crisis by working with scholars, institutions, publishers and funders to transform the scholarly communications system (ACRL, 2003). The principle that publicly funded research 'should be freely accessible in the public domain is a compelling one, and fundamentally unanswerable' (Working Group on Expanding Access to Published Research Findings, 2012, 5). The effective dissemination of research outputs is crucial to realizing this principle, and is the key driver towards open access. Peter Suber (2015) defines open access as literature that 'is digital, online, free of charge, and free of most copyright and licensing restrictions'. The Budapest Open Access Initiative (2012) states that 'the only constraint on reproduction and distribution, and the only role for copyright in this domain, should be to give authors control over the integrity of their work and the right to be properly acknowledged and cited'.

Open access is usually achieved through one of two complementary strategies, self-archiving and open access (OA) journals.

- Self-archiving (green OA): authors deposit their refereed journal articles in searchable online repositories.
- Open access journals (gold OA) publish articles but do not charge for access.

Support for open access has gained momentum through advocacy from scholars, librarians and others and with the support of governments, research funders and institutions. The Taylor & Francis Open Access Survey 2014 (Devine, 2014) showed that 'positive attitudes towards open access, when discussed in general, are growing. Seventy per cent of respondents disagreed or strongly disagreed with the statement "There are no fundamental benefits to open access publication," an increase of 10% year on year and a strong indicator that open access continues to be viewed as a force for good.' Libraries are bringing about changes in scholarly communication by enabling open access through the development of repositories, supporting publishing initiatives, engaging with faculty and advocating for author rights.

CASE STUDY 7.2 University of Salford Institutional Repository (USIR)

The University of Salford launched USIR, its repository, in 2008 to support changes in scholarly communication and to provide open access to research outputs produced by its researchers. The University adopted its first Open Access Policy in 2010 (University of Salford, 2015b). The policy mandated the deposit of journal articles in USIR and encouraged the deposit of all other forms of research output. This was followed in 2013 with a policy mandating students studying for a higher degree to deposit a copy of their thesis in USIR. The introduction of the Higher Education Funding Council for England (HEFCE, 2014) policy for open access in the post-2014 Research Excellence Framework led to the introduction of a revised policy that mandates the deposit of peer-reviewed journal articles and conference papers in USIR within ten weeks of their acceptance.

The impact of these policies and the partnership between the Library and faculty can be seen in the development of the research outputs collection in USIR, which in October 2015 consisted of 11,926 records, of which 7870 have full-text documents attached, with 4055

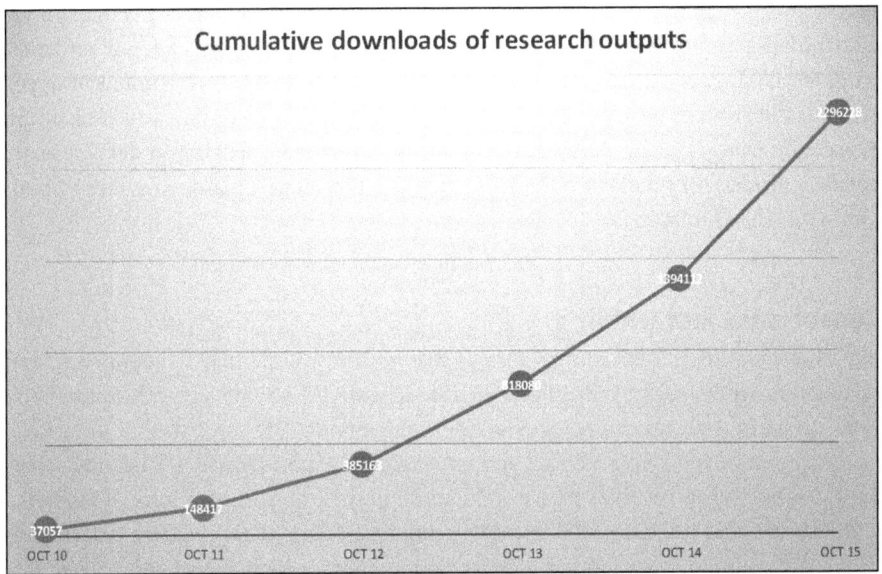

Figure 7.2 *Cumulative downloads of open access research outputs from USIR between October 2010 and October 2015*

available on open access and cumulative downloads totalling 2,296,228 (Figure 7.2).

USIR is capturing, preserving and disseminating research outputs produced at the University of Salford. It is demonstrating the academic quality of research at the institution, increasing its visibility and helping researchers to increase the reach and impact of their work.

Libraries are also increasingly likely to be providing publishing services. The Association of Research Libraries (Hahn, 2008) investigated the provision of publishing services by libraries, finding that 44% of the 80 libraries responding to its survey reported that they were delivering publishing services, while another 21% were planning to develop them. The main focus of library publishing activity was on journals, but libraries were also publishing conference papers and proceedings and monographs. Hahn (2008, 5) noted that libraries were 'focusing on the capabilities and possibilities of new models rather than slavishly duplicating or simply automating traditional models'. Libraries are able to explore these new models as the barriers to offering publishing services have dropped with the development of community-led open source publishing platforms such as Open Journal Systems, closer integration with existing university presses and partnerships with commercial open access publishers such as Ubiquity Press.

The UCL Press is an example of a new library-led publishing initiative. Its website states that its establishment is grounded in the open scholarship agenda and that it seeks 'to use modern technologies and 21st-century means of publishing/ dissemination radically to change the prevailing models for the publication of research outputs' (UCL Press, 2016). Libraries are also supporting the development of open access publishing in other ways, whether by managing funds to pay article or book processing charges or by supporting organizations who are seeking to develop new business models for scholarly publishing such as Knowledge Unlatched and the Open Library of the Humanities.

Consultancy and training

Ben Showers (2012), discussing the roles that libraries might play in supporting the digital humanities, suggests that libraries need to work collaboratively with researchers to understand their needs and provide the right support. He suggests that librarians need to be embedded with scholars and into research teams. Hughes (2014) notes that digital scholarship involves many stakeholders, including researchers, librarians, archivists, IT and technical staff and data scientists. This is recognized by Wolski and Richardson (2014), who suggest that interdisciplinary, collaborative approaches are central to the new ways of doing research made possible by digital technologies.

Libraries are taking different approaches to developing this embedded support for researchers. Lippincott, Hemmasi and Lewis (2014) state that some universities are developing digital scholarship centres, focused on developing relationships and 'extending the ways in which librarians and academic computing professionals relate to and work with faculty (and often students) and their scholarly practices'. The mix of services and resources offered by these centres varies from institution to institution, but includes guidance on intellectual property rights, data management, analysis and visualization, specialized tools and software, digital media creation, project planning, digitization and digital preservation and scholarly communication.

The provision of consultancy and training requires staff with specialized skills, who can work collaboratively with other specialists and with researchers in the digital environment. The Digital Scholarship Librarian at K-State Libraries (2015) is required to 'initiate, build and nurture excellent relationships with a diverse community within the university, as well as external partners, in support of digital scholarship services'. At UCLA (2015), the Digital Scholarship Librarian is asked to 'assist faculty and other clients to plan effective, innovative and sustainable digital projects' and 'develop new workflows to support innovative scholarship around a variety of digital content, including traditional library content, born-digital material, research data and other digital products of scholarship, and other digital materials utilized by faculty in their research'. These roles combine relationship management skills with other specialist skills needed to support digital scholarship.

CASE STUDY 7.3   Consultancy and training at the University of Salford

The University of Salford Library supports the development of digital scholars by providing training and consultancy. The training is offered as part of the University-wide SPORT programme or on discipline-specific school or research centre-based programmes.

The consultancy and training offered by the Library is delivered by a mix of library staff with specialized skills, working collaboratively with liaison librarians and with staff from other areas of the University. Staff with specialized skills have been recruited to support the development of research data management and scholarly communications and to develop the archives and specialized collections, and all are required to contribute to training delivery. They train in areas such as data management planning, data archiving, copyright, information ethics, open access publishing, citation and impact and archival research. The training offered by liaison librarians covers topics such as information management, information retrieval and literature reviews. Training is also provided on generic and specialist software packages for postgraduate research students.

The training is delivered using a range of approaches including face-to-face workshops and seminars, online webinars and stand-alone online learning resources. The training developed to support research data management showcases the different methods used. A key element of the training is a stand-alone online Research Data Management Training Programme. This was adapted from the MANTRA programme created by EDINA (2015) and released under a Creative Commons licence. This enabled the adaptation of a resource that was created by experts and which has been evaluated and revised to local circumstances. This has been complemented with face-to-face workshops on data management planning and data archiving, often delivered in partnership with faculty. The Library has also provided expert advice for research teams embarking on new projects.

The expertise that the Library has developed in working with digital content, whether born digital or digitized, and the relationships it has developed with faculty have led to the Library's being consulted in the development of digital scholarship initiatives. This ranges from specific projects such as the creation of an online imaging resource to the production of interactive e-books and the development of a digital humanities initiative.

The training and consultancy delivered by the Library is helping researchers to integrate new digital tools into their workflows, manage their digital content more effectively and exploit digital content more effectively in their research. It helps to build relationships with researchers, connects them with expert Library staff and shows how the Library can support digital scholarship.

These specialist positions are facilitating deeper engagement with researchers as envisaged by Dempsey, Lavoie and Malpas (2014). Sinclair (2014) cites the journal *Southern Spaces*, a peer-reviewed, multimedia, open access journal published in collaboration with the Robert W. Woodruff Library of Emory University, as an example of what can be achieved by libraries and librarians working with faculty and other specialist staff. This journal takes 'advantage of the Internet's capabilities to deliver audio, video, images, and text and facilitating new ways of organizing and presenting research' and supports 'scholarship that incorporates GIS and other forms of spatialized data projection' (Emory Centre for Digital Scholarship, 2015).

Challenges

While libraries are taking different approaches to the development of digital scholarship services there are some shared challenges. Walters and Skinner (2011, 5–6) discuss the need to build what they call 'the trio of strong infrastructures, content, and services' to support digital scholarship. Libraries need funding and sustainable funding models; a robust technical infrastructure; an understanding of how scholars and researchers work and want to engage with their services and content; and an understanding of intellectual property and licensing. They need to collaborate with others to avoid duplication of effort and unnecessary costs.

Libraries must also recruit and develop staff with the right skills to engage with researchers, develop effective cross-campus partnerships with IT and other technology providers and deliver these new and specialist services. Swan and Brown (2008) noted the shortage of specialized data librarians and the lack of a recognized career path for them as one the key challenges facing libraries seeking to develop support for data management. Jaguszewski and Williams (2013, 15) note that 'a combination of recruiting, retraining, and reskilling is underway at many libraries' in the USA. They report a study carried out by Tito Sierra, who found that 'more than half of the advertised positions were newly created or significantly redefined jobs, and that two-thirds of functional specialist positions were for newly created or redefined roles. About half of the newly created functional specialist positions have a strong digital or technology focus' (Jaguszewski and Williams, 2013, 15). The pressure on library budgets (Bosch and Henderson, 2013) means that many libraries have found it difficult to obtain additional funding to create new posts. At the same time, as Jaguszewski and Williams (2013) noted, there is a scarcity of vacant roles that can be redefined to meet new and emerging support requirements.

CASE STUDY 7.4   Meeting the challenges at the University of Salford

The University of Salford Library has had to address these challenges when developing digital scholarship services. The library uses workforce planning to ensure that it has the right people with the right skills to support new initiatives. This has involved making difficult choices about the composition of the workforce, which roles should be discontinued and what new roles need to be created. The creation of the Research Data Manager position, for example, was one of a series of changes made to the Library's workforce to support the delivery of a new library strategy. The Library has also sought to develop the skills of the workforce to support digital scholarship. Training needs analysis was carried out with library staff to identify areas for development and to inform both individual and service-wide staff development priorities.

Building relationships with scholars and support staff in key areas such as the Research Office and IT has been critical to the development of services to support digital scholarship. This has helped the library to develop an understanding of how researchers work and how they want to engage with the content and services provided. It has also led to recognition of the skills and expertise possessed by the Library and how they can be used to support new initiatives around scholarly communication, copyright and research data management.

The sustainability of these new initiatives is a major challenge. The Library has sought to absorb the cost of developing new services by stopping other activities wherever possible. For other new services, such as the development and maintenance of the technical infrastructure for research data management or the creation of an institutional fund for the payment of article processing charges, a case has had to be made for additional funding. The University of Salford will need to continue to balance making changes to the mix of services and support offered against the need to seek additional funding.

The resources required to develop the trio of infrastructures needed to support digital scholarship are often bound up in existing programmes and positions, leading libraries to seek additional funding or make difficult choices about the services they deliver and their staffing. While libraries are seeking to develop these services, other providers are waiting to step in if they fail. Hawkins (2012) quotes Annette Thomas, CEO of Macmillan Publishing, as saying that in her view 'publishers are here to make the scientific research process more effective by helping them keep up to date, find colleagues, plan experiments, and then share their results'. Scholars and researchers need support to navigate the changing scholarly communications environment, to manage their research data and to create and exploit digital content; and if libraries do not provide it, others will.

Conclusions

Libraries are developing new roles and services to support digital scholarship, through the curation and collection of digital resources and by enabling a range of scholarly activities that have been made possible by digital technologies (Weller, 2011). These changes are being enabled by a shift from a collection-centric approach to one based on engagement across the whole research lifecycle. The focus has shifted from the consumption to the creation of scholarship as libraries become more engaged with the process and application of research and seek to become embedded into research workflows.

The services being developed by libraries to facilitate this shift and support digital scholarship will vary according to their institutional mission and priorities, and through engagement with faculty. They include the development of digital collections, support for boutique digitization, curation and digital preservation; research data management and support for specialist tools and software to enable data analysis and data visualization; supporting the transformation of scholarly communication by: enabling open access through the development of digital repositories; advocating for author rights; developing library publishing programmes; working in partnership with researchers and other support staff; and providing consultancy and training to enable new scholarship.

Developing new services to enable digital scholarship is challenging. Libraries need to recruit or develop staff with the skills to deliver these services and ensure that they are affordable and sustainable. The digitization and preservation of materials, the management and preservation of research data, the development of digital repositories and library publishing programmes require sustained investment in technical infrastructure and staffing. The experience of the University of Salford shows that these challenges can be met and that it is possible to develop staff skills and deliver sustainable and affordable services to support digital scholarship. However, other libraries will approach these challenges in different ways as decisions about what services should be provided and how they might be funded will depend on institutional mission and priorities.

This is an exciting time for libraries as they develop new services and activities to provide support across the research lifecycle. Whilst there are challenges, there are also opportunities for libraries to enable the broader range of scholarly activity that is made possible by digital technologies and to provide services that are of real value to scholars and researchers.

Notes
1 Digital Bodleian Library, http://digital.bodleian.ox.ac.uk/.
2 Europeana, www.europeana.eu/portal/.
3 Hathi Trust, https://www.hathitrust.org/.

References
ACRL (2003) *Principles and Strategies for the Reform of Scholarly Communication 1*, Chicago, ACRL, www.ala.org/acrl/publications/whitepapers/principlesstrategies.
ACRL Research Planning and Review Committee (2012) 2012 Top Ten Trends in Academic Libraries, *College & Research Libraries News*, **73** (6), 311–20, http://crln.acrl.org/content/73/6/311.full.pdf+html.
Alexander, L., Case, D. B., Downing, K. E., Gomis, M. and Maslowski, E. (2014) Librarians and Scholars: partners in digital humanities, *EDUCAUSE Review*, http://er.educause.edu/articles/2014/6/librarians-and-scholars-partners-in-digital-humanities.
American Council of Learned Societies Commission on Cyberinfrastructure for the Humanities and Social Sciences (2006) *What is Digital Scholarship?*, http://cnx.org/contents/PmUZ95-a@1/What-Is-Digital-Scholarship.
Borgman, C. (2007) *Scholarship in the Digital Age: information, infrastructure and the internet*. Cambridge MA, MIT Press.
Bosch, S. and Henderson, K., (2013) The Winds of Change, *Library Journal*, **138** (8), 28–33.
Budapest Open Access Initiative (2012) *Read the Budapest Open Access Initiative*, www.budapestopenaccessinitiative.org/read.
Coble, Z., McCormick, M., and Vinopal, J. (2014) *Getting an Earful: the unexpected services of a digital scholarship unit*, New York, NYU, https://archive.nyu.edu/handle/2451/33806.
Cusworth, A. (2013) Echoes and Traces: a digital approach to Welsh traditional music, *Welsh Initiative for Digital Arts & Humanities Blog*, https://widah.wordpress.com/2013/03/05/echoes-traces-a-digital-approach-to-welsh-traditional-music/.
De Belder, K. (2013) *Transformation of the Academic Library*, OCLC Research Distinguished Seminar, Dublin, Ohio, OCLC, www.oclc.org/research/events/2013/05-10.html.

Dempsey, L. (2010) Outside-in and Inside-out Redux, *Lorcan Dempsey's Weblog*, 6 June, http://orweblog.oclc.org/Outside-in-and-inside-out-redux/.

Dempsey, L. and Malpas, C. (2015) Evolving Collection Directions. Presentation at *Collection Development Strategies in an Evolving Marketplace: an ALCTS Midwinter Symposium*, Slideshare, www.slideshare.net/lisld/alctssymposium.

Dempsey, L., Malpas, C. and Lavoie, B. (2014) Collection Directions: the evolution of library collections and collecting, *portal: Libraries and the Academy*, **14** (3), 393–423, http://muse.jhu.edu/journals/portal_libraries_and_the_academy/summary/v014/14.3.dempsey.html.

Devine, E. (2014) Open Access: what do researchers really think? *Taylor & Francis Editor Resources*, http://editorresources.taylorandfrancisgroup.com/open-access-what-do-researchers-really-think/.

EDINA (2015) *Research Data MANTRA*, Edinburgh: EDINA, http://datalib.edina.ac.uk/mantra/.

Emory Center for Digital Scholarship (2015) *Southern Spaces*, Atlanta, Emory University Libraries and Information Technology, http://digitalscholarship.emory.edu/projects/journal-southernspaces.html.

EPSRC (2014) *EPSRC Policy Framework on Research Data. Expectations*, Swindon, EPSRC, https://www.epsrc.ac.uk/about/standards/researchdata/.

Gross, J. and Ryan, J. C. (2015) Landscapes of Research: perceptions of open access (OA) publishing in the arts and humanities, *Publications*, **3** (2), 65–88, http://dx.doi.org/10.3390/publications3020065.

Hahn, K. (2008) *Research Library Publishing Services: new options for university publishing*, Chicago, Association of Research Libraries, 1–40, www.arl.org/news/arl-news/1172#.Vq4AeFN4ZE4.

Hawkins, D. (2012) A Publisher's New Job Description, *Against the Grain*, **11**, www.against-the-grain.com/2012/11/a-publishers-new-job-description/.

HEFCE (2014) *Policy for Open Access in the post-2014 Research Excellence Framework*, London, HEFCE, www.hefce.ac.uk/rsrch/oa/Policy/.

Hughes, L. (2014) Digital collections as research infrastructure, *EDUCAUSE Review*, http://er.educause.edu/articles/2014/6/digital-collections-as-research-infrastructure.

Jaguszewski, J. M. and Williams, K. (2013) *New Roles for New Times: transforming liaison roles in research libraries*, Washington DC, Association of Research Libraries, 1–17, www.arl.org/publications-resources/2893-new-roles-for-new-times-transforming-liaison-roles-in-research-libraries#.Vq4ccFN4ZE4.

K-State Libraries (2015) *Digital Scholarship Librarian*, Recruitment details, https://www.lib.k-state.edu/digital-scholarship-librarian.

Lippincott, J., Hemmasi, H. and Lewis, V. M. (2014) Trends in Digital Scholarship Centers, *EDUCAUSE Review*, http://er.educause.edu/articles/2014/6/trends-in-digital-scholarship-centers.

Liu, A. and Thomas III, W. G. (2012) Humanities in the Digital Age, *Inside Higher Ed*, https://www.insidehighered.com/views/2012/10/01/essay-opportunities-humanities-programs-digital-era.

Lynch, C. (2014) The 'Digital' Scholarship Disconnect, *EDUCAUSE Review*, **49** (3), 10–15, http://er.educause.edu/articles/2014/5/the-digital-scholarship-disconnect.

National Library of Wales (2011) *Digitisation strategy 2011/12–14/15*, Cardiff, National Library of Wales, 1–17, https://www.llgc.org.uk/fileadmin/fileadmin/docs_gwefan/amdanom_ni/dogfennaeth_gorfforaethol/StrategaethDdigido2012-2015.pdf.

Nature (2013) *Availability of Data, Material and Methods*, London, Nature Publishing Group, www.nature.com/authors/policies/availability.html.

New York University Data Services (2016) *Data Services: what we do*, New York, NYU Libraries, http://guides.nyu.edu/c.php?g=277095&p=1848840.

Rambo, N. (2015) *Research Data Management: roles for libraries*, New York, Ithaka S & R, http://sr.ithaka.org/?p=274643.

RCUK (2011) *RCUK Common Principles on Data Policy*, London, RCUK, www.rcuk.ac.uk/research/datapolicy/.

Royal Society (2012) *Science as an Open Enterprise*, London, Royal Society, 1–105, https://royalsociety.org/topics-policy/projects/science-public-enterprise/report/.

Showers, B. (2012) Does the Library Have a Role to Play in the Digital Humanities? *Digital Infrastructure Team*, London, Jisc, http://infteam.jiscinvolve.org/wp/2012/02/23/does-the-library-have-a-role-to-play-in-the-digital-humanities/.

Sinclair, B. (2014) The University Library as Incubator for Digital Scholarship, *EDUCAUSE Review*, http://er.educause.edu/articles/2014/6/the-university-library-as-incubator-for-digital-scholarship.

Suber, P. (2015) *Open Access Overview*, http://legacy.earlham.edu/~peters/fos/overview.htm.

Swan, A. and Brown, S. (2008) *The Skills, Role and Career Structure of Data Scientists and Curators: an assessment of current practice and future needs*, Report to the JISC, Truro, Key Perspectives, https://www.jisc.ac.uk/media/documents/programmes/digitalrepositories/dataskillscareersfinalreport.pdf.

Tenopir, C., Sandusky, R. J., Allard, S. and Birch, B. (2014) Research Data Management Services in Academic Research Libraries and Perceptions of Librarians, *Library & Information Science Research*, **36** (2), 84–90, http://dx.doi.org/10.1016/j.lisr.2013.11.003.

UCL Press (2016) *About UCL Press*, https://www.ucl.ac.uk/ucl-press/about.

UCLA (2015) *Digital Scholarship Librarian*, Recruitment details, https://recruit.apo.ucla.edu/apply/JPF00820.

University of Salford (2015a) *Research Data Management Policy*, Salford, University of Salford, www.salford.ac.uk/__data/assets/pdf_file/0009/674208/ResearchDataManagementPolicy.pdf.

University of Salford (2015b) *Open Access Policy*, Salford, University of Salford,

www.salford.ac.uk/__data/assets/pdf_file/0007/535426/OpenAccessPolicy.pdf.
USIR (2015) *Management Information* (December), Salford, University of Salford, www.salford.ac.uk/__data/assets/pdf_file/0010/680266/December2015.pdf.
Walters, T. and Skinner, K. (2011) *New Roles for New Times: digital curation for preservation*, Washington DC, ARL, 1–74,
www.arl.org/storage/documents/publications/nrnt_digital_curation17mar11.pdf.
Wang, M. (2013) Supporting the Research Process through Expanded Library Data Services, *Program*, **47** (3), 282–303.
Weller, M. (2011) *The Digital Scholar: how technology is transforming scholarly practice*, London, Bloomsbury Academic.
Wolski, M. and Richardson, J. (2014) A Model for Institutional Infrastructure to Support Digital Scholarship, *Publications*, **2** (4), 83–99,
http://dx.doi.org/10.3390/publications2040083.
Working Group on Expanding Access to Published Research Findings (2012) *Accessibility, Sustainability, Excellence: how to expand access to research publications*, London, RIN, 1–140, www.researchinfonet.org/publish/finch/.

PART 4

Communications and social networking

8

Social networking with the scholarly community: a literature review

Suzanne Parfitt

Introduction

To remain relevant to the ever-changing needs of its patrons, an academic library must have a strategic aim of adapting to the developing technological and information landscape. The establishment of strategies to support digital scholarship is an important step on this journey and librarians must remain engaged with patrons in order to achieve success in this area. This engagement is essential for two reasons: (i) so academic libraries can advise scholars on how digital research activities can be incorporated into their work and (ii) to build close collaborative connections with researchers in order to facilitate the continuous development of relevant library services. Librarians therefore must not only gain knowledge of the new digital tools, systems and processes, but also new ways of engaging patrons. Social networking sites (SNS) have introduced new opportunities for academic libraries to engage with patrons. SNS usually enable information, digital video, audio, photographs and music to be fed into a personal space that can be shared with others. SNS also provide a platform where people can engage with one another. Engagement is a two-way exchange and can be defined as 'some action beyond exposure, and implies an interaction between two or more parties' (The Conclave, 2013, 6). In this chapter, we explore published literature discussing patron engagement using SNS, methods that have a positive impact on patron responsiveness and patrons' views on library engagement through SNS. We will also discuss prevalent themes in the literature. These will cover methods for measuring the success of engagement using SNS and factors that should be considered by libraries wishing to engage with patrons through SNS.

Defining social media and social networking sites

Social media is increasingly popular, and in the USA is used by 90% of young adults aged 18 to 29 (Perrin, 2015). Junco (2012) studied 2368 American college students and found that those who were using Facebook spent an average of 101 minutes on the site each day. The findings of another American study suggest that online engagement is becoming ever more popular with young people; 34% of 12- to 24-year-olds now prefer to collaborate online rather than in person or via phone, as opposed to 19% for older generations (Meeker, 2015). This highlights the importance of online engagement for academic libraries, with many of their patrons being in this sector.

Given the rapid development of a wide range of social media tools, it is not easy to characterize social media and social networking sites. Three categories of social media sites are commonly used: (i) social networking sites (e.g. Facebook, Google+), (ii) microblogging sites (e.g. Twitter, Tumblr) and (iii) social bookmarking/tagging sites (e.g. Delicious, Diigo) (Mon, 2015). While this simple categorization does not accommodate all social media sites, such as Flickr and Instagram for image sharing or YouTube and Vimeo for video sharing, it does give a basic indication of what constitutes a social networking site. The terms social networking sites and social network sites are often used interchangeably, although 'networking' implies that people are looking to meet new people while 'network' suggests communication with people within their existing network (Boyd and Ellison, 2007). In this chapter, we refer to social networking, indicating communication with 'Friends' (i.e. existing academic library SNS connections) but also reaching out to create new connections.

Evolution of social networking site use in academic libraries

Facebook was first launched in 2004, exclusively for Harvard University students (Vassilakaki and Garoufallou, 2014). By 2007 the site was open to everybody over the age of 13 and 58 million people worldwide were using Facebook each month (Sedghi, 2015). At that time, a survey of 126 academic librarians throughout the USA found that only two respondents' libraries had a Facebook profile and the majority of librarians felt fairly apathetic about the site; neither enthusiastic nor disdainful (Charnigo and Barnett-Ellis, 2007). Since then, social media has continued to evolve rapidly, with 'new ideas, tools and developments coming online constantly' (Johnson et al., 2015, 35). SNS attract increasingly large audiences, with Facebook reaching 1.55 billion active monthly users by September 2015 (Facebook, 2015). As social media has evolved, so too has the use of SNS in academic libraries and the outlook of librarians. Chu and Du's (2013) research explored SNS tools being used by academic libraries in Asian, North American and European universities. A total of 140 libraries were approached, but a small sample of 38 responded to the questionnaire, thereby limiting possibilities for generalization. Nevertheless it is interesting to note that librarians had a positive attitude towards the use of SNS; 71.1% of the libraries were using SNS, with Facebook (62.9%) and Twitter (62.9%) being used most frequently. The following year, a survey of 100 American universities found, by using content analysis, that all the libraries studied had a presence on Facebook and Twitter (Boateng and Liu, 2014, 120). Zohoorian-Fooladi and Abrizah (2014) conducted focus groups with 22 librarians from three Malaysian universities, of which all three used Facebook and one used Twitter. In contrast to the apathy shown by the librarians in Charnigo and Barnett-Ellis's (2007) study, these librarians had 'positive perceptions on the usefulness of social media tools in academic libraries'. These studies illustrate how academic libraries and librarians have increasingly embraced the use of SNS in line with the tools' growing popularity. Librarians have traditionally been pioneers in the adoption of new technology for communication, from the telephone to e-mails to online chat, and social media is another advance that holds much potential for library–patron engagement.

Engaging with SNS

SNS offer a dynamic environment where participation and feedback are key benefits (Mercun and Zumer, 2011; Phillips, 2011; Nguyen, Partridge and Edwards, 2012). By enabling patrons to engage, the library can use SNS to help build a participatory library where opinions are welcomed and embraced and library services are user-centred (Nguyen, Partridge and Edwards, 2012). This is important when academic libraries are building services to support digital scholarship, in order to ensure that the services developed are highly relevant to their patrons' needs. The process of achieving patron engagement, however, can be hard work and may take months to achieve, according to Visser and Richardson (2013), whose 'Digital Engagement Framework' suggests that there are four stages in attaining engagement: reached, interested, involved and activated. Patrons must first be *reached* in order to begin to develop a relationship with them. They must be offered something that will *interest* them, they must be invited and inspired to become *involved* and finally *activated* to spread their enthusiasm, share the library's success and be a fully engaged patron. Other similar models have been suggested, based on the same principle, using different terms for the stages. For example, Paine (2011) suggests five stages of engagement: lurking, casual, active, committed and loyalist. By working to achieve the higher stages of engagement through SNS, academic libraries can develop relevant services for patrons who feel valued and involved.

Four areas that are key to successful patron engagement through an academic library Facebook page are:

- collaborating with other departmental social media users throughout the university
- having a flexible strategy
- encouraging contributions to the library's social media from student workers, staff and faculty
- keeping informed about patrons (Ramsey and Vecchione, 2014).

Of these four, the most important factor for patron engagement is keeping informed about patrons (Ramsey and Vecchione, 2014). Student involvement is also very valuable; Ramsey and Vecchione noted a 20% increase in likes during the first year that student workers began posting for the library. In their focus groups in three Malaysian universities, Zohoorian-Fooladi and Abrizah (2014) found that when the chief librarian and senior library managers had overall authority for social media this acted as a barrier to other librarians' becoming involved. This was then an obstacle to the libraries' social media participation and consequently patron engagement opportunities decreased. Both these cases support the view that by actively encouraging SNS contributions from a range of sources, and not just senior management, a library can increase patron engagement.

The literature has revealed a number of other actions that have a positive impact on patron responsiveness, as described below.

Be interesting and interested

In order to progress from *reached* to *interested* it is essential that the library posts content that is interesting to its patrons (Glazer, 2012; King, 2015). Libraries must show interest in their patrons and respond to any contact made, because listening is just as important as broadcasting (Burkhardt, 2010; Koontz, 2014; Smeaton and Davis, 2014; Taylor & Francis, 2014). Patrons like being heard and will participate more if they are part of the conversations (Buono and Kordeliski, 2013). It is also important for libraries to 'like', comment on and share content on other profiles to show interest and to demonstrate that the library has an active profile (Witte, 2014).

Have an active profile

Patrons are more likely to engage with an active library page. This opinion is supported by a study of 14 Malaysian academic library Facebook pages which found that three libraries with the most active profiles (updated daily) received more 'likes', comments and more posts by users (Ayu and Abrizah, 2011). Fiander (2012) urges caution, however, stating that 'too much activity on the page might be viewed by users as spam, or clogging up their newsfeed with too much library'. This is echoed by evidence from the business sector that responses often decrease when there are more than two Facebook posts a day (Rezab, 2011). Another study found that the number for optimal Twitter engagements is three per day (Socialbakers, 2013).

Respond to negative feedback

The importance of responding to negative feedback posted on SNS is widely acknowledged (Burkhardt, 2010; Canty, 2012; Fiander, 2012; Gunton and Davis, 2012; Hagman, 2012). SNS provides a key opportunity for academic libraries to rapidly respond to issues and it is important for several staff to have access to the library's SNS account, in order to increase the speed of response (Fiander, 2012; Hagman, 2012). Twitter hashtags and searches are also useful for finding feedback about the library that is not directly sent to the library, in order to respond accordingly (Hagman, 2012). It is not clear whether these responses encourage further patron engagement but they are certainly important to increase goodwill and patrons' satisfaction with the library. They can also provide valuable indications to the library on how its services can be improved in order to increase patrons' satisfaction.

Patrons' views

The importance of gathering patrons' opinions is highlighted by Huwe (2011), who states that 'we can begin to discover trends in faculty and student use of social media – provided we take time to talk to folks about it'. Nearly all the studies that have directly asked patrons for their opinions on academic library SNS have used questionnaires (Connell, 2009; Epperson and Leffler, 2009; Ismail, 2010; Ayiah and Kumah, 2011; Sachs, Eckel and Langan, 2011; Cassidy et al., 2014; Lwoga, 2014; Kumar Bhatt and Kumar, 2014; Wu et al., 2014). An exception is Burhanna, Seeholzer and Salem (2009), who used focus groups as well as a questionnaire to explore the use of Web 2.0 technologies in their academic library in order to inform the library's decisions on Web 2.0 development. When the student participants were asked what they thought about the library's adding resources in Facebook, the responses were generally quite unenthusiastic, for example, 'I'm sure it wouldn't be too bad a thing to do'. This lack of enthusiasm reflects the initial apathy towards library SNS use, as described earlier. Focus group findings cannot be generalized to a larger population but the findings from Burhanna, Seeholzer and Salem's four focus group sessions were consistent and hence valuable for informing the library's plans.

Questionnaires enable a larger audience to be reached than can be done by a focus group or interviews. They are useful for gathering people's views; however, one of their greatest limitations is the lack of opportunity to talk to respondents (Foddy, 1993 cited in Pickard, 2013, 207). Kumar Bhatt and Kumar's (2014) work is an example of a study using a questionnaire. The questionnaire about SNS use by the library was distributed to a purposive sample of 200 students at Jawaharlal Nehru University, Delhi and 170 responses were received. Findings included 66.4% wanting the library to contact them through SNS and 94.1% believing that chatting or messaging with a librarian is the most useful service that can be provided. The sample is quite small and the results cannot be generalized beyond Jawaharlal Nehru University. However, the study demonstrates that questionnaires in general are useful to libraries for planning their SNS use and ways that libraries can engage with patrons.

When analysing the findings of questionnaires it is important to bear in mind that results may not reflect what students will actually do. It is therefore useful to also look at their actual use of technology. Cassidy et al. (2014) used a questionnaire that was sent to all students at Sam Houston State University in the USA, resulting in 941 usable responses. While not focused solely on social media use, this paper does include findings on SNS; for example 67.5% of students who used Twitter expressed an interest in the library's using Twitter. Students' familiarity with a technology, however, does not necessarily lead to a desire for the library to use it; 90.3% of students recognized Google+ but only 7.3% of these were interested in the library's using it. The issue of potentially misleading questionnaire results is again highlighted in Sachs, Eckel and Langan's (2011) study, which surveyed 136 users at Western Michigan University's Waldo Library and also users at 14 peer institutions. Responses from Waldo Library patrons showed that 63% of respondents were very or somewhat comfortable asking a librarian for research help on Facebook. However, this was countered by the finding that only 4 of 115 respondents had ever asked a librarian a question via Facebook. This illustrates the importance of gaining a deeper understanding of responses. Sachs, Eckel and Langan achieved this by using detailed survey questions; mixed methods research would also be useful by bringing together different methodological approaches to achieve a deeper understanding (Williamson, 2013).

Methods and measures

There are various methods for the measurement of academic libraries' patron engagement through SNS. However, a widely used methodology still does not exist to examine the effectiveness of academic library engagement through SNS in meeting student expectations. Even the business world does not have an established standard for measuring social media performance (Engagement Labs, 2014). González-

Fernández-Villavicencio (2014) establishes a set of social media indicators that aim to provide libraries with standardized indicators to demonstrate return on investment for social media use. The 'Engagement, Interaction' indicator is of particular relevance, as this metric is used to measure the capacity of the relationship between the library and the user. This is measured in terms of retweets, shares, downloads and comments. It is important for each library to set its own goals and take baseline measurements against which milestones and growth can be measured (Dickson and Holley, 2010; Landis, 2010; Glazer, 2012; Solomon, 2013). The following methods described below have been used for measuring the success of engagement via SNS.

Follower and interaction counting

A popular quantitative method involves counting the number of followers or fans and their interactions (Cuddy, Graham and Morton-Owens, 2010; Solomon, 2013; Visser and Richardson, 2013; Stuart, 2014; King, 2015). Counting fans or followers enables a library to assess how many people will potentially see their posts because, as explained earlier, the audience must be *reached* before engagement is possible. It must be remembered, however, that only a small proportion of connections may actually view a post (Stuart, 2014). More meaningful measures therefore involve counting likes, indicating how many users have reached the *interested* phase of engagement. Twitter replies and Facebook comments show they are *involved* and shares, mentions and content contributions indicate fully *activated* patrons (Visser and Richardson, 2013). Stuart (2014) gathered these statistics for the ten most 'liked' academic library Facebook pages in the United Kingdom. He found that they actually raised many questions; for example, 'If the University of Glasgow Library has the most "likes", why are twice as many people talking about LSE?' (Stuart, 2014). This illustrates that although quantitative data is valuable in providing a broad picture, deep understanding is limited.

Questionnaires, focus groups and interviews

As discussed, questionnaires, and occasionally focus groups, are popular methods for collecting patrons' views, with quantitative questionnaires being used most often. When assessing social media use, however, numbers are not enough and it is essential to also collect qualitative evidence (Solomon, 2013). Qualitative methods, such as interviews, focus groups and questionnaires with open questions, can be useful for exploring patrons' views in more depth. It is important to bear in mind, however, that responses may not accurately reflect what a person knows or feels about an experience (Lalmas, O'Brien and Yom-Tov, 2014). Sewell (2013) highlights the value of using a variety of methods. Following a successful study using content analysis to analyse a library's Twitter followers Sewell identified the need to carry out a survey to learn about patrons' SNS preferences and their preferred method of interaction with the library.

Content, interaction and sentiment analysis

Content analysis is a research tool used to quantify and analyse the presence, meanings and relationships of words or concepts within text (Colorado State University, n.d.). It is useful for 'describing and making inferences about the characteristics and patterns of usage, as well as making inferences about the consequences of communication' (Brandtzaeg and Heim, 2009, 145). Interaction analysis provides details about the level of interaction between a system and its users. Content and interaction analysis can be used to study how academic libraries are using SNS and how patrons and other users are responding. Young and Rossmann (2015) aimed to create a community of student participants through Twitter. They used these analysis methods to identify that 'broadcast-drive, personality-devoid content' was causing their community to be disengaged. By refocusing on 'community-driven, personality-rich' content they saw a 46.8% increase in interaction. Phillips (2011) used content analysis to study status messages posted by 17 academic libraries on Facebook and found that libraries are using supportive comments, invitations, humour, pictures and direct questions for interaction. There is currently no information available that combines content/interaction analysis and patrons' opinions on library engagement to enable a deeper understanding of what affects and motivates patron engagement.

Sentiment analysis adds a further dimension by categorizing patrons' comments or responses as positive, negative or neutral. Sentiment opinion analysis is useful for exploring trends and correlations in patron responses. A library could investigate, for example, 'Is there an increase in Facebook Wall comments after you post a link to your library's new DVD list, and are they complaints or compliments?' (Solomon, 2013, 155). Sentiment can, however, be difficult to judge and analysis can be a 'surprisingly complicated endeavor' (Sponder, 2012, 224).

Graph data

NodeXL is open source software that enables networks, and relationships within networks, to be analysed and visualized. This method does not provide any qualitative meaning to the data but it can be useful in visualizing engagement connections. The 'betweenness centrality' can be used as an indicator of engagement within an SNS and is identified as a central node that lies on the shortest route between other pairs of nodes (Stuart, 2014). NodeXL can also be used to create network maps of subsets of followers, such as students or faculty, which may be useful for a library to establish target audiences for potential engagement (Yep and Shulman, 2014, 180).

Anecdotes

Anecdotes are not metrics; however, they can provide convincing examples of achievement (Visser and Richardson, 2013). Glazer (2012) gives an example whereby a library Facebook post about users being able to check out music CDs and DVDs led to the university's television network reporting on the change of policy in its morning news show. This kind of anecdotal evidence can 'help you to convince critics, encourage your team, inspire others and generally create an optimistic feeling about your institution's digital engagement strategy' (Visser and Richardson, 2013, 47).

Issues and implications

There are a number of factors that should be considered by libraries wishing to engage with their patrons through SNS. Issues include low patron usage of the library's SNS page (Sewell, 2013; Zohoorian-Fooladi and Abrizah, 2014) and the need for a policy to define posting protocol and procedures (Lankes et al., 2007; Chen et al., 2011; Sachs, Eckel and Langan, 2011; Fiander, 2012; Nguyen, Partridge and Edwards, 2012). Other issues that are often cited are described below.

Privacy issues

A privacy policy should be considered. Although Charnigo and Barnett-Ellis (2007) found that only 19% of the 126 academic librarians studied had concerns about privacy issues in relation to Facebook, this topic is often mentioned in the literature (Secker, 2008; Burhanna, Seeholzer and Salem, 2009; Dickson and Holley, 2010; Park, 2010; Chen et al., 2011; Fiander, 2012; Nguyen, Partridge and Edwards, 2012; Stoeckel and Sinkinson, 2013). In particular, the ability to engage openly is SNS' key advantage and privacy issues can clash with this openness (Park, 2010; Nguyen, Partridge and Edwards, 2012,).

Time needed for SNS monitoring and creation of quality content

It is important not to fall into the common misconception that the majority of time will be spent in the initial stages of setting up an academic library Facebook page. More time will actually be needed as it becomes established (Chu and Du, 2013).

Monitoring will take more time as the site's popularity grows, because the library must take advantage of the increased opportunities to interact with patrons (Fiander, 2012). There is a need to maintain a high level of monitoring because students expect timely responses and are likely to lose interest in the library's SNS if they don't receive speedy assistance (Dickson and Holley, 2010; Mercun and Zumer, 2011). Additionally, taking time to create good quality content is key to a site's success (King, 2015) and will help to generate conversation (Buono and Kordeliski, 2013).

The need to be adaptable to change

It is important for academic libraries to keep up to date with changing SNS technology. Although Facebook and Twitter have been popular for many years they will not necessarily remain so. Currently, Google+ is gaining popularity, with 540 million active users (Bradley, 2015). A recent study also found that of the 40% of students who use social media to stay in touch with their lecturers, 12% are now using Snapchat, which is rising in popularity too (Jisc, 2015). The popularity of SNS may also vary from country to country. Saw et al. (2013) suggested that a university with Chinese international students should consider using Renren. Xu et al. (2015) also highlight the popularity of WeChat in China.

Librarians in developing countries face a number of general issues, including policy and security; additional problems include inadequate numbers of computers, unstable internet connectivity and insufficient electricity (Lwoga, 2014). Lwoga's (2014) study focuses on a university library in Tanzania where 72.4% of the 76 undergraduate medical students had Facebook accounts, 39.5% had Google+ and 19.7% had Twitter accounts. As a result of the questionnaire findings, a library Facebook page has been implemented, which has improved the promotion of library service and the provision of user-oriented services.

Conclusions

It is essential for an academic library's aims and objectives to reflect the changing technological and information landscape, including strategies to support digital scholarship. It is important to maintain and explore new channels of engagement in order to (i) advise scholars on appropriate digital research tools, systems and processes and (ii) to develop library services that meet scholars' changing needs. SNS are ideal tools for patron engagement by academic libraries and the use of SNS has been increasingly embraced by librarians as their popularity has grown. It can, however, be difficult to achieve patron engagement, and patrons must go through four stages (reached, interested, involved and activated) before full engagement is attained. Key aspects in achieving engagement include keeping informed about patrons, being open to contributions from a range of sources (including students), collaborating with other departmental social media users throughout the university, having a flexible strategy, being interested/interesting and having an active (but not too active) profile.

There is no established standard for measuring social media performance but a number of methods are commonly used to measure engagement. These include follower/interaction counting, questionnaires, focus groups, interviews, content analysis, network graphs and anecdotes. These methods can provide an indication of a library's level of achievement in engaging with its patrons. There are, however, a number of factors that should be considered by libraries who wish to engage with patrons through SNS. These include the need to consider an SNS policy, privacy issues, time needed for content creation and the need to be adaptable to changing SNS technology. Academic libraries that embrace the opportunities afforded to them by SNS for patron engagement increase their potential to enhance support for scholars and to provide relevant services for digital scholarship.

Acknowledgement

The literature review on which this chapter is based was originally written under the supervision of Dr Ying-Hsang Liu as a component of the Applied Research specialization in the Master of Information Studies course at Charles Sturt University.

References

Ayiah, E. M. and Kumah, C. H. (2011) Social Networking: a tool to use for the effective service delivery to clients by African libraries. Presented at *IFLA 2011, International Federation of Library Associations*.

Ayu, A. R. R. and Abrizah, A. (2011) Do you Facebook? Usage and applications of Facebook page among academic libraries in Malaysia, *The International Information & Library Review*, **43** (4), 239-49.

Boateng, F. and Liu, Y. Q. (2014) Web 2.0 Applications' Usage and Trends in Top US Academic Libraries, *Library Hi Tech*, **32** (1), 120-38.

Boyd, D. M. and Ellison, N. B. (2007) Social Network Sites: definition, history, and scholarship, *Journal of Computer-Mediated Communication*, **13** (1), 210-30.

Bradley, P. (2015) Introduction, *Social Media for Creative Libraries*, London, Facet Publishing, 1-16, https://www.youtube.com/watch?v=4zSsloDyvUg.

Brandtzaeg, P. B. and Heim, J. (2009) Why People Use Social Networking Sites. In Ozok, A. A. and Zaphiris, P. (eds), *Online Communities and Social Computing: Third International Conference, OCSC 2009, Held as Part of HCI International 2009, San Diego, CA, USA, July*

19–24, 2009, Proceedings, Springer.

Buono, M. P. and Kordeliski, A. (2013) Connect, Create, Collaborate: how and why social media is good for your library and why you should join the fun, *Young Adult Library Services*, **11** (2), 30–40.

Burhanna, K. J., Seeholzer, J. and Salem, J. (2009) No Natives Here: a focus group study of student perceptions of Web 2.0 and the academic library, *The Journal of Academic Librarianship*, **35** (6), 523–32.

Burkhardt, A. (2010) Social Media: a guide for college and university libraries, *College & Research Libraries News*, 10–24, http://crln.acrl.org/content/71/1/10.full.pdf+html.

Canty, N. (2012) Social Media in Libraries: it's like, complicated, *Alexandria*, **23** (2), 41–54.

Cassidy, E. D., Colmenares, A., Jones, G., Manolovitz, T., Shen, L. and Vieira, S. (2014) Higher Education and emerging technologies: shifting trends in student usage, *The Journal of Academic Librarianship*, **40** (2), 124–33.

Charnigo, L. and Barnett-Ellis, P. (2007) Checking Out Facebook.com: the impact of a digital trend on academic libraries, *Information Technology and Libraries*, **26** (1), 23.

Chen, D. Y.-T., Maxwell, W., Chu, S. K.-W., Li, W. Z. S. and Tang, L. L. C. (2011) Interaction between Libraries and Library Users on Facebook. Presented at *The 2011 Research Symposium of the Center for Information Technology in Education (CITERS 2011)*, Hong Kong, http://hdl.handle.net/10722/161205.

Chu, S. K.-W. and Du, H. S. (2013) Social Networking Tools for Academic Libraries, *Journal of Librarianship and Information Science*, **45** (1), 64–75.

Colorado State University (n.d.) *An Introduction to Content Analysis*, http://writing.colostate.edu/guides/page.cfm?pageid=1305&guideid=61.

Connell, R. S. (2009) Academic Libraries, Facebook and MySpace, and Student Outreach: a survey of student opinion, *portal: Libraries and the Academy*, **9** (1), 25–36.

Cuddy, C., Graham, J. and Morton-Owens, E. G. (2010) Implementing Twitter in a Health Sciences Library, *Medical Reference Services Quarterly*, **29** (4), 320–30.

Dickson, A. and Holley, R. P. (2010) Social Networking in Academic Libraries: the possibilities and the concerns, *New Library World*, **111** (11/12), 468–79.

Engagement Labs (2014) *Defining a Standard Measurement for Social Media Performance*, https://www.engagementlabs.com/wp-content/themes/elabs/files/engagementlabs-whitelist.pdf.

Epperson, A. and Leffler, J. J. (2009) Social Software Programs: student preferences of librarian use, *New Library World*, **110** (7/8), 366–72.

Facebook (2015) *Company Info*, http://newsroom.fb.com/company-info/.

Fiander, D. J. (2012) Social media for academic libraries. In Rasmussen Neal, D. (ed.), *Social Media for Academics*, Oxford, Chandos Publishing.

Glazer, H. (2012) 'Likes' Are Lovely, but do They Lead to More Logins? *College & Research Libraries News*, **73** (1), 18–21.

González-Fernández-Villavicencio, N. (2014) The Profitability of Libraries Using Social Media. Presented at the *Second International Conference on Technological Ecosystems for Enhancing Multiculturality*, New York, ACM Press, 561–66.

Gunton, L. and Davis, K. (2012) Beyond Broadcasting: customer service, community and information experience in the Twittersphere, *Reference Services Review*, **40** (2), 224–7.

Hagman, J. (2012) Joining the Twitter Conversation, *Public Services Quarterly*, **8** (1), 78–85.

Huwe, T. (2011) New Metrics for Academic Social Media Users, *Computers in Libraries*, **31** (4), 30.

Ismail, L. (2010) What Net Generation Students Really Want: determining library help-seeking preferences of undergraduates, *Reference Services Review*, **38** (1), 10–27.

Jisc (2015) *'Just Snapchat me' – the New Way to Stay in Touch with University Tutors*, Jisc, www.jisc.ac.uk/news/just-snapchat-me-the-new-way-to-stay-in-touch-with-university-tutors-26-feb-2015.

Johnson, L., Adams Becker, S., Estrada, V. and Freeman, A. (2015) *NMC Horizon Report: 2015 higher education edition*, The New Media Consortium.

Junco, R. (2012) The Relationship between Frequency of Facebook Use, Participation in Facebook Activities, and Student Engagement, *Computers & Education*, **58** (1), 162–71.

King, D. L. (2015) Managing Your Library's Social Media Channels, *Library Technology Reports*, **51** (1), 6–9

Koontz, C. (2014) *Marketing and Social Media: a guide for libraries, archives, and museums*, Lanham MD, Rowman & Littlefield.

Kumar Bhatt, R. and Kumar, A. (2014) Student Opinion on the Use of Social Networking Tools by Libraries: a case study of Jawaharlal Nehru University, New Delhi, *The Electronic Library*, **32** (5), 594–602.

Lalmas, M., O'Brien, H. and Yom-Tov, E. (2014) Measuring User Engagement, *Synthesis Lectures on Information Concepts, Retrieval, and Services*, **6** (4), 1–132.

Landis, C. (2010) *A Social Networking Primer for Librarians*, London, Facet Publishing.

Lankes, R. D., Silverstein, J., Nicholson, S. and Marshall, T. (2007) Participatory Networks: the library as conversation. *Information Research*, **12** (4), www.informationr.net/ir/12-4/colis/colis05.html.

Lwoga, E. T. (2014) Integrating Web 2.0 into an Academic Library in Tanzania, *The Electronic Library*, **32** (2), 183–202.

Meeker, M. (2015) *Internet Trends 2015 – Code Conference*, www.kpcb.com/internet-trends.

Mercun, T. and Zumer, M. (2011) Making Web 2.0 Work for Users and Libraries. In Gupta, D. and Savard, R. (eds), *Marketing Libraries in a Web 2.0 World*, International Federation of Library Associations, Berlin/Munich, De Gruyter Saur, 13–22.

Mon, L. M. (2015) *Social Media and Library Services*, Chapel Hill, Morgan & Claypool.

Nguyen, L. C., Partridge, H. and Edwards, S. L. (2012) Towards an Understanding of the Participatory Library, *Library Hi Tech*, **30** (2), 335–46.

Paine, K. D. (2011) *Measure What Matters: online tools for understanding customers, social media, engagement, and key relationships*, Chichester, Wiley.

Park, J. (2010) Differences among University Students and Faculties in Social Networking Site Perception and Use: implications for academic library services, *The Electronic Library*, **28** (3), 417–31, http://doi.org/10.1108/02640471011051990.

Perrin, A. (2015) Social Media Usage: 2005–2015, www.pewinternet.org/2015/10/08/social-networking-usage-2005-2015.

Phillips, N. K. (2011) Academic Library Use of Facebook: building relationships with students, *The Journal of Academic Librarianship*, **37** (6), 512–22.

Pickard, A. J. (2013) *Research Methods in Information*, 2nd edn, London, Facet Publishing.

Ramsey, E. and Vecchione, A. (2014) Engaging Library Users through a Social Media Strategy, *Journal of Library Innovation*, **5** (2), 71–82.

Rezab, J. (2011) How Often Should You Post on Your Facebook Pages? www.socialbakers.com/blog/147-how-often-should-you-post-on-your-facebook-pages.

Sachs, D. E., Eckel, E. J. and Langan, K. A. (2011) Striking a Balance: effective use of Facebook in an academic library, *Internet Reference Services Quarterly*, **16** (1–2), 35–54.

Saw, G., Abbott, W., Donaghey, J. and McDonald, C. (2013) Social Media for International Students – it's not all about Facebook, *Library Management*, **34** (3), 156–74.

Secker, J. (2008) Case Study 5: Libraries and Facebook, *LASSIE: Libraries and Social Software in Education*, London, Centre for Distance Education, University of London.

Sedghi, A. (2015) *Facebook: 10 years of social networking, in numbers*, www.theguardian.com/news/datablog/2014/feb/04/facebook-in-numbers-statistics.

Sewell, R. R. (2013) Who Is Following Us? Data mining a library's Twitter followers, *Library Hi Tech*, **31** (1), 160–70.

Smeaton, K. and Davis, K. (2014) Using Social Media to Create a Participatory Library Service: an Australian study, *Library and Information Research*, **38** (117), 54–76.

Socialbakers (2013) Tweeting Too Much? Find out the ideal Tweet frequency for brands, www.socialbakers.com/blog/1847-tweeting-too-much-find-out-the-ideal-tweet-frequency-for-brands.

Solomon, L. (2013) *The Librarian's Nitty-gritty Guide to Social Media*, Chicago, American Library Association.

Sponder, M. (2012) *Social Media Analytics: effective tools for building, intrepreting, and using metrics*, New York, McGraw-Hill.

Stoeckel, S. and Sinkinson, C. (2013) *Tips and Trends: social media*, http://acrl.ala.org/IS/wp-content/uploads/2014/05/2013summer.pdf.

Stuart, D. (2014) *Web Metrics for Library and Information Professionals*, London, Facet Publishing.

Taylor & Francis (2014) *Use of Social Media by the Library: current practices and future opportunities* (White Paper), www.tandf.co.uk/journals/access/white-paper-social-media.pdf.

The Conclave (2013) *The Conclave: complete social media measurement standards,* www.smmstandards.com/wp-content/uploads/2013/06/Complete-standards-document4.pdf.

Vassilakaki, E. and Garoufallou, E. (2014) The Impact of Facebook on Libraries and Librarians: a review of the literature, *Program: Electronic Library and Information Systems,* **48** (3), 226–45.

Visser, J. and Richardson, J. (2013) *Digital Engagement in Culture, Heritage and the Arts,* http://digitalengagementframework.com.

Williamson, K. (2013) Research Concepts. In Williamson, K. and Johanson, G. (eds), *Research Methods: information, systems and contexts,* Prahan, Tilde Publishing.

Witte, G. G. (2014) Content Generation and Social Network Interaction within Academic Library Facebook Pages, *Journal of Electronic Resources Librarianship,* **26** (2), 89–100.

Wu, J., Chatfield, A. J., Hughes, A. M., Kysh, L. and Rosenbloom, M. C. (2014) Measuring Patrons' Technology Habits: an evidence-based approach to tailoring library services, *Journal of the Medical Library Association: JMLA,* **102** (2), 125–29.

Xu, J., Kang, Q., Song, Z. and Clarke, C. P. (2015) Applications of Mobile Social Media: WeChat among academic libraries in China, *The Journal of Academic Librarianship,* **41** (1), 21–30.

Yep, J. and Shulman, J. (2014) Analyzing the Library's Twitter Network: using NodeXL to visualize impact, *College & Research Libraries News,* **75** (4), 177–86.

Young, S. W. H. and Rossmann, D. (2015) Building Library Community through Social Media, *Information Technology and Libraries,* **34** (1), 20–37.

Zohoorian-Fooladi, N. and Abrizah, A. (2014) Academic Librarians and their Social Media Presence: a story of motivations and deterrents, *Information Development,* **30** (2), 159–71.

9

Developing digital scholars: from the ivory tower to the Twittersphere

Alison Hicks

Introduction

Who or what is a digital scholar? Questions such as this are often surprisingly absent from library literature, either being side-lined in our rush to establish a digital scholarship centre or neglected in our push to capitalize upon interest in open access (OA) publishing and, more recently, open educational resources (OER). Yet, while the establishment of physical and financial backing for these efforts is vitally important, our disregard for the underlying (and occasionally contentious) scholarly practices and activities that support these goals is troublesome. Just as we saw with Web 2.0 hype back in the early 2000s, a focus on the shiny new technologies rather than on the practices and individual capacities needed to engage within these new environments runs the risk of reducing digital scholarship to a technical or instrumental skill set and neglecting the broader sociocultural issues that are at play within this arena, including questions about the nature and purpose of scholarship in an era of increased accountability, impact and control. The focus on the tools rather than the people also constitutes a missed opportunity for librarians.

This chapter will explore our changing understandings of digital and open scholarship as well as the librarian's role in supporting the development of the capacities that are needed to engage within these environments. Defining a digital scholar as 'someone who employs digital, networked and open approaches to demonstrate specialism in a field' (Weller, 2011, 5), and digital scholarship as comprising three major forms: open education, open access and networked participation (Veletsianos and Kimmons, 2012a, 168), the chapter will be split into three sections. The first section will start by exploring the concept of digital scholarship, drawing out the connections between digital, networked, participatory and open scholarship. The chapter will then focus more concretely on the idea of networked participation, or the use of online social networks to 'share, reflect upon, critique, improve, validate, and ... develop ... scholarship' (Veletsianos and Kimmons, 2012a, 168), paying particular attention to how changing ideas of academic influence, reputation and identity intersect with the realities of contemporary academia. Finally, the third section of the chapter will use a series of practical examples to explore how librarians can use these ideas to facilitate researcher learning and development as well as further discussion in the field.

What is digital scholarship?

In some respects, it is no wonder that the term 'digital scholarship' has been so confused in recent years – whether a researcher limits themselves to the use of word processing software and the library's online catalogue or engages daily in large-scale, data-intensive collaborative research, there can be few scholars nowadays who fail to use technology when they engage in scholarly practices. In this vein, the concept of digital scholarship may seem tautological, at best. However, when these same activities are seen through the lens of research that has explored the tangled nature of digital scholarship, it becomes obvious that the picture is not so clear cut. The meaning of scholarship, for example, is complex, being defined in 1990 by Ernest Boyer in terms of discovery, integration, application and teaching rather than just as the generation of new knowledge. Viewed in this light, digital scholarship must be understood as going beyond the adoption of new research methods to engage more deeply with personal habits as well as ideas of outreach, engagement and education.

The definition of digitality is equally complicated. While the term could refer to the use of new technologies to enhance research, for example, making scholarship faster or more collaborative (Veletsianos and Kimmons, 2012b, 767), it is clear that the social and networked affordances of new technologies open up a number of different opportunities within the field. Social media, for example, helps scholars to share their research, including through blogging or social network sites such as Twitter. However, while the ability to make connections and communicate is useful, it is the value of openness as well as the concepts of participation and informal collaboration that are inherent within this act of sharing that can be seen as more remarkable. These ideas mean that, in effect, it is an embracing of the 'open values, ideology and potential of technologies born of peer-to-peer networking and wiki ways of working in order to benefit both the academy and society', or the *affordances* rather than the *use* of these technologies (Pearce et al., 2010) that can be seen as constituting the focus on the digital within this definition. This has a number of repercussions for our understanding of digital scholarship.

One of the most important consequences centres on the nature of digital scholarship. As Veletsianos and Kimmons point out, the practices that are invoked as scholars use these new technologies in their research suggest that, rather than replicating or merely amplifying old scholarly norms, digital scholarship has the potential to enhance or to transform its very shape and structure (2012b, 768). In other words, digital scholarship cannot be characterized by the translation of old norms (such as publishing models) into new technological infrastructures. Instead, as Greenhow and Gleason highlight, digital scholarship 'leverage[s] social media affordances (ie, promotion of users, their inter-connections and user-generated content) and potential values (ie, knowledge as decentralized, co-constructed, accessible and connective) to evolve the ways in which scholarship is accomplished in academia' (2014, 3). These practices transform both the reach and the meaning of scholarship. A secondary consequence relates to the development of digital scholars; the evolution of new forms of scholarly communication, outputs and networks (Weller, 2011) means that digital scholarship cannot just be limited to functional, skill-based literacy. Instead, as communities negotiate and work to integrate these new values into shared meaning making and understandings, teaching and learning must centre on the development of dynamic capacities or the ability to act and make decisions within these environments rather than on fixed sets of skills.

Emerging from social constructivist understandings of knowledge that position the development of meaning as decentralized, accessible and socially mediated, digital scholarship can thereby be linked to the goal of encouraging more inclusive research as well as reacting against 'the hierarchies and elitism of traditional academia, with its gatekeepers and its exclusionary literacy practices and strategies of preferment' (Goodfellow, 2013a, 2). These ideas have led Veletsianos and Kimmons to characterize digital scholarship as being enacted through three major forms: OA and open publishing; open education, including OER and open teaching; and networked participation (2012a). While OA and OER need no introduction for librarians, it is the idea of networked participation, or 'scholars' use of participatory technologies and online social networks to share, reflect upon, critique, improve, validate, and further their scholarship' (Veletsianos and Kimmons, 2012b, 768) that remains less well known in the field, despite the direct relevance to many aspects of library practice. Centred upon the idea that scholars now have the capacity to 'collaborate, build academic community, solicit feedback, and develop public relevance for their work' through digital networks (Glass, 2015, 2), it is clear that the openness engendered within these practices could be both a source of opportunity as well as a point of tension as academics adjust and adapt to the changing realities of higher education. The chapter will now turn to exploring these ideas in more detail.

Networked participation: opportunity and tension

Centring on a number of emergent practices, networked participation has generally referred to the use of technologies such as video-sharing sites, blogging and micro-blogging tools as well as social media services in order to communicate, discuss, publish and reflect on ideas in an open, public space (Greenhow and Gleason, 2014, 3). This means that a scholar who has uploaded a manuscript for feedback to academia.edu can be seen to be sharing ideas with broader audiences before formal publication, or an educator who is using Twitter to engage in professional or social commentary with others in the field and a PhD student who is using a WordPress blog to discuss emerging ideas from her thesis can be said to be engaging in networked participatory scholarship. Structured around research development and bringing in connectivist ideas of learning as network building (Siemens, 2005), these practices seem particularly worthy, being grounded in a push to democratize education and scholarship.

Yet, despite the admirable educational aims, it is clear that these ideas about research activity often exist in a certain state of tension. Digital scholarship does not exist in a vacuum and this vision of networked participation could be seen as somewhat idealized. Or, as Goodfellow (2013a) so astutely puts it: do the ideas of open, scholarly and digital form an impossible triangle? Scholars work in a 'context of relatively conservative value and reward systems that have the practice of peer review at their core' (Harley et al., 2010, 13), a system that has been built on notions of exclusivity as well as the premise of knowledge scarcity rather than abundance (Stewart, 2015). They also tend to be employed in a system that, increasingly, links the value of education to economic productivity and measures academic achievement and output in similar terms of quality assessment (Greenhow and Gleason, 2014, 2). Viewed in this light, it is apparent that the idea of networked participatory scholarship, with its focus on openness and sharing, can be seen neither as straightforward nor as unproblematic. It also raises a number of important questions about the essence of scholarly work within these new realities, as well as the concept of a digital scholar and the nature of the very technologies themselves.

One of the most commonly cited tensions regarding networked participation centres on the positioning and the impact of these scholarly practices within '"entrenched" academic reward and promotion structures' (Veletsianos, 2013, 642). In other words, while new, participatory practices may reach new communities or have created new forms of peer evaluation, academia does not currently have a way of measuring or valuing this impact and engagement. In fact, blogging work may still be considered secondary for many administrations, even while it is used as the basis for published or peer-reviewed work (Skallerup Besette, 2015). Coupled with reports that bloggers have occasionally either been treated with 'disdain' during promotion and tenure reviews (Lupton, 2014, 4) or have felt like they were jeopardizing future job prospects (Lupton, 2014, 24), these ideas mean that scholars may consider that they need to refrain from publishing work openly (Goodfellow, 2013a, 7) or, at the very least, engage more discretely online. The experiences of Steven Salaita, a professor whose appointment at the University of Illinois was rescinded for comments made from his personal Twitter account, form a case in point (Stoytcheva, 2015). In effect, academics are often using these new technologies to build influence and reputation, or in very similar ways to traditional academic purposes, for instance to build influence and reputation. However, because these interactions look very different within new, participatory networks (that are built upon and emphasize open sharing and collaboration), academia does not yet have a way to recognize or value contributions (Stewart, 2015, 18).

The emphasis on influence also highlights another area of growing interest and concern; what do these new developments mean for the digital scholar's identity? Engagement on social media requires that academics value 'transparency and responsiveness, a willingness to work in public and to help others feel comfortable doing the same' as well as multi-platform, multi-identity academic selves (Utell, 2015). Yet, the fact that social networks were originally designed and employed for the maintenance of personal relationships raises a number of questions about boundaries between both personal and professional identities, as well as the need to negotiate these practices when the technology is often expressly designed to discourage these competing identifications (Lupton, 2014, 6). This lack of privacy has further led many academics to question whether their academic identities may be 'undermined' by their forays into networked participation, with several of Lupton's research participants wondering about the credibility or the perceived quality of their online work (2014, 22). Similarly, it is clear that for academics who identify with a minority gender, sexual, racial or ethnic identity, the risks of participating online or the costs of the emotional labour may not outweigh the benefits, with scholars expressing concern about misogynistic (Mitchell, 2013) or racial (Cottom McMillan, 2012) online harassment, amongst other issues. These aggressions are compounded by the existence of easily accessible internet archives.

Lastly, it is clear that the very tools that we use for participatory scholarship cannot be considered as neutral platforms from which we can engage in networked practices. For some, technologies reinforce existing structures rather than opening up social norms, with personalizing algorithms within social media services (Bucher, 2012) or search engines (Umoja Noble, 2012) leading to filter bubbles of like-minded individuals or relevant information (Pariser, 2011). For others, the instability of digital publications and networks makes them, ironically, less accessible to a global readership (Goodfellow, 2013b). In addition, the for-profit or venture capitalist funding that is behind common social media or repository sites such as academia.edu and Facebook means that many are starting to question and draw attention to these sites' commitment to the open values of networked participation, their appearance of educational status notwithstanding (Fitzpatrick, 2015). Even Wikipedia, whose values of collaborative accessibility often position it as the poster child of the networked participation movement, can be critiqued for its limited representation of certain countries, communities and their knowledges (Graham et al., 2014) as well as for its inherent gender bias (Wagner et al., 2015). Bias is not limited to tools, either. The methods chosen to research the current state of networked participation may exclude a number of participants (Fransman, 2013), with Veletsianos and Kimmons (2012b) warning that future research may find that the ideals of educational justice that are assumed to drive networked participatory scholarship may, in fact, be characteristics of early adopters rather than intrinsic to these practices.

In sum, there are a number of admirable aims within emerging scholarly practices. Notwithstanding, the issues highlighted here demonstrate the importance of taking a critical approach to the use and development of new technologies and practices. While this may seem overly negative, it is clear that an uncritically positive depiction of new tools and devices can lead to the problematic narratives of technology's revolutionary, disruptive or 'emancipatory' potential within education that are currently seen in both academic and popular writing (Hall, 2011; Veletsianos, 2013). A critical gaze can help to draw attention to these issues and, as educators who are actively immersed in today's information landscapes, librarians are perfectly placed to lead and contribute meaningfully to these conversations.

Librarian roles

Librarian involvement within questions of digital scholarship can take a number of forms and formats but generally tends to centre on the role of a repository manager or a scholarly communication librarian. In focusing on the idea of networked participation, however, this chapter argues that digital scholarship is also an area of interest for instruction librarians, dovetailing neatly with existing researcher education initiatives. As a consequence, this chapter will highlight a number of instructional outreach and engagement activities that centre on these ideas of digital scholarship and networked participation. Unlike traditional library trainings, though, which may tend to centre on a specific tool, for example EndNote or Impact Story, the focus within this section will be on education related to the practices, or the explicit and implicit activities that afford digital scholarship. This approach is far less common within librarianship, yet, as Veletsianos and Kimmons (2012a) point out, scholars need to be able to 'develop an understanding of the affordances of the participatory web for scholarship and consider the implications of online identity and digital participation' or the literacies that are needed to engage with these networks, rather than just the technical expertise. At the same time, these practices should not be taught as if they were a fixed or a limited skill set. Instead, they should be seen as dynamic, flexible and subject to change, as communities engage with both the possibilities and the pitfalls of networked participation. Illustrative examples of these ideas will be drawn from work at the author's home institution, the University of Colorado, Boulder (UCB).

One way that librarians can integrate questions of digital scholarship into their teaching and researcher-outreach initiatives and efforts is through re-centring existing workshops on the practices of networked participation rather than merely highlighting the software. In other words, rather than focusing on demo-ing the nuts and bolts of a useful tool, a session could be reimagined around an exploration of how this tool might fit into the researcher's existing individual and disciplinary or community-based practices, as well as in conjunction with other technologies that they are using. These ideas are borne out by research demonstrating that, rather than experiencing problems with the technical functionality of these tools, scholars often struggle with the integration of the tools into their existing workflow or when they are faced with competing disciplinary demands and norms (Hicks and Sinkinson, 2015). A recent study of the reference manager Mendeley, for example, found that while researchers often wanted to use the social and networked capacity of Mendeley to share and work collaboratively, they were frequently hobbled by local norms for citation sharing and storage (that build upon e-mail networks and existing libraries of references) as well as dominant disciplinary practices, for example preference for the use of a Facebook group for networking (Hicks and Sinkinson, 2015).

At UCB, these ideas have directly led to the creation of workshops that focus on workflow and software feature comparison rather than on technical features. A reference manager workshop, for example, is now structured around a comparison of Mendeley, Zotero, EndNote and Papers, rather than immediately siphoning learners into learning one specific or institutionally mandated technology. Most importantly, however, the workshop is centred on attendees' needs, starting with a series of questions about participants' research and study practices, as well as their disciplinary norms or constraints, rather than the software's features and affordances. Having sensitized workshop attendees to the importance of reflecting on their current habits and practices (including their preferred study location, as well as how they find, organize, read and share research materials), the workshop then highlights how each tool could match participants' needs rather than vice versa. This simple switch has been welcomed by participants, with one attendee noting that 'It was very helpful to have a brief overview of each system, then an assessment to help me choose which one would work best for me, then more in-depth information about the one I chose'. Comments like this demonstrate how the workshop now helps learners to match their needs to a tool rather than vice versa and make an informed decision about their research practice needs and development. These ideas can also be seen in Coonan's use of animal metaphors (for example, Zotero for 'squirrel' researchers who need to be able to capture their references on the move) to explore reference management workflow and practice (2013).

Research into networked participation and digital scholarship has also led to the creation of a series of new workshops at UCB. Focusing on complex questions about digital scholars' practices within a networked world, these workshops have been explicitly designed to develop learners' awareness such as the development of online identities or the measurement and improvement of impact. Rather than listing potential sites for researcher profiles, however, these workshops are centred, as above, on researcher practices rather than on tools. They are further characterized by their emphasis on the pitfalls as well as the opportunities of digital technologies, or the need to provide a critical appraisal of these tools. Thus, the Creating a Digital Identity workshop spends considerable time questioning the purpose and goals of an online identity, as well as discussing the benefits and drawbacks of using commercial sites for networking and as a research portfolio. Similarly, the workshop that focuses on Improving Your Impact critically engages with the concepts of outreach, public discourse and measurement, asking participants to reflect on the nature of 'impact' and the forces behind the sudden interest in this topic, as well as serving as a how-to primer about ways to open up and share personal and collaborative research practices.

Many participants mention that they find the focus on practical details useful, including scholar profiles, the measurement of impact and advice about sharing research and teaching materials. Others find that this workshop forms a neutral space that can help to uncover assumptions as well as legitimate fears and concerns among the participants. This often helps them to join the dots between scraps of information they have absorbed, for instance, between their knowledge that they can put published articles online and a vague understanding of the rules that govern this by developing specific knowledge about negotiating contracts, permission and institutional or commercial repository sites. Attendees also mention that the workshop forms a space to discuss and experiment with questions of digital identity in an open way, rather than solely relying on confused advice from a supervisor or dire warnings about the value of engaging on social media from a PhD committee member. We have found that many participants, for example, are urged to stay away from public engagement for fear of someone stealing either their ideas or their work. Others are cautioned against publishing OA because it may later harm their ability to negotiate a book contract. While these concerns are important, participants appreciate this workshop because it presents a rounded picture of both the benefits and the drawbacks of engaging online and enables individuals to make their own informed decision about their next academic steps. In turn, the open and questioning nature of workshops such as these has enabled librarians to become more sensitive to these issues and to temper their enthusiasm for online engagement and OA with a measured appraisal of the reality of academic pressures and disciplinary norms. This format has also helped to foreground the structural constraints that can affect the notion of success in the academy, or the idea that we cannot assume that the use of different technologies or metrics will automatically lead to greater representation or quality of opportunity within higher education. There are many factors that affect visibility and prestige in the academy and it is clear that the focus on unpacking these ideas contributes to both the honesty and the success of this workshop.

Beyond workshops, librarians at UCB have also partnered with educational technology staff in order to create public digital scholarship discussion fora. These events, which are open to the entire campus, acknowledge that digital scholarship is still developing and that scholars and their communities may need to work through a number of complex questions related to identity, participation and impact. Academics Online week, which was held at UCB in 2014, is one such example of a public discussion event, where scholars and librarians came together to exchange ideas about the nature of digital scholarship and its potential impact on their work. On one level, this event served as a drop-in technology testing zone, where librarians and faculty gave mini overviews of a number of digital scholarship tools in the field, including Impact Story, Mendeley, Twitter and more. This half of the event allowed faculty and librarians to sit down in a one-on-one setting and try out the tools, while also hearing about how local experts on campus used these tools in their daily, academic lives. On another level, this event also included several open discussions about the nature of digital scholarship and what this means to campus faculty, educational technology staff and librarians, including panels entitled 'What is Open Scholarship' and 'What is Open Access'. These events facilitated a number of discussions and broader debates about the nature of openness and digitality. They also served to raise awareness about these issues on campus, further sparking a number of follow-up workshops and consultations about questions of digital scholarship. We found that a discursive approach to changing academic realities was particularly helpful because it grounded practices within the messy everyday nature of digital scholarship, rather than presenting it in theoretical or ideal terms. This made the topic approachable to a wide variety of campus faculty and graduate students as well as serving to draw attention to the 'in-progress' nature of practices and the need for further discussion and work in the area. Our emphasis on including a wide variety of interdisciplinary perspectives, or a mix of speakers from different disciplines, also helped us to break this topic down for our campus; the variety of perspectives meant that discussion was lively and participants were able to make a number of useful comparisons and connections across scholarly traditions. In addition, and while this wasn't our original goal, we found that these events also served as a site of professional development for librarians, many of whom had started to receive questions about altmetrics or the legality of using academic social media sites, and wanted to improve their knowledge in the area.

Lastly, but most importantly, undergraduates, too, can be included in these conversations around digital scholarship. OA is an obvious starting point, with many universities now making undergraduate theses and senior projects available through institutional repositories. Undergraduate research is often seen as 'immature and unpolished, drafts not-ready-for-primetime', as well as liable to undermine the faculty member's reputation (Miller, 2013). Yet, as Hicks and Howkins point out, 'if we believe that undergraduate students have nothing to contribute to a particular field, it is worth asking ourselves what such an attitude communicates to students about the nature of the ... discipline and their place within it' (2015, 355). OA undergraduate publishing can thereby be seen as a way for students to exercise their academic agency by both entering into and participating within broader conversations around their interests. As libraries start to become more involved with digital publishing (Michigan Publishing, for example, forms a part of the University of Michigan Libraries), as well as with scholarly communication and other initiatives that focus on broadening the reach and the visibility of OA publishing, it is clear that undergraduate research can play an important part within the library's goals of making information accessible for all (Miller, 2013). Beyond the technological implications for making undergraduate research available, the inherent focus on research accountability reinforces everyday meanings of information literacy (Booth and Miller, 2014), and instruction sessions may need to take a different shape when undergraduate research forms part of scholarly conversations. Librarians involved in information literacy instruction can help to scaffold undergraduate student researchers' needs by focusing on information privilege, or the need for OA publishing, as well as on paying greater attention to attribution, copyright and permissions (Booth, 2013).

The concept of networked participation also forms a useful way to think about redesigning undergraduate research assignments, which, like in traditional academic reward systems, tend to focus exclusively on the final essay or the product of research. In our role as subject specialists and liaisons, a number of scholars and practitioners have started conversations with interested faculty about the nature of research assignments and ways in which we can break or slow down the research process (Blackwell-Starnes, 2011; Deitering and Gronemyer, 2011; Sinkinson and Hicks, 2013; Mihailidis and Cohen, 2013; Hicks and Howkins, 2015). By working with faculty to redesign assignments around the intermediary academic practices that may eventually lead to a final paper (for example, by following a Twitter hashtag, or mapping a scholar's informal online conversations), we make questions of enquiry, as well as authority and evaluation, more visible to students, as well as scaffolding their participation in and exploration of today's complex information landscapes. And, while this idea is not yet scalable, it is clear that the process of working with faculty as co-designers of educational experiences has also led to a number of benefits, including a greater understanding of each other's role and a more relevant and responsive research assignment. Students react well to these new ideas, too, with one student in the Hicks and Howkins study pointing out that 'having been forced to look at largely primary sources, make inferences, and draw conclusions to connect dots that haven't necessarily been connected before was a very different kind of experience (but a good one)' (2015, 353). While this study found that students may initially be cautious about the idea of analysing contemporary media such as blogs and tweets in a history class, it was clear that by the end of the class, students were engaging in far more sophisticated evaluation of the information environments that surrounds them.

Conclusion

Digital scholarship and the idea of the digital scholar form complex concepts that are constantly in flux as academic and scholarly researchers react to, make sense of and create new disciplinary norms related to teaching, scholarship and individual research practices. In recent studies, digital scholarship has thereby referred to a number of related ideas, including:

1. Building a digital collection of information for further study and analysis
2. Creating appropriate tools for collection building
3. Creating appropriate tools for the analysis and study of collections
4. Using digital collections and analytical tools to generate new intellectual products
5. Creating authoring tools for these new intellectual products, either in traditional form or in digital form

(American Council of Learned Societies Commission on Cyberinfrastructure for the Humanities and Social Sciences, n.d.)

This chapter has argued, however, that it is the change in the scholarly practices around these tools and collections that is both noteworthy and a neglected opportunity for librarians. In other words, by seeing digital scholarship as constituting and being constitutive of a number of new, scholarly activities that are centred on principles of openness or social and networked participation, rather than just as the use of new technologies, we open up the potential for more meaningful and necessary conversation about the changing nature of academia. This approach also dovetails nicely with the drive (Accardi, Drabinski and Kumbier, 2010) to broaden the way that we think of information literacy; as Crissinger points out, 'asking faculty and graduate students to think critically about how we evaluate scholarship and what impact really means to them as scholars and information consumers is information literacy' (2015). These ideas can also be seen through the work of Jisc in the UK, which has carried out significant research into digital capabilities, and includes digital communication and collaboration as well as traditional information literacy skills as a key part of a researcher's digital capacity. In effect, these ideas illustrate both the dynamic nature of and the critical need for information literacy within today's complex information landscapes.

At the same time, it is clear that communities who explore both the role and the place of these new practices may not always recognize or even share the open ideals from which the concept of networked participation was born. Just as Massive Open Online Courses were transformed from their radically open, connectivist beginnings into more traditional models of online education, digital scholarship runs the risk of becoming distanced from ideas of openness and failing to transform inherited scholarly practices. For some, interest in alternative systems of measurement has neglected to broaden the idea of research impact, continuing to treat 'knowledge diffusion as a "black box" with only inputs and outputs' or removing the concept of meaning from questions of public value (Budz Pedersen, 2015). For others, the focus on impact, for example in the Research Excellence Framework, which is a programme that assesses the research of British higher education institutions, has been critiqued for over-simplifying or marginalizing the value and worth of non-immediately popular research (Mulholland, 2015). While it may be frustrating to see how easily goals of openness can be subverted, these issues could also be seen as demonstrating the emerging nature of the field, as well as highlighting the pressures that scholars and institutions face in an era of increased accountability. More positively, developments could also be seen as helping to create impetus for continued engagement; as open scholar Bonnie Stewart points out, 'we are part of a flawed system and open research is an important approach to solve it' (Notsosternlib, 2015). It is in this spirit that librarians should approach digital scholarship, drawing upon their core professional values to continue advocating for the creation of academic practices that are as open, as accessible and as diverse as they can possibly make them.

References

Accardi, M. T., Drabinski, E. and Kumbier, A. (2010) *Critical Library Instruction: theories and methods*, Duluth MN, Library Juice Press.

American Council of Learned Societies Commission on Cyberinfrastructure for the Humanities and Social Sciences (n.d.) What is Digital Scholarship? *Open Stax*, http://cnx.org/contents/3e6519f7-9f9a-4060-a5af-567a8e959f2c@1/What-Is-Digital-Scholarship.

Blackwell-Starnes, A. (2011) Academic Research, Professional Discourse: social bookmarking as a catalyst for rhetorical research pedagogies, PhD Thesis, Texas Woman's University.

Booth, C. (2013) Open Access as Pedagogy, *Info-mational*, https://infomational.wordpress.com/2013/07/29/open-access-as-pedagogy/.

Booth, C. and Miller, C. (2014) Open Access as Undergraduate Pedagogy, *Library Journal*, http://lj.libraryjournal.com/2014/03/opinion/backtalk/open-access-as-undergraduate-pedagogy-backtalk/#_.

Boyer, E. L. (1990) *Scholarship Reconsidered: priorities of the professoriate.* Princeton NJ, Carnegie Foundation for the Advancement of Teaching.

Bucher, T. (2012) Want to Be on the Top? Algorithmic power and the threat of invisibility on Facebook, *New Media & Society*, **14** (7), 1164–80.

Budz Pedersen, D. (2015) Real Impact Is about Influence, Meaning and Value: mapping contributions for a new impact agenda in the humanities, *The Impact Blog*, http://blogs.lse.ac.uk/impactofsocialsciences/2015/07/27/mapping-the-public-influence-of-the-humanities/.

Coonan, E. (2013) Referencing without Tears, *Research Skills Central*, https://researchcentral.wordpress.com/2013/11/13/referencing/.

Cottom McMillan, T. (2012) Risk and Ethics in Public Scholarship, *University of Venus*, https://www.insidehighered.com/blogs/university-venus/risk-and-ethics-public-scholarship.

Crissinger, S. (2015) The Best Work I Do Is at Intersections, *ACRLog*, http://acrlog.org/2015/12/07/intersections/.

Deitering, A. M. and Gronemyer, K. (2011) Beyond Peer-reviewed Articles: using blogs to enrich students' understanding of scholarly work, *portal: Libraries and the Academy*, **11** (1), 489–503.

Fitzpatrick, K. (2015) Academia, not Edu, *Planned Obsolescence*, www.plannedobsolescence.net/academia-not-edu/.

Fransman, J. (2013) Researching Academic Literacy Practices around Twitter: performative methods and their onto-ethical implications. In Goodfellow, R. and Lea, M. (eds), *Literacy in the Digital University: critical perspectives on learning, scholarship and technology*, London, Routledge, 27–41.

Glass, E. (2015) Social Paper: retooling student consciousness, *Scholarly and Research*

Communication, **6** (4), 10pp.

Goodfellow, R. (2013a) Scholarly, Digital, Open: an impossible triangle? *Research in Learning Technology*, **21**, 1–15.

Goodfellow, R. (2013b) The Literacies of Digital Scholarship – truth and use values. In Goodfellow, R. and Lea, M. (eds), *Literacy in the Digital University: critical perspectives on learning, scholarship and technology*, London, Routledge, 67–78.

Graham, M., Hogan, B., Straumann, R. and Medhat, A. (2014) Uneven Geographies of User-Generated Information: patterns of increasing informational poverty, *Annals of the Association of American Geographers*, **104** (4), 746–64.

Greenhow, C. and Gleason, B. (2014) Social Scholarship: reconsidering scholarly practices in the age of social media, *British Journal of Educational Technology*, **45** (3), 392–402.

Hall, R. (2011) Revealing the Transformatory Moment of Learning Technology: the place of critical social theory, *Research in Learning Technology*, **19** (3), 273–84.

Harley, D., Krysz Acord, S., Earl-Novell, S., Lawrence, S. and Judson King, C. (2010) *Assessing the Future Landscape of Scholarly Communication: an exploration of faculty values and needs in seven disciplines*, Center for Studies in Higher Education, UC Berkeley.

Hicks, A. and Howkins, A. (2015) Tipping the Iceberg: a collaborative approach to redesigning the undergraduate research assignment in an Antarctic history capstone seminar, *The History Teacher*, **48** (2), 339–70.

Hicks, A. and Sinkinson, C. (2015) Examining Mendeley: designing learning opportunities for digital scholarship, *portal: Libraries and the Academy*, **15** (3), 531–49.

Lupton, D. (2014) *'Feeling Better Connected': academics' use of social media*, Canberra, News & Media Research Centre, University of Canberra.

Mihailidis, P. and Cohen, J. N. (2013) Exploring Curation as a Core Competency in Digital and Media Literacy Education, *Journal of Interactive Media in Education*, **1**, p.Art. 2, doi:http://doi.org/10.5334/2013-02.

Miller, C. (2013) Riding the Wave: open access, digital publishing, and the undergraduate thesis. Presentation at *USETDA 2013 Conference*, http://scholarship.claremont.edu/pomona_fac_pub/377/.

Mitchell, A. (2013) Take Back the Net: institutions must develop collective strategies to tackle online abuse aimed at female academics, *LSE Impact of the Social Sciences*, http://blogs.lse.ac.uk/impactofsocialsciences/2013/07/24/take-back-the-net-female-academics-online-abuse/.

Mulholland, J. (2015) Academics: forget about public engagement, stay in your ivory towers, *The Guardian Higher Education Network*, www.theguardian.com/higher-education-network/2015/dec/10/academics-forget-about-public-engagement-stay-in-your-ivory-towers.

Noble, S. U. (2012) Missed Connections: what search engines say about women, *Bitch*, **12** (54), 36–41.

Notsosternlib (2015) We Are Part of a Flawed System and Open Research is an Important

Approach to Solve It, [Twitter post, 8 October], https://twitter.com/notsosternlib/status/652097968317706243.

Pariser, E. (2011) *The Filter Bubble*, New York NY, Penguin Press.

Pearce, N., Weller, M., Scanlon, E. and Kinsley, S. (2010) Digital Scholarship Considered: how new technologies could transform academic work, *in education*, **16** (1), 33–44.

Siemens, G. (2005) Connectivism: a learning theory for the digital age, *International Journal of Instructional Technology and Distance Learning*, **2** (10), 3–10.

Sinkinson, C. and Hicks, A. (2013) Unraveling the Research Process: social bookmarking and collaborative learning. In Pixy Ferris, S. and Wilder, H. (eds), *The Plugged-in Professor: tips and techniques for teaching with social media*, Oxford, Chandos, 49–60.

Skallerup Besette, L. (2015) Social Media, Service and the Perils of Scholarly Affect, *Hybrid Pedagogy*, www.hybridpedagogy.com/journal/social-media-service-and-the-perils-of-scholarly-affect/.

Stewart, B. (2015) Open to Influence: what counts as academic influence in scholarly networked Twitter participation, *Learning, Media and Technology* **40** (3), 1–23.

Stoytcheva, S. (2015) Steven Salaita and the Critical Importance of Context: contingency and the ALA code of ethics. Paper presented at the *Canadian Association of Professional Academic Librarians (CAPAL)*.

Utell, J. (2015) Redefining Service for the Digital Academic: scholarship, social media, and silos, *Hybrid Pedagogy*, www.hybridpedagogy.com/journal/redefining-service-for-the-digital-academic/.

Veletsianos, G. (2013) Open Practices and Identity: evidence from researchers and educators' social media participation, *British Journal of Educational Technology*, **44** (4), 639–51.

Veletsianos, G. and Kimmons, R. (2012a) Assumptions and Challenges of Open Scholarship, *The International Review of Research in Open and Distributed Learning*, **13** (4), 166–89.

Veletsianos, G., and Kimmons, R. (2012b) Networked Participatory Scholarship: emergent techno-cultural pressures toward open and digital scholarship in online networks, *Computers & Education*, **58** (2), 766–74.

Wagner, C., Garcia, D., Jadidi, M. and Strohmaier, M. (2015) It's a Man's Wikipedia? Assessing gender inequality in an online encyclopedia, *Proceedings of The International AAAI Conference on Web and Social Media (ICWSM2015), Oxford, UK*.

Weller, M. (2011) *The Digital Scholar: how technology is transforming scholarly practice*, London, Bloomsbury Academic.

10

Reflections on digital scholarship: so many reasons to be cheerful

Alison Mackenzie and Lindsey Martin

This book captures many of the reasons why library and information professionals working in academic libraries everywhere have reason to be optimistic about their future. It provides timely examples of libraries and librarians reimagining their working environments and themselves; demonstrating relevance, resilience and innovation both within their libraries and across their institutions.

As discussed in the opening chapter, librarians have long been aware of the challenges posed by digital scholarship. Indeed, we have observed that the opening gambit for much of the published literature is to rehearse concerns around the continuing relevance of academic libraries and academic librarians. Thankfully, most of the ensuing discussions then go on to demonstrate how the profession is, in the face of these challenges, successfully adapting, innovating and generally navigating its way through disruptive change. Even so, you could be forgiven for internalizing the continuing sub-text that an academic librarian's lot is one of constant tension and struggle in the face of what are often portrayed as indifferent institutions and higher education sectors.

Much of the content of this book showcases examples of where, from an organizational to an individual perspective, libraries are demonstrating flexibility and stretch through the remodelling of services and through innovation in forging new partnerships and carving out new roles or applying existing expertise to new situations, and are making these moves with the confidence that their contribution will provide added value. This boldness is welcome; it is grounded in a clear sense of self-worth, informed by the ongoing belief that the work of the library remains key to the success of all educational institutions.

This is in contrast to the anxiety expressed by some colleagues over the loss of professional identity, when the association between the library and the librarian becomes less tangible. We have observed two almost opposing developments, offering opportunities but also challenge. The first is where the role of the librarian is taken out of the library and becomes more completely engaged in 'outreach' activities, illustrating participation in a networked environment, rather than simply providing a demonstration. The second is where, as Bergstrom describes, new, non-traditional roles are created within the library; for example, data curation librarians and digital scholarship co-ordinators. There is also evidence in the literature of the emergence of this new breed of 'hybrid' professionals with discipline, research and information expertise who are not necessarily recruited from within the library profession and yet who work in a library setting.

What we are witnessing and is explicit in this book is an increase in diversity of professional roles. It is impossible to draw anything more than a dotted line to the impact of digital scholarship, but the roles that are emerging are closely aligned to the needs of that environment, coupled with, in some countries, research funders' requirements. They span all activities, from undergraduate support to specialist research activities, and all are bound by a common characteristic, to improve scholarly practice through the use of technology.

The anxiety of disintermediation, the intervention of third-party providers (Auckland, 2012) and what has been described as the 'Googling of Education' (Weller, 2011, 172) have perhaps spurred action amongst senior managers – many of the roles and activities described in this book could very easily sit with other professional services within a university environment, but, as is evident from Mackenzie, Howard and Fitzgibbons's chapters (amongst others), examples of partnership go beyond collaboration, to become a new way of working.

A recurring theme throughout the chapters is the need for librarians to demonstrate digital resilience in the face of the rapid development and expansion of digital technologies and their impact on digital scholarship and scholars. The shifts in the research behaviours of academics and their views of libraries and support services were recently captured in a UK report (Wolff, Rod and Schonfield, 2016). The key findings of the report suggest that the contribution of academic libraries in support of the activities of discovery, access, research practices and dissemination is in good health. This is likely to continue as a growth area as, according to Bosman and Kramer, 2015), there has been a surge of new scholarly communication tools in recent years, with over half of the 400+ tracked by them created since 2013. Their global survey of researchers across all disciplines and career stages has attracted 20,670 respondents to date and has looked at how researchers use tools across their research workflows, and also at their use of academic social media sites; for example, they found that two-thirds of respondents use ResearchGate and nearly a third use academia.edu for dissemination of research publications (Matthews, 2016). Whilst researchers across the globe are clearly adopting digital tools and platforms to manage their research workflows independently from libraries, the blurring of the lines between publishers' platforms and academic social media sites, whilst presenting a challenge, also provides many opportunities for librarians who understand the territory and can advise on the difficult grey areas around copyright and paid-for publishing models. This positive view is echoed by Lankes (2014): 'Librarians have long been at the birth of ideas (feeding researchers through reference and resources) and at the entombment of research (gathering and fixing research in static documents). Now we are presented with the vast rich chaos of the interim which to me is a fundamental area of investigation for librarians.'

Auckland (2012, 3), in her report based on a survey of libraries in research-intensive institutions in the UK, identified skills gaps in nine key areas of research support. Although anecdotal, it is evident that significant progress has been made across many of the areas identified, managing the research publication workflow and preserving outputs; developing expertise on managing data, use of metadata and knowledge of funders' requirements. Equally striking is that the emphasis in 2012 was on the need to develop new technical expertise in order to bridge perceived skills 'gaps'. While this is still essential, we would argue that equal if not more emphasis should be paid to developing career and digital resilience.

The biggest digital scholarship challenge we face, therefore, is not actually the technology or associated skills. It is to develop a mindset which is collectively comfortable with the dynamism of scholarship in the digital environment and which understands the need for staff to be adaptable, outward looking and forward thinking – in other words, resilient. These attributes are arguably more important than any technical skills, which although necessary are subject to regular and unpredictable change. But what do we mean by resilience when applied to human behaviour? According to Pemberton, writing from the perspective of career coaching, it 'is about being open to learning and growth, being able to take risks because of a sense of being able to deal with the consequences of that risk. Resilience does not protect us from setback, but it ensures we are able to manage our way through it' (2015, 3) and as a means of responding to an unpredictable working life, stability, flexibility and stretch provide a successful base to build on:

Stability: those things that the individual knows to be true. In library terms it would be our core values that imbue our profession with purpose and meaning.

Flexibility: the ability to acknowledge change in the professional and working environment.
Stretch: willingness to move beyond a comfort point to unknown territory, to take risks and, if necessary, leave behind skills and ways of doing things that are no longer relevant.

The concepts of career resilience and what we are here describing as digital resilience go beyond librarians' being technically capable and confident partners and practitioners of digital scholarship, to incorporate a range of behaviours and attributes which will deliver on sustainable organizational relevance and individual career progression. It is the ability to be true to our stable, professional values whilst demonstrating flexibility in responding to change and uncertainty, and recognizing when and how to stretch into new skills and new roles. Bremner illustrates this from an organizational perspective where, at Macquarie University, the Library has introduced a new approach to working that is better suited to the ebb and flow of the digital environment, while Bergstrom describes how staff in Notre Dame's Center for Digital Scholarship are actively encouraged to engage with innovation, take risks and learn from failure. Hicks, Howard and Fitzgibbons, meanwhile, personify these traits in practice. In each of these instances, the groundwork for success is rooted in the resilient attitudes and behaviours of individuals in relation to the digital environment.

References

Auckland, M. (2012) *Re-skilling for Research: an investigation into the role and skills of subject and liaison librarians required to effectively support the evolving information needs of researchers*, Research Libraries UK,
www.rluk.ac.uk/wp-content/uploads/2014/02/RLUK-Re-skilling.pdf.

Bosman, J. and Kramer, B. (2015) *101 Innovations in Scholarly Communication: how researchers are getting to grip* [sic}*with the myriad of new tools*,
http://blogs.lse.ac.uk/impactofsocialsciences/2015/11/11/101-innovations-in-scholarly-communication/.

Lankes, R. D. (2014) *On Productivity: introducing a blog series on reinventing the academic library*, http://davidlankes.org/?p=6510,

Matthews, D. (2016) Do Academic Social Networks Share Academics' Interests?, *Times Higher Education*, 7–13 April, 249, 39–43.

Pemberton, C. (2015) *Resilience: a practical guide for coaches*, Maidenhead, Open University Press.

Weller, M. (2011) *The Digital Scholar: how technology is transforming scholarly practice*, London, Bloomsbury Academic.

Wolff, C., Rod, A. B. and Schonfield, R. C. (2016) *Ithaka S+R, JISC and RLUK Survey of Academics 2016*,
https://repository.jisc.ac.uk/6437/1/ithaka-survey-of-academics-2015.pdf.

Index

academic librarianship, University of Western Australia (UWA) 48–49
American Historical Association (AHA), guidelines 12–13
anecdotes, social networking sites (SNS) 149
application, scholarship component 4–5, 19
Association of Research Libraries (ARL), survey 14

bespoke digital scholarship services 26–8
Blackboard Learn LMS/VLE 51–54
Boyer's model of scholarship components 4–5, 19
BPII *see* Business Process Improvement Initiative
Bucknell University
  defining xiii–xiv
  digital scholarship annual conference 105–106
Business Process Improvement Initiative (BPPI), Macquarie University 83–4

career resilience, library/librarian roles 175–6
Carpe Diem, learning design initiative 49–51

case study
  Center for Digital Scholarship (CDS) 110–18
  communication and documentation of scholarship 33–5
  consultancy and training 131–2
  Coventry University 37–40
  data services 125–7
  digital scholarship centre 110–18
  digitization of the Abbey Theatre Archive 35–7
  Disruptive Media Learning Lab (DMLL) 37–40
  funding 30–2
  library enquiry process 97–9
  library scanning and copying process 99–100
  library shelving process 95–7
  library/librarian roles 29–30
  Macquarie University 95–100
  National University of Ireland 35–7
  Newcastle University 33–5
  research support 125–7, 129–30, 133–4
  scholarly communication 33–5, 129–130
  University of Hull 29–30

180   DEVELOPING DIGITAL SCHOLARSHIP

University of Notre Dame 110–18
University of Salford 125–7, 131–2, 133–4
University of Salford Institutional Repository (USIR) 129–30
University of Sussex 30–2
University of Western Australia (UWA) 43–58
CDS see Center for Digital Scholarship
CEF see Centre for Education Futures
Center for Digital Scholarship (CDS) 110–18
  see also centres for digital scholarship
  institutional needs 110–11
  marketing 115–16
  research support 111–13
  staffing model 111
  sustainability vs. innovation 117–18
  technology 116–17
  University of Notre Dame 110–18
  web presence 114–15
Centre for Education Futures (CEF)
  skills development 57
  University of Western Australia (UWA) 45, 55–7
centres for digital scholarship 14, 64, 106–10
  case study 110–18
  Center for Digital Scholarship (CDS) 110–18
  institutional needs 109–11
  skills development 108
  space and resources 108–9
  technical infrastructure 109
  University of Notre Dame 110–18
chapter summaries xv–xx
collaboration 17
collection-centric approach, vs. engagement with users 122–3
communication, scholarly see scholarly communication
communication and documentation of scholarship, case study 33–5
consultancy and training
  case study 131–2
  research support 130–2
  University of Salford 131–2
content analysis, social networking sites (SNS) 148
content networks/networking 7–8
continuing professional development (CPD) 65, 71

continuous improvement, Lean in Higher Education approach 88
Coventry University, case study 37–40
CPD see continuing professional development
curation, research support 123–4

data services
  case study 125–7
  research support 125–7
  University of Salford 125–7
Developing Digital Literacies (DDL) 66, 67, 70, 71, 74
developing librarians see skills development; training and development
digital humanities 6
digital literacies 63–4
  defining 63
  Exeter University 64
  Research Information Literacy and Digital Scholarship (RILADS) 66
  SCONUL survey 66–70
  strategy 49–52, 66, 67, 69
digital pervasiveness 3, 6
digital resilience, library/librarian roles 175–6
digital scholarship
  consequences 159–60
  defining 6–7, 62, 122, 158–9
  features 158–60
  forms 159
  as an ideology 7–8
  related ideas 167
digital scholarship annual conference, Bucknell University 105–6
digital scholarship centres see centres for digital scholarship
digital technology effects, university practices xiv–xv
digitization 7–8
  Abbey Theatre Archive, case study 35–7
  National Library of Wales, strategy 124
  research support 123–4
  strategy 123–4
discovery, scholarship component 4–5, 19
Disruptive Media Learning Lab (DMLL), case study 37–40

engagement with users 105–106
  vs. collection-centric approach 122–3

library engagement, digital scholarship services and systems 23-8
research support 122-3
social networking sites (SNS) 143-9
enquiry process, library, case study 97-9
Exeter University, digital literacies 64
experimental digital scholarship 32-3

Facebook *see* social networking sites
focus groups, social networking sites (SNS) 147-8
funding, case study 30-2

graph data, social networking sites (SNS) 148-9

'hybrid information jobs' 63

innovation, 'islands of innovation' 7-10
innovation vs. sustainability 17-18
  Center for Digital Scholarship (CDS) 117-18
institutional needs, centres for digital scholarship 109-11
institution-wide business systems 25
integration
  digital scholarship 163
  scholarship component 4-5, 19
interaction analysis, social networking sites (SNS) 147, 148
interviews, social networking sites (SNS) 147-8
'islands of innovation' 8-10
  values-led 7-8

Jisc (Joint Information Systems Committee)
  defining digital literacies 63
  defining digital scholarship 62
  Developing Digital Literacies (DDL) 66, 67, 70, 71, 74
  training and development 61

leadership 17-18
Lean in Higher Education approach 83-4
  Macquarie University 86-90
learning design initiatives
  Carpe Diem 49-51
  library/librarian roles 49-51
learning management system (LMS)

Blackboard Learn LMS/VLE 51-4
University of Western Australia (UWA) 47, 51-4
Libraries of the Future, strategy 16
library engagement, digital scholarship services and systems 23-8
library/librarian roles 14-16, 23-30
  see also research support; skills development; training and development
  academic librarianship 48-9
  bespoke digital scholarship services 26-8
  Blackboard Learn LMS/VLE 51-4
  career resilience 175-6
  Carpe Diem 49-51
  case study 29-30
  Centre for Education Futures (CEF) 55-7
  digital resilience 175-6
  digital scholarship 162-7
  flexibility 175-6
  learning design initiatives 49-51
  mindset 175-6
  new/non-traditional 174
  open access (OA) 165-6
  professional development 49
  skills gaps 14-16
  stablity 175-6
  stretch 175-6
  University of Colorado, Boulder (UCB) 163-7
  University of Western Australia (UWA) 48-9
literature review 3-19
LMS *see* learning management system

Macquarie University
  Business Process Improvement Initiative (BPPI) 83-4
  case study 95-100
  Lean in Higher Education approach 86-90
  library enquiry process 97-9
  library scanning and copying process 99-100
  library shelving process 95-7
  Quality Enhancement Framework and Service Model 84-90
  strategy 82, 101-2

What We Do Matters programme 90–4
makerspace environment 19, 27, 106–7
marketing, Center for Digital Scholarship (CDS) 115–16
Massive Open Online Courses (MOOCs), training and development 56–7
mindset, library/librarian roles 175–6
MOOCs *see* Massive Open Online Courses

National Library of Wales, digitization strategy 124
National University of Ireland, case study 35–7
networks/networking
  content 7–8
  library/librarian roles 162–7
  networked participation 160–2
  peer evaluation 160–1
  peer-to-peer 7–8
  tensions 160–2
Newcastle University, case study 33–5

open access (OA) 159
  library/librarian roles 165–6
  scholarly communication 128
Open Scholar 7
openness
  approaches to 8–10
  scholarly practices 10–12
  technical-led 7–8
  technology 10–11
opportunities, University of Western Australia (UWA) 58
ownership, digital scholarship services and systems 25–6

partnerships 17
  digital scholarship services and systems 25–6
  University of Western Australia (UWA) 46–8, 58
peer evaluation 160–1
peer-to-peer networks/networking 7–8
preservation, research support 123–4
privacy issues, social networking sites (SNS) 149
professional development, University of Western Australia (UWA) 49

Quality Enhancement Framework and Service Model, Macquarie University 84–90
questionnaires, social networking sites (SNS) 145–6, 147–8

RDM *see* research data management
REF *see* Research Excellence Framework
related ideas, digital scholarship 167
repositioning of libraries 13–14
research data management (RDM) 63
Research Excellence Framework (REF) 9, 168
Research Information Literacy and Digital Scholarship (RILADS), digital literacies 66
research support 121–35, 174–5
  see also library/librarian roles
  case study 125–27, 129–30, 133–4
  Center for Digital Scholarship (CDS) 111–13
  challenges 132–4
  consultancy and training 130–2
  curation 123–4
  data services 125–7
  digitization 123–4
  engagement with users vs. collection-centric approach 122–3
  preservation 123–4
  scholarly communication 127–30
  skills gaps 175
  training and development 130–2
  University of Salford 125–7
resources
  centres for digital scholarship 108–9
  training and development 71–2
respect for people, Lean in Higher Education approach 87–8
RILADS *see* Research Information Literacy and Digital Scholarship
roles, library/librarian *see* library/librarian roles

scanning and copying process, case study 99–100
scholarly communication
  case study 33–5, 129–30
  defining 127–8
  open access (OA) 128
  research support 127–30

scholarly practices
  changing 10–13
  openness 10–12
  shaping 10–13
scholars' use of technology 8–10
scholarship
  categories 4–5, 19
  components 4–5, 19
  scope 4–7
SCONUL *see* Society of College, National and University Libraries
sentiment analysis, social networking sites (SNS) 148
shelving, library, case study 95–7
skills development 23, 63–4
  see also library/librarian roles; training and development
  Blackboard Learn LMS/VLE 51–4
  Centre for Education Futures (CEF) 57
  centres for digital scholarship 27
  skills and competencies 65–6
  University of Western Australia (UWA) 51–4, 57, 58
skills gaps 14–16, 63, 66
  research support 175
social networking sites (SNS) 141–51, 161
  active profiles 144–5
  adaptability 150
  anecdotes 149
  categories 142
  content analysis 148
  defining 142
  engagement with users 143–9
  focus groups 147–8
  follower counting 147
  graph data 148–9
  interaction analysis 147, 148
  interest 144
  interviews 147–8
  monitoring 149–50
  negative feedback 145
  networked participation 162
  patrons' views 145–6
  privacy issues 149
  quality content, creating 149–50
  questionnaires 145–6, 147–8
  sentiment analysis 148
  technology 150
  use in academic libraries 142–3

Society of College, National and University Libraries (SCONUL)
  digital literacies survey 66–70
  SCONUL's Seven Pillars of Information Literacy framework 67
strategy 17–19
  digital literacies 49–52, 66, 67, 69
  digitization 123–4
  Libraries of the Future 16
  Macquarie University 82, 101
  technology 26, 27
  Universities Australia 81–2
  University of Western Australia (UWA) 44–6
sustainability vs. innovation 17–18
  Center for Digital Scholarship (CDS) 117–18

teaching, scholarship component 4–5, 19
technical infrastructure, centres for digital scholarship 109
technology
  adapting to change 150
  Center for Digital Scholarship (CDS) 116–17
  impact 174–5
  piloting/testing 27
  scholars' use of 8–10
  social networking sites (SNS) 150
  strategy 26, 27
training and development 14–16, 61–75
  see also library/librarian roles; skills development
  academic librarianship 48–9
  Carpe Diem 49–51
  Centre for Education Futures (CEF) 45, 55–7
  consultancy and training 130–2
  continuing professional development (CPD) 65, 71
  Developing Digital Literacies (DDL) 66, 67, 70, 71, 74
  Jisc (Joint Information Systems Committee) 61, 66, 67, 70, 71, 74
  Massive Open Online Courses (MOOCs) 56–7
  professional development 49
  research support 130–2
  resources 71–2
  University of Salford 130–2

Twitter 161

UCA *see* University for the Creative Arts
UCB *see* University of Colorado, Boulder
Universities Australia, strategy 81–2
University College London (UCLDH), centre for digital scholarship 64
University for the Creative Arts (UCA), centre for digital scholarship 64
University of Colorado, Boulder (UCB), library/librarian roles 163–7
University of Edinburgh, centre for digital scholarship 64
University of Hull, case study 29–30
University of Notre Dame
    Center for Digital Scholarship (CDS) 110–18
    digital scholarship centre 110–18
University of Oxford, centre for digital scholarship 64
University of Salford
    challenges case study 133–4
    consultancy and training case study 131–2
    research data management case study 125–7
University of Salford Institutional Repository (USIR), case study 129–30
University of St Andrews, Lean in Higher Education approach 84
University of Sussex, case study 30–2
University of Western Australia (UWA)
    academic librarianship 48–9
    Carpe Diem, learning design initiative 49–51
    case study 43–58
    Centre for Education Futures (CEF) 45, 55–7
    educational principles 44
    future of education 44
    learning management system (LMS) 47, 51–4
    library/librarian roles 48–9, 55–7
    Massive Open Online Courses (MOOCs) 56–7
    opportunities 58
    partnerships 46–8, 58
    professional development 49
    recommendations 58
    skills development 51–4, 57, 58
    strategy 44–6
    University Library 45–6
    virtual learning environment (VLE) 47, 51–4
university practices, digital technology effects xiv–xv
USIR *see* University of Salford Institutional Repository
UWA *see* University of Western Australia

value maximization, Lean in Higher Education approach 88–90
virtual learning environment (VLE)
    Blackboard Learn LMS/VLE 51–4
    University of Western Australia (UWA) 47, 51–4

waste reduction, Lean in Higher Education approach 90
web presence, Center for Digital Scholarship (CDS) 114–15
What We Do Matters programme, Macquarie University 90–4